fourth edition

Strategic Communications Planning

FOR EFFECTIVE PUBLIC RELATIONS AND MARKETING

D1572976

Dr. Laurie J. Wilson, APR, PRSA Fellow, Professor
Department of Communications, Brigham Young University

Joseph D. Ogden, Assistant Dean
Marriott School of Management, Brigham Young University

KENDALL/HUNT PUBLISHING COMPANY
4050 Westmark Drive   Dubuque, Iowa 52002

Copyright © 2004 by Kendall/Hunt Publishing Company

ISBN 0-7575-1208-9

Printed in the United States of America
10   9   8   7   6   5   4   3   2   1

TABLE OF CONTENTS

ACKNOWLEDGMENTS

I n the 10 years since the first edition of this book was published, the Strategic Communications Planning Matrix has proven to be not only a valuable professional tool but also an invaluable teaching tool. The matrix provides a structure for effective communications that inherently teaches analytical skills that are too often missing from education today. For our success, we owe a great debt to those who first conceived "the matrix" as it has come to be known by students and practitioners across the country. And, we owe thanks to many graduates of our program who lent their skills in editing and designing past editions. Their contributions enabled us to continue to provide camera-ready copy to the publisher — keeping the cost of the text within a student's budget.

In this new edition, one of those graduates, Joseph Ogden, has become a co-author. His successful 12-year career in public relations, investor communications and marketing qualified him to teach as an adjunct professor in our public relations program while he directs external relations and a host of other efforts for the Marriott School of Management at Brigham Young University. For past editions he assisted in the design and layout, which in this edition was created by two other graduates of our program, Duff Tittle and Brett Pyne, who own a communications and graphic design firm and teach as adjunct professors in the BYU public relations program. For this edition we brought on as an editor and content consultant another graduate of our program, Jerry Gowen. Jerry has nearly eight years of experience in public relations, trade media relations and marketing, and has also begun teaching as an adjunct professor in the public relations program at BYU. Finally, Emily Smurthwaite, who recently received her master's in mass communications from BYU, proofread the text for Associated Press style and consistency.

Still, we acknowledge that without the foresight of those original BYU faculty members, the strategic communications planning matrix would not exist. Lacking an analytical tool for students to use in solving public relations problems within the RACE model, they collaborated on a process that specifically outlined the type of research needed and how that research and its subsequent analysis should direct the planning and communication steps. Bruce Olsen, APR, Fellow PRSA, came up with the original tool with input from Ray Beckham and Brad Hainsworth. Dr. Beckham then initiated the use of the copy outlines for specific communication products resulting from matrix planning. In the early 1990s, Larry Macfarlane and I refined and further developed the matrix and JoAnn Valenti refined the copy outlines.

We also cannot ignore the suggestions and contributions of our students and graduates over the years. As a result of years of teaching and using the matrix, Joseph and I have significantly streamlined it and enhanced the copy outlines. We also demonstrate the applicability of the matrix for all organizational communication with publics whether it be marketing, public relations or advertising.

While the authors bear sole responsibility for the content and any inaccuracies, this book expounds a solid strategic planning approach which owes much to the contributions and suggestions of professionals, faculty and students across the nation. Nevertheless, the matrix and copy outlines were born of a desire on the part of those original BYU professors to excel in preparing their students for successful careers in public relations. The publication of this new edition is a credit to their dedication to students and to the profession. I gratefully recognize their initial work and their continued support and mentorship.

As the Strategic Communications Planning Matrix evolves and moves into a new era of application across the communication functions of organizations, we salute those who first had the vision to create the process.

Laurie J. Wilson
Sandy, Utah
June 2004

ABOUT THE AUTHORS

Laurie J. Wilson is an award-winning professor of communications at Brigham Young University. In 2001, she was named the Public Relations Society of America Outstanding Educator. In 1990, she was recognized as the Public Relations Student Society of America Outstanding Faculty Advisor. Five years later, she was inducted into the PRSSA Hall of Fame. She also received the Karl G. Maeser Teaching Award and three Student Alumni Association Excellence in Teaching Awards from BYU.

Wilson received her Ph.D. from The American University in Washington, D.C. After working in public relations and marketing for several years, she joined the BYU faculty in 1989 where she has served as chair of the Communications Department, the public relations program and the department's diversity task force.

Wilson currently serves as national chair for a number of education initiatives in PRSA, has served in the Public Relations Division of the Association for Education in Journalism and Mass Communication and served on the diversity task force of the Association of Schools of Journalism and Mass Communication. She serves on site teams accrediting communications programs for the Accrediting Council for Education in Journalism and Mass Communication and certifying schools in public relations education for PRSA.

Wilson's areas of expertise, research and publication include strategic planning and issue management, corporate social responsibility and building community partnerships. She consults regularly in those areas. In addition to this book, Wilson has co-authored two other communication books. She also serves as a member of the Executive Board of the United Way of Utah County.

J oseph D. Ogden is assistant dean for external relations at Brigham Young University's Marriott School of Management, an internationally ranked business school. His areas of expertise include persuasive writing, media relations, strategic planning, investor communications and marketing. Ogden has taught public relations case studies and advanced media writing courses for BYU's Department of Communications and has served as a member of the department's national advisory board.

Before coming to BYU, Ogden worked as corporate communications director for a nearly $1 billion-a-year personal care and nutrition products company. He was the company's spokesperson, oversaw public relations and marketing in Asia and managed investor communications for the publicly traded firm.

In 1995, he founded JDO Consulting, a strategic marketing and PR firm. The firm has worked with a wide range of clients including a candidate for U.S. Congress, a music retailer, and a New Jersey-based Chinese Internet service provider.

Ogden earned his MBA from the Marriott School and his BA in communications with a minor in music from Brigham Young University.

PREFACE

This new edition is prompted by two important worldwide trends. The first is the dramatic change resulting from corporate and investment scandals during the first few years of this century. The second is the staggering rate of technological innovation and advance.

The former trend has impact far beyond the change in regulation and business reporting. For the first time since public relations was established as a corporate function, unprecedented numbers of corporate executives have begun to recognize the necessity of establishing and maintaining long-term relationships with key organizational publics. This crisis of trust and reputation has finally demonstrated the direct bottom-line effect public relations professionals have been trying for decades to measure and prove to management. With relationship building, all organizational publics are now a key focus — communication is becoming an integrated function, whether it is for the purpose of advertising and marketing, human resources or public relations.

The rate of technological change is also a positive trend, although one we have been less prepared to manage. It isn't that the basic principles and purposes of communicating messages to publics have changed or have the fundamentals of communication to establish and maintain mutually beneficial relationships. The fundamentals and principles are as salient now as ever. Rather, the capacity to monitor and manage the explosion of messages, many from less than credible sources, has not developed at the same rate as the technology to deliver them. The environment within which we deliver messages to key organizational publics is unbelievably cluttered with unpredictable competing messages. This phenomenon underscores the necessity of continual reputation building and social reporting, and it makes the public information function of an organization's communications more important than ever.

While these two trends are dramatically influencing the way organizations communicate, they have not changed the basic principles upon which the Strategic Communications Planning Matrix was built. The planning process outlined in the matrix is as viable as ever and, in fact, has become an even more crucial tool. Although slightly modified for this edition, it still provides the framework to integrate solid research to drive the establishment of objectives, the selection of key organizational publics, the design of messages to those publics and the use of channels and tools to deliver those messages. The Strategic Communications Planning Matrix, developed nearly two decades ago by the faculty at Brigham Young University, is a systematic, analytical model expanding the four-step public relations process — research, action planning, communication and evaluation (RACE) — to a step-by-step research-based communications planning and programming tool. It has been proven — in education and industry alike — to be a valuable analytical problem-solving tool enabling the integration of information and translation of knowledge into sound communications practice. One of the key advantages of the Strategic Communications Planning Matrix continues to be that it links research to problem-solving action.

While the first three editions of this text focused the matrix process on public relations planning, this fourth edition expands its application to all of an organization's communications. It is assumed that the reader already has a basic foundation in and understanding of communication and persuasion principles. The goal of this text is not to present the principles, concepts and skills taught elsewhere. For added detail on specific topics, readers are referred to supporting references at the end of each chapter. The goal of this text is to synthesize information and provide a methodology to successfully apply it in an integrated communication environment representative of our rapidly changing world. The Strategic Communications Planning Matrix is that methodological tool.

This strategic approach to communication planning and implementation must be appropriately placed in the overall context of long-term, relationship-based communication. Chapter one addresses the crisis of trust in our society and briefly traces the stages in the development of the communication function. It elevates relationship building to equal status with strategic planning and shows its application across all organizational communication. Chapter two reviews the principles of public information, public opinion and persuasion, and it discusses the ethical basis for an organization's communication within society. With this foundation laid, we can proceed to integrate the principles, concepts and skills of communications using the Strategic Communications Planning Matrix.

Chapter three discusses the methodologies of communication research and the diverse sources of information. Chapter four demonstrates how research is effectively used in planning and implementing communication. Chapter five turns our attention to setting the goals and objectives to accomplish any task or challenge set before us. Chapter six helps us understand and select those publics key to an organization's success and to develop the messages to build trust-based relationships with those publics necessary to our success. Chapter seven discusses the design of strategies and tactics to deliver messages and facilitate two-way communication with the organization's publics. Chapter eight demonstrates effective calendaring and budgeting. Chapter nine provides tips for effective implementation of our strategic communications plan. Chapter 10 focuses on what has been the very elusive methodology of evaluation and measurement of the effect of communications. Chapter 11 provides tips for giving business presentations. Chapter twelve addresses the importance of ethics and professionalism in effective communication. The text concludes with a sample campaign plan, found in Appendix A, that illustrates the effective use of the Strategic Communications Planning Matrix outlined in this text.

Appendix B provides 20 copy outlines for various communications tools and Appendix C contains the professional codes of ethics from the Public Relations Society of America, the American Marketing Association and the American Advertising Federation.

Although not the only approach to systematic and analytical communications problem solving, the Strategic Communications Planning Matrix is a highly effective and proven tool. The matrix approach provides a sound methodology for students and professionals alike to ensure communications planning is driven by research and analysis to reach and build relationships of trust with critical publics. The matrix also ensures the use of effective messages and delivery channels to meet an organization's communications challenges and opportunities.

fourth edition

STRATEGIC COMMUNICATIONS PLANNING

FOR EFFECTIVE PUBLIC RELATIONS AND MARKETING

COMMUNITY AND THE RELATIONSHIP-BUILDING APPROACH TO COMMUNICATIONS

> "Trust is the most basic element of
> social contact — the great intangible at
> the heart of truly long-term success."
> — Al Golin

40-year veteran of the public relations industry
and founder of Golin/Harris International

LEARNING IMPERATIVES

▸ To understand that an organization's survival is dependent upon establishing trust among key publics

▸ To understand the characteristics of a relationship-building approach to organizational communications

▸ To be introduced to the Strategic Communications Planning Matrix as a tool for planning and implementing organizational communication

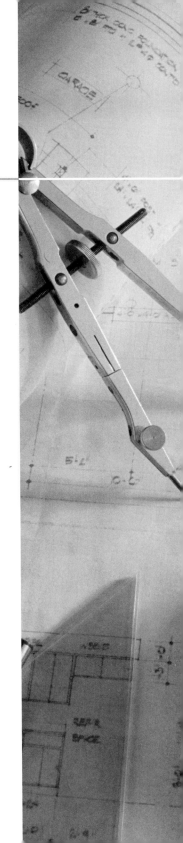

W̲e are in a new century, and the issue is trust. Actually, the issue has always been trust. Communication scholars, particularly those in the relationship-building school of public relations scholarship, have been telling us for decades that the issue is trust. And many public relations practitioners have been trying to convince corporate managers of that fact for years. Some executives followed that advice. But it took the events of the early part of this century — 9/11 and its effect on the economy, the demise of Enron, Worldcom, Arthur Andersen and others; the security brokers' scandal; mismanagement by mutual fund managers and many other similar events — for all sectors of our economy to finally realize that trust among an organization's publics is the single most important factor in organizational survival.

Now, in a crisis of trust, organizations are looking to their professional communicators for counsel on rebuilding the relationships that have eroded along with public trust. The bad news is that damage control is always more costly than damage prevention. The good news is that we finally have the top tier of executives in all kinds of organizations recognizing the need for an integrated approach to communication. No longer can we afford to separate marketing and advertising, human resources and public relations. Those organizational functions — all based in communication — require a strategic and integrated approach. All organizational communication must build — or rebuild — relationships with publics key to the organization's success.

> Trust

An emotional judgment of a person's credibility and performance on issues of importance.

In his recent book, "Trust or Consequences" (2004), Al Golin, a respected senior public relations professional, discusses his decades-long career counseling Chief Executive Officers (CEOs) of major corporations to be intimately involved in building relationships with all organizational publics. He asserts that trust is the key element of strong relationships that ensure organizational success in the long run. Mr. Golin's success with CEOs has been mixed. Many, like Ray Kroc of McDonald's, have followed his advice, making regular deposits in the "trust bank" and reaping significant benefits over the long-term. Others have disregarded his counsel in favor of short-term gains, leaving them ill-prepared and at risk when crises hit.

Nevertheless, in post-9/11 America, Mr. Golin's relationship-building approach is suddenly in high demand. And relationship building is fundamentally based on establishing trust with all organizational publics. That trust is established only when it becomes an organizational value tied to honesty and openness — a value that permeates the entire organization from the highest paid top executives through the lowest paid support and service people. It is an effort that integrates all the organization's communications functions — internal and external.

Fortunately, because we have been researching and preaching relationship building for years, public relations scholars and practitioners know how to integrate efforts to do what needs to be done. Rather than being fragmented by public as organizational functions have been in the past, we can integrate our approach to all the publics — both internal and external — for the organization to thrive over the long term. The roots of trust-based relationship building are in the literature and practice of public relations.

In the early 1900s when public relations emerged from the journalism profession as press representation for corporations, the public relations counselor was positioned as a key adviser to the CEO. As the administrative and management functions and staffing within business organizations grew, public relations became a "staff" function, rather than a more strategic line position. The loss of stature was in part due to early inability to demonstrate concretely, in terms of profits, the contribution of public relations to the organization's bottom line. Attorneys and accountants assumed the key advisory positions because communication with publics, with no tangible short-term benefit, was a luxury to be eliminated in times of financial difficulty. It was not viewed as strategic to the accomplishment of organizational goals. The logic was that products sold because consumers wanted them, not because of any organizational communication effort. Once relegated to a staff position public relations stayed there, even when business entered an era of keen market competition for products and services where communication now plays a primary role in sales.

> Public Relations

An organization's efforts to establish and maintain mutually beneficial relationships in order to communicate and cooperate with the publics upon whom long-term success depends.

In the last two decades, public relations professionals have been waging a battle to regain a strategic role. Part of that effort is a strong emphasis on research and evaluation to justify communications efforts in terms of their specific benefit to the accomplishment of the organizational mission. Another emerging value to organizations is the ability of communicators to manage issues that have affected the organization's focus on its primary business. And corporate management is recognizing the ability of communicators to manage certain organizational issues that do not respond to traditional economic and business principles and practices (Wilson, 1996; Wilson 1994a and 1994b). As a result of the crisis of trust, we have finally demonstrated the bottom-line effect of building relationships with publics. And we have justified our argument that ultimate organizational survival may depend upon building relationships over the long term.

What does it mean to be a "strategic" function?

In this chapter, we introduce the strategic planning process that drives the tactical decisions made by communications professionals. But first, we must understand what it means to be a strategic function.

Very simply, strategy is a well-coordinated approach to reaching an overall goal. It may be helpful to draw an analogy to military strategy. In a given battle, the overall goal may be to secure a certain piece of ground or a particular town. The strategy is the coordinated effort of all participants to achieve that goal. When an organization sets a particular goal in support of its mission, strategy serves to integrate the efforts of all departments to achieve the goal. Communications is strategic when it aids in formulating the organization's approach to accomplishing overall goals and then supports those efforts in a coordinated and consistent manner, working in concert with all other organizational entities.

To effectively function in that role requires solid research with results that drive decision making. It requires vision or a long-term rather than short-term mentality. Strategic functioning necessitates a broad perspective of the organizational environment and all contributing members. It

> ### > Strategic Function

One that contributes significantly to the accomplishment of an organization's mission and goals.

demands incisive understanding of the organizational mission and the goals that directly support the accomplishment of that mission. Finally, strategic functioning means that the communications and marketing efforts are driven by an understanding of the organization and where communications fits and coordinates with all other organizational functions. Strategic managers are analytical, pragmatic, visionary and perspicacious.

The development of communications and public relations functions in business organizations

Business organizations began giving serious attention to communication with publics in the early 1900s. Journalists began serving as press agents and publicists for major corporations such as Ford Motors and AT&T. By mid-century, public relations practitioners were organizational counselors, who responded to traditional American business management practices by manipulating the organization's environment, oftentimes in ways that might now be considered ethically questionable. By the 1960s, conflicts over issues important to key organizational publics gave birth to crisis management as a key function of the organization's communicators. Rather than just reacting to crises, good managers began to anticipate problems and mediate them before they could affect the organization's environment and profitability.

Issue management was born as a long-term approach to identifying and resolving issues before they became problems or crises. The very concept of issue management fit well into traditional American business management techniques, based almost entirely on economic principles. Nevertheless, there was obvious conflict between the long-term nature of issue management and the short-term orientation of American business management. Further, there was a more critical conflict between the self-interested rather than public-interested approach of American business communication and the publics who were beginning to demand accountability.

> **Crisis Management**

The process of anticipating and preparing to mediate problems that could affect an organization's environment and profitability.

> **Issue Management**

A long-term approach to identifying and resolving issues before they become problems or crises.

In spite of the conflict, issue management techniques became popular in business communications practice, and gave birth to the role of communication in strategic management, which evaluates all proposed action through a focus on organizational goals, usually defined in short-term contributions to the bottom line. Even though issues must be identified years in advance to be effectively mediated, as depicted in Hainsworth's issue cycle (1990), the purpose is to save the organization future difficulty, not to address the needs of organizational publics because they are intrinsically valued. This focus in communication brought us squarely into the camp of purely economically based rationalist business management.

It is not surprising that the organizational communications ended up here. Throughout its history, public relations and business communications have consistently moved away from a "relations" orientation. Even with all of our technological advances, we have been slow to recognize the limitations of mass communication and mass media. We resisted a shift from using mass media to more targeted media, which means we have not been accessing appropriate message channels to reach many of our publics. Some of us still tend to see publics as an inert mass, hypnotized by mass media, mindlessly absorbing our messages and acting on them.

Dramatic social changes in our society and the increasing influence of publics have been ignored almost entirely. Partially as a reaction to the economic (bottom line) orientation of strategic management and partially as a result of international trends in business, some scholars in the 1990s attempted to shift our emphasis in public relations to relationship building, particularly those in the critical school (Creedon, 1991; Kruckeberg and Starck, 1988; Wilson, 1996 and 2001). They have returned to the roots of human communication and persuasion in devising approaches that build more personal relationships based on trust and cooperation, viewing segmented and personalized communication as more viable approaches to publics than mass communication.

> **Strategic Management**

The process of evaluating all proposed action by focusing on organizational goals, usually defined in short-term contributions to the bottom line.

The synthesis of strategic planning and relationship building

The limitations of the strategic management approach to communications are in its ties to traditional American business management. Nevertheless, that approach made sense in what has been a prevailing mood in American business and in communications to control the environment and organizational influences to maintain or increase bottom-line profits.

Although the business environment of the past few decades has been imperative in the growth and development of our society and is responsible for our high standard of living, the social problems resulting from the loss of "community" are affecting American business in ways that prohibit it from operating as it has. In the 1990s, the negative effects of social problems changed the environment that business had controlled and within which it operated relatively untouched. Then as the new century opened and we experienced the crisis of trust, business has had to pay attention to relationships with publics that are imperative for organizational survival.

> Relationship Building

A return to the roots of human communication and persuasion that focuses on personal trust and mutual cooperation.

Societal trends affecting the practice of business, communications and public relations

Five trends in society should have led us to our roots in communication and relationships long ago, instead of causing us to align as we have with rationalist business management methods with their singular focus on profit.

The first trend is increasingly segmented publics requiring alternatives to traditional media channels for the dissemination of messages. In fact, our study of audience has indicated that even within the groups segmented by demographics and psychographics, we find smaller segments which have been labeled interpretive communities (Lindloff, 1988) because of differences among them in the ways they receive, interpret and act upon messages.

The second trend is dramatically escalating social problems that no longer affect only fringe or marginalized groups in society. The productivity of the workforce of corporate America is seriously jeopardized by problems affecting families such as drug abuse, physical abuse, gangs, teen pregnancy and the declining quality of education. When such problems begin to affect the workforce — as they do now — they threaten the profit potential of the organization and must be addressed.

The third trend is an increased reliance on organizational communicators to establish relationships with publics to mediate issues. The business environment has become increasingly burdened with social issues and problems that corporations have failed to control using traditional management techniques. They are beginning to form alliances with communities, government and special interest groups to address societal problems. These actions are ostensibly in the name of social responsibility, but a more accurate justification of the establishment of cooperative efforts is probably that corporations have been unable to solve those problems unilaterally.

The fourth trend leading us to a relationship-based approach to business management and communications is that business entities in the United States now face a more knowledgeable and business-savvy public that is demanding corporate commitment of resources to solve the problems affecting the community, employees and their families. In fact, some would say that the public understands just enough about the operation of business to be dangerous. They are aware of corporate profits (although not always cognizant of net profits versus gross revenues), and are applying pressure for organizations to provide resources to solve the problems faced by communities.

> **Misinformation**

Information that is unintentionally inaccurate or misleading.

The fifth and final trend requiring mutually beneficial relationships with our publics is their previously mentioned control over access to information. Whereas more limited channels of mass media place control in the organization, today's consumer has more personal control over what information he/she receives. Withholding information in today's technological society is virtually impossible. Controlling information or the "spin" on information is also unlikely when publics have multiple sources from which to secure information. This makes misinformation and disinformation from external sources a significant concern for organizations. Building trust-based relationships with publics is the only approach that results in sustained credibility.

Essentially, then, we in communications and marketing must begin to think of our publics in terms of strategic communities. Wilson (1996 and 2001) contends we must begin to approach our publics as strategic cooperative communities, focusing on relationship-based interaction among all members of a community to achieve individual and collective goals.

Building relationships with publics

From the synthesis of the strategic management approach and the strategic cooperative communities model, five characteristics emerge to typify organizations operating within this style of management.

1. The first characteristic is **long-range vision**. Rather than selecting key publics and critical issues by their immediate effect on the organization, companies are beginning to identify all potential organizational publics and systematically establishing relationships. They are using their relationships to identify the issues that will be critical in the next century, not just the next decade. They are implementation-oriented and have a respect for people. They work toward a consensus for action.

2. Next is a **commitment to community**, not just to profit. Companies involved in the community are often led by a CEO who is personally committed to charitable work. Commitment at this high level gives the organization's community involvement strength and integrity because it is based on a sincere desire to serve rather than to manipulate for the sake of profit alone. It is understood that what is good for or improves the community almost always benefits the company as well.

3. Underlying this community commitment is an organizational value orientation emphasizing the **importance of people**. Progressive policies and initiatives based on trust of and respect for employees

> Disinformation

Information that is intentionally inaccurate or misleading.

are usually evidence of a people-first orientation. Human dignity is highly valued and policies and procedures are designed accordingly.

4. The fourth characteristic is **cooperative problem-solving**. The company values employees who will work together to solve problems. Employees are given the latitude to design and implement solutions within their work areas, relying on management to provide an overall vision. In such an environment, employees are not afraid to make a mistake because management understands that mistakes are indicative of an effort to progressively solve problems.

5. Lastly, such organizations build **relationships with all of their publics** based on mutual respect, trust and human dignity, not just on self-interested gain. These relationships engender an environment in which community members seek solutions where all participants win. The community begins to look out for the best interests of the organization because it is in the community's best interest for the organization to thrive.

> Strategic
Cooperative
Communities

Relationship-based interaction among all members of a community to achieve individual and collective goals.

Relationships with an organization's public are based on critical values that have little to do with profit motivation. The values of service, respect and concern for community are at the base of the relationships we establish with people. Whether we build a relationship with an individual, or with an individual representing an organization, does not change the fact that the strength of the association is determined by the salience of shared values that place a priority on people.

It is important to note that durable relationships are not created out of rationalist, bottom-line business management techniques. They are created and strengthened through mutual trust, respect, cooperation and benefit. Trust of a community actor is based on honest communication and cooperation. Trust is a prerequisite of cooperative relationships as well as a tangible result. It naturally follows that an actor's credibility is based on the perceptions of other community members regarding the trustworthiness of that actor's words and actions. Theirs is an inherently emotional judgment of the actor's performance on the issues of importance to the community.

The Strategic Communications Planning Matrix

Given this framework for approaching integrated organizational communications within an overarching scheme of relationships cultivated with all publics, we can now turn to planning specific initiatives to solve specific challenges or take advantage of emergent opportunities. Now that we have established a strategic role for communications in developing relationships, or cooperative communities, we are able to implement the planning that will accomplish specific objectives and is targeted at specific publics immediately important to the organization. If we have worked to identify and assess our strategic relationships, the selection of key publics for any particular communications or marketing effort will be simplified and much more accurate. We have less chance of omitting a critical public, and we know more about all of our publics so part of our research is already done. We are also better prepared to send messages because our relationships with organizational publics have been maintained and strengthened in our overall approach to marketing and communications.

A strategic, analytical approach to an organization's communication has long been needed. Public relations has used the four-step RACE model — research, action planning, communications and evaluation — but making that process truly analytical, so that each step is determined by the information acquired and decisions made in previous steps, has been a challenge. Incorporating feedback during implementation and making needed alterations to ensure success has been even more difficult. We have struggled in communications to become research-based. We have succeeded somewhat in becoming research-oriented. But until the research obtained has been saliently interpreted and applied to the decision making processes in our planning and implementation, we are not research-based.

It is not enough to discover the attitudes, values and beliefs of a segmented demographic public; we must interpret those in terms of the issue or problem at hand and predict behavior. Determining that a public's self-interest regarding a certain issue is the health and welfare of its children

> **Strategic Communications Planning**

An approach to communications planning that focuses actions on the accomplishment of organizational goals.

> **Research-based**

When decision making in the planning and implementation process is based on the acquisition, interpretation and application of relevant facts.

10–STEP STRATEGIC COMMUNICATIONS PLANNING MATRIX

> Research

1. Background	Planning begins with a synthesis of primary and secondary research providing background information on the industry, external environment, product or program, market situation and current trends in opinions and attitudes. The background section also identifies and profiles potential publics that may be affected by the problem/opportunity or could aid in its resolution/accomplishment. Intervening publics and available resources are also identified.
2. Situation Analysis	The situation analysis consists of two paragraphs. The first paragraph is a statement of the current situation and a description of the challenge or opportunity based on research. The second paragraph identifies the potential difficulties and related problems.
3. Core Problem/ Opportunity	The core problem/opportunity is a one-sentence statement of the main difficulty or prospect — including potential consequences if not resolved or realized.

> Action Planning

4. Goal and Objectives	The goal is a one-sentence statement of the end to be achieved to resolve the core problem or seize a significant opportunity. The goal does not have to be stated in quantifiable terms. Objectives are numbered or bulleted statements of specific results that will lead to the achievement of the goal. Objectives must be: specific, measurable, attainable, time-bound and mission-driven.
5. Key Publics and Messages	Key publics include a description of each audience that must be reached to achieve the goal and objectives. Four elements should be identified for each public or audience: 1. Demographic and psychographic profile 2. Motivating self-interests 3. Status of current relationship with the organization and issue 4. Third party influentials and other opinion leaders Messages are public-specific and appeal to the public's self-interests. They are designed to be primary or secondary. Primary messages are one or two sentence summary statements similar to sound bites. Secondary messages are bulleted details that add credibility to and support the primary messages with facts, testimonials, examples, etc.

matrix

| 6. Strategies and Tactics | Strategies identify approaches to send messages to each public through specific channels in order to motivate action. Multiple strategies may be required for each public.

Tactics are communications tools and tasks required to support each strategy. Each strategy is supported by a number of tactics designed to convey key messages to a specific public through the communications channel outlined in the strategy. |
|---|---|
| 7. Calendar | Calendaring should be done with a time-task matrix (such as a Gantt chart) used to plan and strategically integrate the timing of implementation. The calendar should be organized by public and strategy with scheduling for each tactic. |
| 8. Budget | Budgets should also be organized by public and strategy. The budget projects the specific cost of each tactic. It should also indicate where costs will be offset by donations or sponsorships. Subtotals should be provided for each strategy and public. |

> Communication

9. Communication Confirmation	The communications confirmation table confirms the logic of the plan by converting it into short statements for each public in tabular form. This format (see below) aids in checking strategies and tactics to make sure they are appropriate to reach the public, that messages appeal to the public's self-interest and that the planning for each public meets the objectives.

Key Public	Self-Interests	Primary Messages	Influentials	Objectives	Strategies	Tactics

> Evaluation

10. Evaluation Criteria and Tools	Evaluation criteria are the specific measures used to determine the success of each objective. Evaluation tools are the specific methods used to gather the data identified by each criterion. The evaluation tools should be included in the calendar and budget.

> Analytical Process

A process in which action in
each step is determined by
the information acquired
and decisions made
in previous steps.

is of no use unless we then formulate messages that emphasize the health and welfare of the public's children. Identifying certain targeted media as the best channels to deliver messages to a segmented public does us no good if we then shotgun the message through mass media anyway.

The Strategic Communications Planning Matrix introduced in this chapter was developed by the faculty at Brigham Young University. It was designed to direct problem solving analytically, using research to make decisions in each step of communication planning and implementation. The matrix is the tool we use throughout this book to support the strategic communications planning process. The process begins with the identification of a problem or opportunity that sets the stage for background research and a situation analysis based on the research. It outlines additional research necessary for decision making that will take place in the planning and implementation processes.

The planning process then starts with setting a goal that directly resolves the identified challenge. This goal may or may not be a tangible measurable outcome. You next move forward to determine objectives — specific and measurable outcomes — that will ensure the accomplishment of the goal. Based on research, key publics are selected, messages determined and strategies and tactics designed to send those messages. Calendaring, budgeting and evaluation are also addressed in a strategic way, using research as the foundation for decisions in each step.

The Strategic Communications Planning Matrix enables professionals in communications and marketing to address problems and issues of concern to organizations in a strategic way, in concert with the overall organizational goals and objectives. It is enhanced by the understanding of how each organizational public forms a strategic relationship. Planning is simplified because of the nature and direction of the cooperative relationships already established, and implementation is made easier because of established channels of interaction and a predisposition on the part of the publics within cooperative communities to give heed to the organization's messages.

SUMMARY

The world business community is in a crisis of trust. We arrived at this position by neglecting the relationships that are key to our success. We neglected those relationships because we were so focused on short-term profit measures that we were unable to see the necessity of strong, trust-based relationships as crucial to long-term survival.

In the past few years, public relations scholars and communications professionals have been struggling to return the practice of the organization's communication to its strategic role and function. Recognizing that we evolved away from, rather than toward, the strategic counseling role we should be serving, we have examined our roots in communication as well as current trends in business, society and technology.

Essentially, we are now at a point of synthesis where we may finally accept our role as builders of relationships strategic to the organization. We must systematically track the status of those relationships to ensure appropriate allocation of resources over the long term. Within the context of those relationships, we can more effectively use traditional analytical and strategic planning to solve organizational problems. The Strategic Communications Planning Matrix provides the tool to approach all communications problems, challenges and opportunities within the trust-based relationship framework of today's successful organizations.

CHAPTER ONE EXERCISES

1. Discuss the corporations in your community and the national and international issues they have become active in resolving. Why do you think they selected those particular issues to address?

2. Select one or two local corporations actively doing business in your locality. Imagine yourself in the position of the corporate communications counselor and identify the strategic relationships of those organizations, and assess the status of those relationships.

REFERENCES AND ADDITIONAL READINGS

Creedon, P.J. (1991). "Public relations and 'women's work:' Toward a feminist analysis of public relations roles." *Public Relations Research Annual*, 3, 67-84. Hillsdale, NJ: Lawrence Erlbaum Associates.

Cutlip, S., Center, A., & Broom, G. (2000). *Effective Public Relations* (8th ed.). Englewood Cliffs, NJ: Prentice-Hall, Inc.

Golin, A. (2004). *Trust or Consequences: Build Trust Today or Lose Your Market Tomorrow*. New York: AMACOM.

Grunig, J. E., & Hunt, T. (1984). *Managing Public Relations*. Fort Worth, Texas: Holt Rinehart & Winston.

Grunig, J.E., & Repper, F. (1992). "Strategic management, publics, and issues." In J.E. Grunig (ed.), *Excellence In Public Relations and Communication Management* (pp. 117-158). Hillsdale, NJ: Lawrence Erlbaum Associates.

Hainsworth, B.E. (1990). "The distribution of advantages and disadvantages." *Public Relations Review*, 16:1, 33-39.

Hainsworth, B.E. & Wilson, L.J. (1992). *Strategic program planning. Public Relations Review*, 18:1, 9-15.

Heath, R.L., & Cousino, K.R. (1990). "Issues management: End of first decade progress report." *Public Relations Review*, 16:1, 6-18.

Kruckeberg, D. & Starck, K. (1988). *Public Relations and Community: A Reconstructed Theory*. New York: Praeger.

Lindloff, T.R. (1988). "Media audiences as interpretive communities." N.J. Anderson (ed.), *Communication Yearbook*, 11, 81-107. Newbury Park, CA: Sage Publications.

Lukaszewski, J.E., & Serie, T.L. (1993b). "Relationships built on understanding core values." *Waste Age,* March, 83-94.

Newsom, D., Turk J.V., & Kruckeberg, D. (2004). *This Is PR: The Realities of Public Relations* (8th ed.). Belmont, CA: Wadsworth Publishing Company.

Norris, J.S. (1984). *Public Relations*. Englewood Cliffs, N.J.: Prentice-Hall, Inc.

Wilcox, D. L., Ault, P. H., & Agee, W. K. (2002). *Public Relations: Strategies and Tactics* (7th ed.). New York: Harper and Row.

Wilson, L.J. (1994a). "Excellent companies and coalition-building among the Fortune 500: A value- and relationship-based theory." *Public Relations Review*, 20:4.

Wilson, L.J. (1994b). "The return to gemeinschaft: Toward a theory of public relations and corporate community relations as relationship-building." In A.F. Alkhafaji (ed.), *Business Research Yearbook: Global Business Perspectives*, Vol. I (pp. 135-141). Lanham, Maryland: International Academy of Business Disciplines and University Press of America.

Wilson, L.J. (1996). "Strategic cooperative communities: A synthesis of strategic, issue management, and relationship-building approaches in public relations." In H.M. Culbertson and N. Chen (eds.), *International Public Relations: A Comparative Analysis*. Hillsdale, N.J.: Lawrence Erlbaum Associates.

Wilson, L.J. (2001). "Relationships within communities: Public relations for the next century." In R. Heath (ed.), *Handbook of Public Relations*. Newbury Park, Calif.: Sage Publications, pp. 521-526.

chapter **2**

PUBLIC INFORMATION AND PERSUASIVE COMMUNICATION

"Public sentiment is everything. With
public sentiment, nothing can fail; without it, nothing can succeed."
— Abraham Lincoln

16th President of the United States

LEARNING IMPERATIVES

▸ To understand the role of public opinion and its impact on successful communication with an organization's publics

▸ To understand the principles underlying persuasion and how to use
them to change behavior

▸ To understand the legitimate role of advocacy in a free market economy and the ethical standards that apply to persuasive communication

A s communications professionals, we are in the public information and persuasion business. The ethical basis of marketing and public relations is in advocacy. We play a critical role in the free marketplace of ideas as we provide information and advocate products, services or issues honestly, responsibly and in accordance with public and consumer interest.

Because we are engaged in public information and persuasion, what we do is inextricably tied to public opinion. What publics think and believe directly affects how they behave. As we established in the previous chapter, an organization that ignores the opinions of its publics simply will not build sufficient trust to survive in today's society. Although this text is not designed to be a comprehensive treatment of the theories and models of public opinion and persuasion, understanding some of the basic principles identified in that literature is requisite to successful persuasive communications efforts. Here we mention and synthesize relevant ideas. The references will provide the reader more depth and detail. Nevertheless, because our circumstances and our actions are so shaped by the force of this phenomenon, we should understand what public opinion is, how it is formed, who influences it and how we should deal with it.

Behavior: the ultimate objective

As important as public opinion is, the savvy communications professional will always remember that behavior is the final evaluation. According to practitioner Larry Newman, in public relations we are ultimately trying to get people to do something we want them to do, not to do something we don't want them to do, or to let us do something we want to do. Knowing what our publics think is only useful insofar as it leads us to accurately predict what they will do. Even when we simply disseminate information in the public interest, we do so with some behavioral expectation in mind. We must determine what behavior we are trying to influence, and then lay the groundwork to get there. The late Pat Jackson (1990) developed the Behavioral Public Relations Model (figure 2.1) that is equally applicable to all motivational communication efforts.

> Triggering Event

An event that transforms readiness to act into actual behavior.

The awareness stage is the communication process itself. Publicity, advertising, publications and other communication tools help to create awareness and reinforcement. They should be designed to tie the message into people's existing perceptions and attitudes, or to adjust those attitudes if necessary. Awareness efforts must be based on quality research to determine the attitudes and perceptions that are the foundation for a certain public's behavior or potential behavior. From this awareness, people begin to formulate a readiness to act according to their attitudes and the influence of the communication. Action itself requires some kind of triggering event such as Election Day in a political campaign or a sale at a clothing store. The event thus transforms readiness into actual behavior.

Studies done by James Grunig (1983) in the early 1980s concluded that publics can be identified by similarities in their communication behavior, but that the behavioral characteristics that segment them are unrelated to demographics. In his research, he consistently identified four types of situational behavioral publics:

- All-issue publics (active on any and all issues)
- Apathetic publics (inactive and disinterested)
- Single-issue publics (active on one or a few issues)
- Hot-issue publics (bandwagon jumpers)

The notion that publics coalesce and emerge from situations is an important one, particularly as we deal with crisis communication and

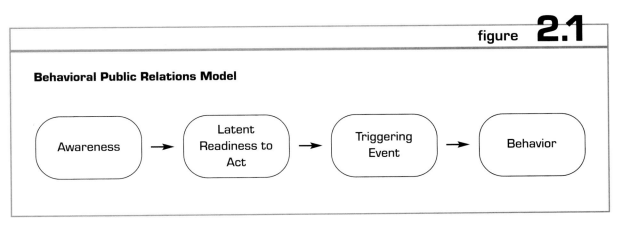

figure **2.1**

Behavioral Public Relations Model

Awareness → Latent Readiness to Act → Triggering Event → Behavior

management. Psychographics may be of more help in profiling these kinds of publics than demographics, but even psychographics may be of limited worth when segmenting publics by issue.

As we will see in the next several chapters, behavior is the ultimate objective. The Strategic Communications Planning Matrix leads us through the steps to motivate behavior. It helps to determine which publics we need to target and what messages will shape their latent readiness to act. It also aids in designing the specific strategies and tactics to deliver those messages and to provide the triggering event. And, it helps us use opinion leaders or a public's "influentials" in the persuasion process.

What is public opinion?

> **Public Opinion**

Attitudes expressed by a majority of people in a particular group about an issue that affects them.

Before we address motivating behavior, let's first investigate the communication process beginning with what people think and how opinions and attitudes translate to behavior. Extensive psychological and sociological studies have been done on the phenomenon of public opinion. Its measurement in an attempt to predict behavior has become not only a science but also a highly profitable business. Most of the descriptions of the phenomenon contain similar elements and can be synthesized into a straightforward definition: Public opinion is the collection of beliefs, attitudes and opinions expressed by the majority of individuals within a particular group or public about a particular issue or topic of current interest to the individuals in that group.

Let's examine the elements of this definition:

- Public opinion is collective. It is not what just one individual thinks, it is the collection of what several people think.
- The beliefs and ideas must be expressed to be public opinion. Public discussion usually crystallizes opinion into something that can be expressed.
- The opinion must be held by the majority of individuals within the group.
- The opinion is identified with a certain group or public, not the mass

or "whoever" is out there. The particular public holding the opinion is identifiable from the mass.

- The opinion is centered on a particular issue or topic.
- The masses are segmented into publics differently from topic to topic. The issue of abortion will create within the mass audience certain public segmentations that will be different than those created by the issue of Palestinian sovereignty in Israel.
- The topic must hold a particular interest to the individuals within the group, or it must involve their self-interest.
- Interest is typically aroused and sustained by events relating to the topic or issue. The abortion debate heats up when pro-life advocates picket abortion clinics. At some point the picketing becomes so common it no longer draws attention. But the debate is again fueled when a doctor practicing at an abortion clinic is attacked by the group.

Opinion formation

Because public opinion is a collection of individual opinions, the logical place for us to begin in determining how public opinion is formed is with the individual. A review of the basic models and principles of human communication will aid us in determining how individuals form opinions.

Opinion is basically a thought process. We attach meaning to the world around us based on a collection of our past experience, knowledge, culture and environment. This collection is often referred to as our frame of reference. It is within this frame of reference that we establish our own personal beliefs, values and attitudes. All of our thoughts, ideas and communicative acts are processed through our frame of reference, and no two individual frames of reference are identical. Our frame of reference determines how we perceive or sense our world, and the communication of others directed toward us.

In the mid-1940s, Hadley Cantril (1944) proposed 15 "laws" of public opinion that are still relevant today. Those laws can be synthesized into a few basic observations that serve as guidelines in persuasive communication aimed at shaping public opinion.

> Frame of Reference

The collection of experiences, knowledge, culture and environment that forms our perceptual screen.

- Opinions are more easily influenced by events than words, but opinion changed by events requires subsequent reinforcement.
- Opinion is basically determined by self-interest, and persuasion is only effective if it maintains a consistent appeal to self-interest over time. Opinion rooted in self-interest is extremely difficult to change.
- Information is most effective when opinion is in formative stages.
- If people already trust their leaders, they will allow them the opportunity to handle sensitive situations. People trust their leaders' decision making more when they feel they (the people) have had a part in shaping the decision.
- Public opinion is focused more on expected results than in methods to achieve those results. People care more about an outcome than the process to reach the outcome.

Elisabeth Noelle-Neumann (1984) has identified another phenomenon of public opinion we characterize here as the "sleeper" effect. An individual's fear of social rejection or isolation may cause him/her not to verbalize opinion he/she perceives to be in the minority. In other words, vocal groups may suppress mainstream or majority opinions because the majority believes itself to be in the minority and, therefore, remains silent. This "spiral of silence" as Noelle-Neumann termed it, or the "silent majority" as Richard Nixon called it, is a sleeper factor usually unaccounted for in our research unless we dig for it. Noelle-Neumann identified mass media as an accomplice in the spiral of silence because their own voice may often reflect the minority opinion, but it has become one of the loudest and most dominant voices in the free marketplace of ideas.

Once the spiral of silence is broken, the silenced opinion flows forth like water from a breached dam. The authors believe this phenomenon was observed recently with the establishment of the "Do Not Call" registry. Prior to the registry, most people tolerated unwanted phone calls from telemarketers, opinion researchers, fund-raisers and other phone solicitors because they felt they needed to be polite. Once the idea of a Do Not Call list drew national attention, people began refusing any unwanted call, whether it was prohibited by the registry or not. Once people found out that the majority of people felt the same way, they gave themselves permission to refuse to be disturbed by unwanted phone calls. They no longer suppressed their opinion and the result is the probable collapse of phone solicitation as an industry.

The phenomenon of perception

Perception is an unpredictable phenomenon, largely because it is so individually determined. Unless you have a solid understanding of an individual's frame of reference, it is impossible to predict how he/she will perceive an event, experience or message. In communication we sometimes forget that meaning is in people. Our words and messages do not transfer meaning; they can only invoke images in the minds of our public that we hope will have similar individual meanings.

In addition to being very individual, perception also carries with it the power of truth. What is perceived by an individual is what he/she believes to be true. We express this in clichés such as "seeing is believing," but the impact of perception is far greater than we usually realize. Whether or not a perception is accurate has no bearing on its existence as truth to the perceiver. Like the blind men who encountered the elephant, each perceived the animal through senses other than sight, and each was certain in his perceptions and descriptions.

Sometimes perception is so intimately tied to an individual's belief and value system that it is difficult, if not impossible, to alter it even when it is flawed. Norris calls these "cast-iron" perceptions. He comments:

> Galileo once got himself into a great deal of trouble with the hierarchy of the Catholic Church. Despite his scientific proof, it was simply inconvenient for the Church at that time to accept the perception of the earth as revolving around the [sun]. And you remember the trouble Columbus had with his sailors? They had the unshakable perception of the world as being flat, and had no desire to discover where the outer edge was (1984, p. 5).

Some perceptions are shared with others in a group and are "pre-formed." We have already decided how certain things should be and that is the way we perceive them. We call these stereotypes. We often stereotype people (i.e., dumb blondes or computer nerds), but other phenomena can be stereotyped as well (i.e., government is wasteful or political revolution is bad). Stereotypes are often useful in helping us deal with the world around us, but they become dangerous when they prevent us from perceiving things as they really are, and when they create an environment in which people are denied the opportunity to reach their potential.

As public relations professionals, we should also be aware of Klapper's concepts of selective exposure, selective perception and selective retention. Because of the barrage of stimuli we receive from our environment, including increasing numbers of messages from people trying to persuade us to do something, our perceptual mechanism also works as a screen or a filter to keep us from experiencing overload. We choose the media we pay attention to and those stimuli we want to perceive as well as those we want to retain. This is a critical principle in marketing, advertising and public relations. Our professions depend on channels to get messages to target publics, but if those publics are electing not to perceive or retain our messages, our efforts are useless.

> **Selective
Perception**

The inherent human function of selecting from the millions of daily stimuli only those messages one chooses to perceive.

For example, think about how you read a newspaper. Few people read a newspaper word for word, first page to last. As you flip through the pages, you read headlines or look at pictures to decide which stories you want to read. In advertising, you pay attention to those ads that interest you for some reason or another. Individuals selectively perceive far fewer messages than are targeted at them in a given day, and they actually retain even less of the content once those messages have been filtered through the perceptual screen to determine whether or not they are useful. In fact, studies of selective perception in advertising demonstrated that people actually pay more attention to ads and consume more information about a product after they have purchased it than before. Just as agenda setting theory predicts, they are looking for reinforcement of their purchase decision.

Selective perception becomes an even more poignant phenomenon when we consider how new technologies have given the consumer, or public, control over how and if he/she receives information. As people seek information less from mass media and more from increasingly specialized and segmented sources, we must become more sophisticated in appealing to their self-interests. The uses and gratifications theory identifies three motives for media use: environmental surveillance, environmental diversion and environmental interaction. A basic assumption of the theory is that people choose how media will serve them and use media for those purposes.

What all this means for communications professionals is that we must make a greater effort to understand the frames of reference of our target publics, use good research to try to predict how messages and events will be perceived by those publics and design messages that those publics will select, retain and act upon.

Attitudes, values and beliefs

Integral to our frame of reference is the value and belief system upon which attitudes are based. One of the best explanations of human behavior and possibly the finest theory on attitude and attitude change was developed by Milton Rokeach. In this theory, beliefs are the fundamental building blocks of attitudes. Beliefs are inferences we make about ourselves and about the world. Rokeach asserted that some beliefs are more central to an individual's cognitive system than others. These core beliefs, or values, are typically well-established and relatively stable. They are very difficult to change because they are most salient to the individual and his/her belief system. They function as "life guides," determining both our daily behavior and our life goals.

According to Rokeach, collections of beliefs organized around a focal point (like an issue, an event or a person) constitute an attitude. He identifies two kinds: attitudes toward objects and attitudes toward situations. The combination of these two kinds of attitudes will determine an individual's behavior in any given situation. Rokeach uses gardening as an example. The collection of an individual's beliefs — that gardening is fun,

> **> Selective Retention**

The inherent human function of selecting from the hundreds of stimuli perceived only those messages one chooses to retain.

that it saves money, that it releases tension and that it produces beautiful flowers — will result in a favorable attitude toward gardening. Given the absence of intervening attitudes, a person's collection of beliefs and resultant attitudes will motivate his/her gardening behavior.

> Beliefs

Inferences we make about ourselves and the world around us.

For communications professionals to motivate behavior then, requires that they understand and tap into core beliefs and values that shape attitudes. In some cases, we may need to change beliefs and attitudes. Remembering that core beliefs are difficult to change, we may try to tap into a value and base the alteration of peripheral beliefs on that central belief. We may also need to motivate people to change the depth of a belief or value to help us build a foundation for attitude change. At any rate, it is important for us to recognize that people do not do something just because we want them to do it. They behave in their own self-interest according to their own beliefs and attitudes. Changing behavior requires addressing those beliefs and attitudes.

Another set of theories that aid us in understanding how to change attitudes are the balance or cognitive consistency theories. Basically this body of research has found that people are comfortable when their beliefs, attitudes, knowledge and behaviors are consistent. The presence of conflict among those cognitive elements creates discomfort or dissonance. Leon Festinger contends that when the cognitive elements are in conflict, people tend to reduce or eliminate the dissonance by changing the elements or introducing new elements (like new information).

> Values

Core beliefs or beliefs central to an individual's cognitive system.

The classic example is that of a smoker. In today's environment with today's information, smoking behavior potentially causes great dissonance or conflict in the cognitive processes. The smoker will try to reduce the dissonance. One way would be to change one or more of the cognitive elements (like behavior) by stopping smoking. Another way would be to add a new element, like switching to a pipe which is perceived to be less harmful. A third way is to see the cognitive elements as less important than they used to be (i.e., longer life isn't such a desirable belief if I have to give up pleasure to achieve it). A fourth method would be to seek consonant information such as evidence contradicting the health hazard studies. Fifth, you might reduce the conflict among cognitive elements by distorting or misinterpreting (misperceiving) the information available on the ill effects of smoking. Finally, you have the option to flee the situation, or simply refuse to contemplate the conflict thereby avoiding the dissonance.

If we understand these cognitive processes, we are better able to work with people to bring about cognitive consonance. The process of changing the cognitive elements is the process of persuasion. We may conclude that the art of persuasion, to be effective in motivating behavior, must be implemented at the most basic level of public opinion: at the level of individual beliefs and attitudes.

> Attitudes

Collections of beliefs organized around a focal point that predisposes behavior.

Measuring public opinion

Saturday Review/World columnist Charles Frankel said, "Majority opinion is a curious and elusive thing." It is certainly not stable. It changes from moment to moment as circumstances are constantly changing. For that reason alone, any measure of public opinion is never absolutely accurate. The moment the survey is completed, the interviews are concluded and the focus groups are dismissed, the results are dated material.

James Stimson (1991), a well-known scholar in the field of public opinion measurement, contends that most measures are not accurate predictors of behavior because they measure attitudes and opinions in isolation from other members of the social group. He points out that individuals may formulate opinions on issues when approached, but those opinions are altered, refined and crystallized through discussion and interaction with others. Additionally, people do not behave in isolation; they are part of social systems that strongly influence behavior.

The Coca-Cola Company learned this lesson the hard way when they introduced "new" Coke in 1985 (Schindler, 1992). Taste tests demonstrated a taste preference for the new formula. In opinion surveys, people expressed the belief that if the majority preferred the new formula then Coke should change to it. But a curious phenomenon occurred in the focus groups. When the groups began discussion, participants favored a formula change as they did in the opinion surveys. Then, as some members of the groups began to voice their preference for the old formula, the overriding value of personal choice caused individuals within the focus groups to change their attitudes to support the rights of those who preferred the old formula (either because of taste or out of habit) to purchase it.

Because quantitative opinion surveys were judged to provide more credible data than qualitative research, Coca-Cola trusted them instead of the focus groups, changed the formula and scheduled a phasing out of the old. For the first couple of weeks people accepted the new formula; then the outcry of the masses for the right of the old Coke loyalists forced the company not only to create "Classic Coke" to leave the old formula on the market but also to eventually scale back its production of new Coke. That is exactly what should have been predicted from observing the focus groups. Opinion surveys that measure opinion and predict behavior in isolation from the group may be inherently flawed.

Further, the opinion expressed by individuals in a public may reflect a number of realities other than the opinion on that particular issue. The expression may be indicative of party or organizational loyalty, peer group pressure to conform or a reflection of the opinion of an influential whose judgment the respondent may trust more than his/her own. And, the combination of beliefs and attitudes that are the basis for behavior are far more complex and multidimensional than a singular opinion on a particular topic. Opinions do not necessarily directly lead to behavior. Too many other factors, events and attitudes intervene. Unless the measuring device is carefully designed and implemented, it may not measure the most salient opinion and resultant behavior. The results will be misleading, causing costly strategic errors.

In spite of the difficulties, we must still do our best to measure public attitudes and opinions as a foundation for persuasive efforts. Measurement problems are identified to aid us in designing research that corrects for and minimizes the difficulties, to help us understand and better interpret results, and to design programs that are flexible enough to respond to changing opinion ascertained either through feedback or continuing research. The methods for measuring public attitudes and opinion are described more fully in the next chapter. The most typical are survey research, which yields statistical results, and personal interviews and focus group research, which provide qualitative results.

METHODS OF PERSUASION

More often than not in today's environment, public relations engages in disseminating information rather than in persuasion. Knowledge and information are key cognitive elements that help shape attitudes and opinion. Further, public information provides the awareness foundation necessary for persuasion to effectively motivate publics. Nevertheless, sometimes even objective information of benefit to a public must be designed and delivered in such a way as to draw the attention of publics accustomed to filtering out messages to prevent overload. The message itself may not be designed to persuade, but the targeted publics may need to be persuaded to pay attention to the message.

Newsom, Turk and Kruckeberg (2004) contend that people are motivated to action through power, patronage or persuasion. Power may be legitimate authority, peer group pressure or informal status. Patronage is simply paying for the desired behavior, either monetarily, in kind or by favor. Persuasion, the method most used by public relations, typically involves information dissemination and devises appeals to change attitudes and opinions to achieve the desired behavior.

Methods and approaches to persuading typically focus on getting a public to pay attention to a message, accept it and retain it. Yet persuasive attempts fall short if they do not address motivating behavior. Carl Hovland's Yale Approach suffers from just such a shortfall. His four-step approach addresses persuading people to a particular opinion first through gaining attention; designing the message for comprehension (understanding); creating acceptance through appeal to self-interest; and finally, ensuring retention through well-organized and presented arguments. Hovland believed attitudes change if you change opinion. But, as

> **> Persuasion**
>
> Disseminating information to appeal for a change in attitudes, opinions and/or behavior.

we have seen, merely changing opinions is insufficient. Unless attitudes and opinions are changed in such a way that they motivate the behavior we are seeking, we have expended valuable resources (time and money) to no avail. Behavior change is not only the ultimate measure of success; it provides the reinforcement necessary to retain an attitude change.

The group dynamics approach recognizes the powerful influence of conformity. The pressure to be accepted into certain social groups is often a motivator even when attitudes and opinions have not been altered through persuasive communication. The power of opinion leaders and other influentials is a manifestation of this approach.

An opinion leader is someone we turn to for advice and counsel, typically because he/she has more knowledge or information about the issue in question. We all have a number of opinion leaders in our lives. They may be authority figures of some kind, or they may be our next door neighbor. When you get ready to buy a car, whom do you talk to about the best value? Before voting on a local referendum, whom do you usually call for information? When you register for classes, whom do you ask about which teachers to take? All of these people are opinion leaders for those particular issues or decisions. Whether their knowledge and information comes from personal experience, special training, extensive reading or any other source, you trust their judgment.

> **Opinion Leader**

A trusted individual to whom one turns for advice because of his/her greater knowledge or experience regarding the issue at hand.

Studies of opinion leaders show that they are usually heavy consumers of media. In the 1940s, Katz and Lazarsfeld conducted studies of voting behavior that led to their landmark two-step flow theory of opinion leadership. They found that certain individuals within a community search out information from the mass media and other channels and pass it on to their peers. (Subsequent research has altered this hypothesis to a multiple-step flow, finding that the number of relays between the media and the final receiver is variable.) Reaching opinion leaders with media messages is one of the most effective persuasive methods used in public relations today.

This idea introduces the effect of media in persuasion. Agenda setting theory contends that media do not tell people what to think, rather they tell people what to think about. Media sets the agenda or determines what is important, and, as Lazarsfeld reiterates, they serve to reinforce existing attitudes and opinions. Remember the uses and gratifications theory? People choose the media they pay attention to based on their own purposes. Agenda setting studies have shown that people select what they pay attention to for the purpose of reinforcing their existing beliefs or the decisions they have already made. Remember also the previously mentioned study on product advertising? People who had already purchased a certain product were the heaviest consumers of ads for that product; they were looking for reinforcement of their decision. The same phenomenon is true across the board. People choose newspapers that project their same political and social opinions. The vast majority of Sean Hannity's listeners are people who agree with his political, social and economic attitudes. For all of these reasons, media have not traditionally been considered to be capable of changing opinion.

Nevertheless, we live in a changing world where some media personalities seem to have transcended the role of information giver and agenda setter; certain commentators and newscasters seem to be influential in shaping public opinion. The riots in Los Angeles following the verdict in the Rodney King case in the 1990s are a poignant warning that media (and the 30-second sound bite) may have more power than previously thought in shaping opinion. Although a jury in a trusted judicial system weighed all the available evidence and rendered its conclusion, most of America had already determined guilt based on more limited information provided by newscasters, news magazines and talk show hosts. As advancing technology exacerbates the isolation of individuals in our publics, media celebrities like Oprah Winfrey, Dan Rather and Katie Couric have become increasingly influential.

Another change in our technological world is the effect of opinion polling in setting the public agenda. A frequently used tactic in political campaigns, pollsters tell America what to think about by the questions they ask. And the phenomenon is put to good use. Part of good campaign strategy is to determine what issues the candidate can win with and then to put those issues on the agenda by polling people for their opinions. People then believe that the issue must be important because the pollster is collecting public opinion about it. Other successful techniques for influencing opinions are shown in figure 2.2.

Persuasive appeals

Perhaps the most effective of persuasive appeals dates back more than two millennia to the philosopher and rhetorician Aristotle. His classic logos (logical argument), pathos (emotional appeal) and ethos (source credibility) are as salient today as they were in ancient Greece. These three appeals constitute the majority of persuasive appeals used in communications, either singly or in combination. Nevertheless, they must be appropriately formulated with specific, well-researched target publics in mind.

To Aristotle's three appeals we should add the appeal to self-interest. One of the most important keys to motivating people is convincing them the desired behavior is in their best interest. Again, people don't do what you want them to do just because you want them to do it. They will be persuaded to behave as you want only if it is in their self-interest to do so.

The message itself is a key element of persuasive appeal. It should appeal to an individual's self-interest and use other appropriate appeals based on target public research. Equally as important, the medium or channel for delivery must be carefully selected. The medium must be credible and believable, capable of reaching the target public and technologically suited to the message itself. For example, television has high credibility and mass viewership, but it is suitable only for short, simple messages. Detailed messages are better conveyed through print media. Robert Cialdini has developed an intriguing persuasion strategy he calls self-persuasion. He identifies five key elements.

1. **Consistency**. Once committed to an opinion, people behave accordingly. And those commitments are reinforced through behavior. Studies show that volunteers serving a cause are much more likely to donate to that cause than those who are not involved.
2. **Reciprocity**. People will actively support something if they feel they owe something to the person or organization inviting their support.

figure **2.2**

Tips for Changing Attitudes and Opinions

- When opposite views are presented one after another, the one presented last will probably be more effective.
- Desired opinion change is more likely if you explicitly state your conclusions rather than letting the audience draw its own.
- Analysis of your target public and the message to be sent should determine the persuasive appeal or combination of appeals used.
- A strong threat may be less effective than a mild threat in inducing the desired attitude change.
- Opinions and attitudes are strongly influenced by groups to which a person belongs or wants to belong.
- A person is typically rewarded for conforming to the standards of the group and punished for deviating from them.
- People with the strongest ties to a group are probably the least influenced by messages which conflict with group standards.
- Opinions expressed or shared with others are typically harder to change than opinions held privately.
- Audience participation helps overcome resistance.
- Over time, the effects of a persuasive communication tend to wear off, but repeating a message tends to prolong its influence.
- The people you most want to reach in your target audience are the least likely to be present or to elect to perceive your communication.
- Successful persuasion considers the beliefs and values underlying attitudes as well as attitudes and opinions themselves.
- A highly credible communicator is more likely to persuade opinion change than someone with low credibility; nevertheless, the communicator's credibility is less of a factor over time since people tend to remember ideas longer than they remember sources.
- The communicator's motives affect his/her ability to persuade and motivate.
- A communicator is more effective if he/she expresses some views shared by the audience.
- The audience's opinion of the persuader is often directly influenced by its attitude toward the message.
- The more extreme the opinion change requested the more actual change is likely to result.

3. **Social validation**. This is the bandwagon effect. People are influenced by others who believe or behave in that way. Get a lot of people to use a product and everyone thinks they have to have it.

4. **Authority (influentials or opinion leaders)**. People follow the advice of someone they trust and has knowledge on the subject.

5. **Scarcity**. People rush to support or obtain something that is disappearing. If the availability is limited, people want to get it before it is gone.

THE ETHICS OF PERSUASION

At the heart of much of the conflict between journalists and marketing, advertising and public relations professionals is the question of ethical practice. Whereas ethical codes for journalists are based in objectivity, the ethical basis for our communication efforts is in advocacy. That foundation does not make the practice of persuasive communication less ethical. In fact, because of the influence of marketing, advertising, and public relations in our society, it is of primary importance that persuasive appeals be used in an honest and ethical manner. The Institute for Propaganda Analysis has formulated a list of persuasive appeals designed to mislead (figure 2.3). Sometimes called "propaganda devices," these appeals raise the question of the difference between persuasion and propaganda. Some consider persuasion ethical and propaganda unethical because of its attempt to distort or mislead. Others contend they are the same, the judgment of propriety being a matter of perception. For example, "name calling" is widely used as labeling an issue or event for ease in reference. A short label reference is selected based on the perception or image it conveys. The same revolutionaries in a Third World nation are alternately considered both terrorists and freedom fighters, depending upon your point of view. The label is consistent with the labeler's perception, not necessarily intended to mislead. To detractors, such a label is considered "propaganda;" to supporters it is an accurate depiction of reality.

In fact, persuasion actually began as propaganda and was not considered "evil" until World War II when Nazi Germany engaged in the practice. In the seventeenth century, Pope Gregory XV established the College of Propaganda to train priests to proselyte. The United States itself engaged in propaganda efforts in both World Wars, not only directed at

---

figure **2.3**

Persuasive Appeals or Propaganda Devices
Source: The Institute for Propaganda Analysis

Name calling
Giving an idea a label, either good or bad, to encourage the public to accept and praise or reject and condemn the idea without examining evidence.

Glittering generality
Associating something with a "virtue word" that is not specifically defined to encourage the public to accept and approve the idea without examining the evidence.

Transfer
Transferring the aura of authority, sanction and prestige of a celebrity or someone respected or revered to a less-well known product, person or idea to persuade the public to accept or reject it.

Testimonial
Endorsement of a product by a celebrity or someone respected or revered who actually uses it.

Plain folks
The method by which a speaker (often a politician) attempts to convince the public that his/her ideas are good because they are "of the people," or that he/she is "one of us."

Card stacking
Selective use of facts to tell only one side of the story, often obscuring the other side.

Bandwagon
An appeal to conformity with the majority, this method tries to persuade by encouraging the public to join their friends and neighbors because "everybody's doing it."

Emotional stereotypes
Designed to evoke an emotional image like the "ugly American" or a "homemaker."

Illicit silence
This device falls in the category of omission, or withholding information that would clarify a situation or correct an incorrect impression or assumption.

Subversive rhetoric
A device frequently used in political campaigns, this appeal involves attacking the spokesperson rather than the idea.

the populations of Europe but also at Americans. Perhaps the most reasonable approach to evaluating persuasive methods and appeals is to avoid the persuasion versus propaganda debate and to simply follow ethical standards that prevent us from manipulating information and publics. Appendix B contains the codes of ethics from three advocacy-based professional associations — the American Marketing Association (AMA), the American Advertising Federation (AAF) and the Public Relations Society of America (PRSA). Following those ethical codes will help us engage in ethical persuasive communication.

According to retired television commentator Bill Moyers, the challenge for communications professionals engaged in persuasion is to do so ethically. Although many practitioners are held to ethical codes of conduct either through their employers or professions, anyone using persuasive devices should meticulously exam the integrity of his/her methods. In his book, "Persuasion: Reception and Responsibility" (1983), Charles Larson identifies a number of ethical criteria that can guide the communications professional. They can basically be reduced to the following guidelines:

- Do not use false, distorted or irrelevant evidence or reasoning, or diversionary tactics.
- Do not deceive or mislead your audience or conceal your purpose.
- Do not oversimplify complex issues or minimize detrimental effects.
- Do not engage in advocacy for something or someone you do not trust or believe in personally.

Ethical decision making is critical to our reputation as professionals. Although ethical codes and behavior are addressed more fully in Chapter 12, it should be noted here that all decisions we make as communications professionals affect the profession itself as well as our own status and professionalism. No decisions are free from ethical considerations; every decision we make as practitioners has ethical consequences. Being aware of those consequences and carefully examining our proposed plans and behaviors according to sound ethical principles will help us avoid the ethical land mines that some of our colleagues unwittingly encounter.

Persuasion in and of itself is not unethical. Advocacy has a strong history and important role in our free society. Nevertheless, it must be conducted according to principles that support not only the public interest but also the public's right to know and choose for itself.

SUMMARY

Marketing and public relations is the business of disseminating information, persuading opinion change and motivating behavior. Since behavior is based on values, beliefs and attitudes, it is imperative we understand how to influence those cognitive elements or we will not meet with success. Sometimes providing public information is enough; often it is not. Persuasive methods, used ethically and responsibly, are inextricable elements of advocacy communication.

CHAPTER TWO EXERCISES

1. Examine a local fund-raising effort for persuasive appeals. What types of appeals are being used? How effective are they in this instance? What recommendations would you make for improving the effectiveness of the persuasive appeals?

2. Describe your own personal frame of reference in terms of basic beliefs, values and attitudes that motivate your behavior.

3. Identify an issue of importance in your community. Identify three publics directly affected by that issue and the opinion leaders for those publics.

REFERENCES AND ADDITIONAL READINGS

Baran, S.J., & Davis, D.K. (1995). *Mass Communication Theory: Foundations, Ferment, and Future.*

Cantril, H. (1944). *Gauging Public Opinion.* Princeton, N.J.: Princeton University Press.

Cialdini, R. (1993). In Newsom, D., Scott, A., & Turk, J.V. (2004). *This Is PR: The Realities of Public Relations* (5th ed.). Belmont, Calif.: Wadsworth Publishing Company., pp. 205-206.

Cutlip, S., Center, A., & Broom, G. (2000). *Effective Public Relations* (8th ed.). Englewood Cliffs, N.J.: Prentice-Hall, Inc.

Grunig, J. E. (1993). "Communication behaviors and attitudes of environmental publics: Two studies." *Journalism Monographs,* 81(March):40-41

Jackson, P. (1990). "Behavioral public relations model." *PR Reporter,* 33:30, 1-2.

Larson, C. (1983). *Persuasion: Reception and Responsibility.* Belmont, Calif.: Wadsworth Publishing Company.

Littlejohn, S.W. (1992). *Theories of Human Communication* (4th ed.). Belmont, Calif.: Wadsworth Publishing Company.

Newsom, D., Turk, J.V., & Kruckeberg, D. (2004). *This Is PR: The Realities of Public Relations* (8th ed.). Belmont, Calif.: Wadsworth Publishing Company.

Noelle-Neumann, E. (1984). *The Spiral of Silence.* Chicago: University of Chicago Press.

Norris, J.S. (1984). *Public Relations.* Englewood Cliffs, N.J.: Prentice-Hall, Inc.

Schindler, R.M. (1992). "The real lesson of new Coke: The value of focus groups for predicting the effects of social influence." *Marketing Research,* December, 22-27.

Stimson, J. A. (1991). *Public Opinion in America: Moods, Cycles, and Swings.* Boulder, Colo.: Westview Press.

Wilcox, D. L., Ault, P. H., & Agee, W. K. (2002). *Public Relations: Strategies and Tactics* (7th ed.). New York: Harper and Row.

chapter 3

COMMUNICATIONS
RESEARCH METHODS

"...digital media collectively provide
searchable access to a wealth of experiences and insights, the quantity and
diversity of which seems likely to
increase substantially."

— Jonathan M. Levitt

Contributor to the Journal of Digital Information

LEARNING IMPERATIVES

▸ To understand the necessity of research as a foundation for decision making

▸ To recognize the variety of information available

▸ To understand the basic research methodologies for effective communication research

For years in the communications field, research has been an unaffordable luxury seldom engaged. Not so in the field of marketing. Market research has been fairly common for the last several decades. But in one of the most critical functions of the organization — the function that builds the relationships and creates the environment within which all other organizational functions thrive — there has been little money for research. For years, public relations practitioners had to find their way in the dark.

Finally, somebody turned on the lights. Not only do most successful organizations now do research, there are a plethora of specialized consultants and research firms which have taken market, environmental, communications and organizational research to levels of sophistication never before dreamed. Whereas in the past, communications practitioners found themselves begging for a pittance to find out what their publics thought, they now have executives whose first question is, "What does the research tell us?"

As a result, our challenge here is no longer to convince the reader to do research and then painstakingly examine all the different methods and kinds of information available. At this point in your education or career, you have learned the value of research and how to do it or how to buy it. Further, there are now in publication dozens of texts and handbooks on conducting research. The challenge here is to provide the basic framework for thinking about and organizing research and analysis, and then, in the next chapter, to apply it in the strategic planning process.

The role of research in communication

Research is only as good as its application to the problem-solving process. To be research-oriented means gathering information is a natural part of your daily routine. Continually gathering and analyzing information means your decisions will be research-based. To be effective in communicating with an organization's publics we must be constantly listening, scanning the environment for information. We should establish good communication channels so information is constantly flowing to us

— resulting in adjustments and refinements of our efforts as plans proceed. Research helps us to:

- Save time and money
- Understand our publics
- Make sound decisions
- Avoid mistakes
- Discover new ideas
- Identify potential publics
- Justify plans
- Connect with communities

Knowing what we know about how people perceive and misperceive, as professional communicators we should be wary of "gut reactions." Always test the information that leads to conclusions and especially to key decisions. The next chapter provides a checklist of the information you need to meet the various challenges of an organization and to plan strategically to seize opportunities. In this chapter, we identify some of the best sources of information and the methodologies used to obtain it.

Research methods and the diversity of tools

Research methods are often categorized as formal and informal, quantitative and qualitative, and primary and secondary. Nevertheless, these categorizations are not parallel. For example, formal research is not necessarily quantitative research, nor is it always primary research. A few definitions regarding research will help to avoid confusion.

Formal and informal research. Formal research implies a structured study. It is governed by rules of research that include previously identifying what you hope to learn, how and from whom. Informal research is less structured and more exploratory. It does not follow specific rules.

Quantitative and qualitative research. Quantitative research involves data analysis of some kind. Qualitative research is focused on individual cases or groups not statistically representative of a given pop-

> Research

Gathering information to clarify an issue and solve a problem.

> Formal Research

Data gathering structured according to accepted rules of research.

ulation. While qualitative research may be supported by some statistical data analysis, it is not governed by laws of probability. It may, however, be governed by rules of research. Focus groups, for example, are a qualitative tool. They used to be considered informal research. Now, that focus group methodology has actually become a dominant method of research, the rules of research governing this methodology are meticulously followed to ensure the most reliable results. Although the method is classified as formal research because it follows rules and structure, it is still a qualitative approach.

Primary and secondary research. Primary research implies gathering the information first-hand, for a specifically identified purpose. It doesn't necessarily refer to survey research. Personal interviews as well as mail and telephone analysis also yield primary information. Survey research that you implement yourself or contract out for a particular purpose is primary research. Secondary research is primary research data originally collected by someone else for a different purpose that is now being drawn upon for a new use. Typically, it is cheaper and faster to use secondary research. You should exhaust secondary sources before embarking on any costly primary research efforts.

> Primary Research

Firsthand information gathered specifically for your current purpose.

Given these definitions, the research tools become more difficult to categorize. Focus groups may be formal or informal. They are typically qualitative, but if enough groups are conducted some data analysis may be done on the results. They are primary research when you organize and conduct them for the immediate purpose, but reviewing transcripts and analysis of focus groups conducted for other purposes is secondary research that may shed light on the problem you are trying to solve.

Similarly, personal interviews may be informal and qualitative research. They may be one of your "listening" techniques. Or, given more structure and an appropriate design, they may be formal and quantitative, allowing statistical analysis with a high degree of confidence. They would be a primary research tool if conducted for the project at hand, yet may be useful as secondary data in subsequent programs.

Whether the research you do is formal or informal, quantitative or qualitative, primary or secondary depends largely on what you need and how you structure it. You should determine your purpose (what you are hoping to accomplish with the research) and what you are trying to find out from whom, before you decide on the best tools to use and how to structure the effort.

SECONDARY RESEARCH

Organizational research

The first place to begin in gathering information is within the organization itself. Many kinds of research tools are available to help gather and assess the information available to you. A communication audit examines all of the organization's communication to see if it is on mission and message. Environmental scanning within an organization monitors the mood and feelings that exist among the workers, customers, investors, suppliers and many other publics of the organization. Mail and telephone analysis, including e-mail, helps you track what issues cause concern among your publics. Certainly customer service and complaint lines help you track opinion trends and potential problems.

Important background information about your company or your client is found in the publications of the organization. Employee publications, annual reports, brochures and marketing material, policies and procedures manuals, organizational charts, sales and accounting records, histories and any other material available from the organization in hard copy or electronically can be valuable research. Keep in mind that such material usually possesses an inherent bias, and you need to look outside the organization as well as inside to make sure you have the complete picture. Organizations do not often open their closets to display the skeletons through their own printed and electronic material. You will get rich information about the organization through its material, but you will not often get the bad news. And, not knowing the bad news may sabotage your communication efforts.

> Secondary
  Research

Information previously assimilated for other purposes that can be adapted to your needs.

The organization may also have data from past surveys or research. You may need some primary research to determine the mood and opinion of employees. Most organizations would benefit by taking a searching look inside before focusing research efforts externally.

Internet and library research

Information technology and the computer revolution have given us access to incredible resources for research. Information that would take weeks or months to find from original sources is now readily available at our fingertips. The communication professional of today and of the future must understand how to get good data from the Internet to compete in this new environment.

Online research has, in most cases, replaced a personal visit to the library. It gives the researcher access to the collections held by thousands of libraries and to databases full of information and references. Much is available in library documents that may be difficult to find or expensive to secure elsewhere. Most of us underestimate the value of the data available in our local college and public libraries. And unless you actually take the time to investigate, to talk to a resource librarian or just to explore the collection, you will not appreciate the vast amount of information at your fingertips.

Remember the latest census? It's available on the Internet. In that census, some people received a more in-depth questionnaire than the rest of us and their psychographic data is accessible as well. Also accessible is a host of government documents and studies published every year, and many private research studies. You can find national and local newspapers and magazines that date back years, sometimes to the beginning of publication. Often the results of opinion polls can be found and rich economic data on local, state, national and international markets.

Some universities have separate libraries for their business schools. In that case, the business library probably contains detailed market analysis and other such valuable information as well. While most of this information may be available electronically, there are volumes of information that can only be accessed by visiting a library in person. The more current the information, the more likely you will be able to get it via the Internet. Nevertheless, there may be significant risks in ignoring the deeper background that older documents contain.

The World Wide Web is another source the Internet provides us. Everything from current news to management structure and policies can be found through an organization's web site. Nevertheless, it should be remembered that these official web sites are designed by the organization itself and the bias found in the information is on a par with organizational newsletters and press releases.

Increasingly, you will find many independent web sites that contain valuable information. Be careful of the source of the information and seek secondary confirmation when possible. The information may be credible, such as that from an industry analyst with a professional responsibility to provide such information, or it may be a site constructed by a disgruntled customer or employee containing extremely biased, if not inaccurate, information, rumor and innuendo.

External organizations

Our tax dollars support local, state and national government offices which have a charge to operate in the public interest. Providing public information is often an integral part of that responsibility. Much of the information is now available over the Internet, but some of the valuable information you seek may only be available upon request, or by digging through studies and papers. Sometimes the bureaucracy can be difficult, and getting information can take weeks or even months. Nevertheless, the information available is often critical.

Most cities and states have economic development offices of some kind that collect invaluable information on industries and markets. State, and sometimes local, governments have information on population, wages, education, unemployment, health and just about everything else you can imagine. Be persistent; the information you want may be part of something else. You will have to do most of the searching, so start specific but be ready to broaden your search until you find documents and reports that will provide the information you need.

If you examine the purpose of associations, pressure groups or professional societies, tapping them in the research step becomes a tool of obvious value. The functions of these organizations are based primarily on gathering and disseminating information. One of the most valuable benefits of membership may be access to the research they gather. You may be able to access the information you want from them through their publications or resource libraries. You may have to pay a search or use fee to access the material. In some cases, you may need to get the material through an association member. But the data available is generally very rich, current and valuable. Environmental data is readily available from area Chambers of Commerce and Travel Councils.

A word of caution is appropriate here. When you receive data from these kinds of organizations, especially from activist groups, check the sources and methodologies used. Be aware that any information published by an interest group of any kind will be inherently biased to some degree. Make sure you understand and allow for that bias, and seek confirming and/or disputing information from other sources or carefully examine the research methodology used and adjust for distortion.

Media research

A number of publishing houses produce Internet-accessible media guides that provide current and valuable information about media throughout the nation by category: newspapers, magazines, radio stations, television stations, cable stations and so on. Online media guides such as Bacon's Media Map (mediamap.com) and Burrells (burrells.com) list editors and reporters by assignment, how to submit pieces and what is typically accepted. The guides also indicate readership, viewership or listenership and will sometimes provide additional demographic information that may be of help in profiling key publics. They at least provide a way to contact the media organization to request more detailed information. Most media organizations can provide detailed viewer, listener or reader profiles because they sell advertising. And, advertisers want to know who they're buying access to.

Media analysis and clips are a critical part of communications research and evaluation. Whether in-house or a contracted service, tracking media coverage is essential. Nevertheless, because of the time it takes to be thorough, you will usually get more comprehensive and cost-effective clipping and analysis if you contract to a clipping service. Clipping services may do as little as simply clip anything (print, broadcast and other electronic media) that mentions the company or an issue of interest to the company. At the other end of the spectrum they may engage in extensive analysis and evaluate the positive or negative impact of the pieces that discuss the organization and its competitors or any of the issues faced by the industry. You can specify the level of service you want and pay accordingly.

PRIMARY RESEARCH

Focus groups

Focus group research has become one of the most important and reliable sources of data to understand publics. A focus group is a moderator-led discussion with four to 15 participants. The moderator asks open-ended questions to garner qualitative responses on attitudes and behavior. The moderator must be careful not to bias the discussion by injecting personal opinion or information into the group. He/she should encourage participation from all members of the group and probe for in-depth understanding. The moderator must also create an atmosphere of openness, honesty, safety and confidentiality in order to engender free and open discussion. With the permission and knowledge of the participants, the session is usually recorded, either by a scribe or by electronic means (audio or video), and the discussion transcribed for further evaluation and data tabulation.

> Focus Group
Research

Moderator-led discussions with fewer than 15 participants providing in-depth information on attitudes and behaviors.

The increasing popularity of focus group research is partially because it is generally easier to conduct than survey research, because it can provide more rapid results, and because it provides more depth of opinion and attitudes within the group where those opinions and attitudes are shaped, refined and crystallized (see figure 3.1). Further, while not always less expensive than other kinds of research it is often more cost effective. Focus groups used to be conducted in communications and marketing research primarily as discussion forums for advisory committees or idea panels to supplement quantitative research. The information was often used as a precursor to survey research to assist in developing a questionnaire that adequately probed attitudes and opinions. In today's research-oriented marketplace, many practitioners recognize that, whereas survey research is becoming less credible as an accurate representation of publics, focus groups provide the kind of information needed to immediately address and resolve problems.

As discussed in the previous chapter, people do not behave in isolation. The discussion and refinement of opinions and attitudes which occur in focus groups often provide the kind of problem-solving behavioral information that surveys cannot. The example cited in the previous chapter of the new Coke formula introduction is a case in point. Both research techniques were used, yielding opposite results. Yet because of the reputation for validity of survey research over focus group responses, the company chose to rely on predictions of behavior based on attitudes expressed in isolation. They should have more carefully considered the group behavior that emerged from the focus groups.

Further, focus group research can demonstrate the process of opinion formation. While not representative, the group is a social microcosm of a larger public. The analysis of attitude and opinion changes based on the flow of the discussion can help us know what information people need to make sound decisions and what appeals will be most effective in the larger arena. Innovations in focus group research now allow quantification of results if certain conditions are met. Conducting large numbers of groups and employing some content analysis techniques can make the data statistically reliable.

figure **3.1**

Uses and Abuses of Focus Group Research

USES

Immediate results. Focus group research is relatively easy to organize, implement and analyze. That often makes it much less costly as well.

Comfort in numbers. A group is usually less intimidating than the attention paid the individual in other research methods. People feel more comfortable expressing opinions.

Flexible and response-oriented. Because the structure is less rigid, the group takes the discussion where it wants to go and a broader investigation of the topic is possible. The focus is on responses (attitudes and opinions), not on the questions, so information emerges on salient topics through the natural flow of discussion.

Gauge of group behavior. Rather than researching individual behavior or potential behavior, focus groups explore attitudes and behavior influenced by the group or society, a far more reliable measure and predictor.

Issues explored and opinion crystallized. Because the group is discovering and examining attitudes and behaviors they may not have thought about before, it allows time for discussion and rumination to discover motivations.

Sensitive issues addressed. When members of the group can empathize with one another because of similar experiences, they are more open in the discussion of sensitive, value-laden issues like stem cell research or spouse/child abuse.

Attitudes of activists included. A focus group provides a cooperative atmosphere which may encourage the participation of activists and organizational detractors not willing to participate in other kinds of research.

Issues and jargon identified. The responses from a focus group identify the issues of most concern to the group as well as the language they use and can understand in discussing those topics. Such a foundation provides solid ground for subsequent research and message development.

ABUSES

Weak or dominant moderator. If the moderator is weak, he/she may allow some members of the group to dominate and others may be intimidated or refrain from offering opinions. The group result will be biased and probably useless. If the moderator dominates the group, he/she will impose opinions and attitudes rather than probing the attitudes of the group.

Not homogenous. A focus group should be homogenous or the members will be intimidated and uncomfortable with sharing their attitudes. Broad representation is achieved by conducting focus groups among several homogenous publics, rather than mixing representation within a single group.

Too few groups. For the research to be valid, a number of groups must be conducted among various homogenous publics. Then the information can be consolidated to provide a more comprehensive look.

Generalizing to population. Focus group research is qualitative, not statistical. You cannot generalize your conclusions to any "general public." Your conclusions are very much issue- and group-specific. They may be indications that will lead you in problem solving or in designing quantitative research, but they do not represent public opinion.

The Internet provides an interesting new resource to traditional focus group research. Scheduled online chats can produce similar results without the geographic restrictions. Nevertheless, care must be taken that participants are invited and known. Otherwise, the data may be inappropriate for the researcher's purpose.

Copy and product testing

One classic use of focus groups is for copy and/or product testing. But this is not the only method by which to test. Copy testing simply selects individuals within your target publics and requests their review of copy, whether survey copy or communication copy (brochures, advertising and the like). In product testing, individuals are asked to examine and use a product — providing feedback on everything from packaging and sales methods to product quality. Product tests may be done individually by personal interview, by mail, in focus groups or online.

Honest responses in copy and product testing help avoid costly mistakes. Survey research instruments should always be tested before being implemented. Testing copy helps ensure that the messages are coming across in such a way as to produce the desired result. Marketers test promotional campaigns or products in areas representative of the overall market. Sometimes, two or three different versions of a product or a campaign will be tested in similar areas to determine which is most effective. Copy and product testing is one of the most valuable kinds of research available to the practitioner. Their greatest value lies in their ability to prevent mistakes — saving money, effort and time.

> Demographic Data

Information used to segment publics according to tangible characteristics such as age, gender and socioeconomic status.

Psychographic studies

Values and Lifestyles Segmenting (VALS), developed by SRI International in the mid-1970s, is research methodology that classifies publics by psychographics or attitudes, beliefs and lifestyles. Found to be far more effective in segmenting publics than demographics alone, psychographic studies help us to know what motivates individuals within a particular public. The VALS categories — achievers, survivors and sustainers, belongers, and so on — have been used extensively in advertising and marketing to segment and tailor messages to specific target publics. They provide the same valuable segmentation for communication with all the organization's publics. Communicators should know the VALS categories, both the original and the more recently revised segmentations, and understand the motivations tied to the differences in attitudes and lifestyles.

> ## Psychographic Data

Information used to segment publics according to values, attitudes and lifestyles.

Oftentimes, local media and other similar organizations will have segmented and profiled their own target audiences using a combination of demographic and psychographic information. Whereas some will be unwilling to disclose the information, which is quite costly to compile, others may be persuaded to share the data especially if the request comes from a nonprofit organization or is for a charitable purpose.

Another valuable tool for understanding key publics is Values in Strategy Assessment (VISTA), a process developed by Wirthlin Worldwide. This tool's premise is that values are the fundamental determinant of an individual's behavior and decisions. Understanding the fundamental values of a public provides the strategy to motivate action.

Survey research and opinion sampling

A popular quantitative research method is survey research, although its credibility has declined in recent years. Several events have affected the ability of researchers to secure truly random and representative samples. Mail surveys have always been extremely unreliable not only because of low response rates but also because of skewing. Only certain kinds of people will take the time to respond to a mail survey, making it anything but representative.

Telephone surveys have also declined in credibility for the same reason. And the "Do Not Call" registry has made telephone surveying more difficult than ever. Although telephone surveys are not prohibited by the registry, the very existence of a "do not call" list seems to have given people the courage to refuse calls they would have previously endured.

Nevertheless, survey research has been a popular research technique in communications and will probably continue to be in some form or another. For example, researchers may find the personal drop-off method to still be effective because of the personal contact involved in dropping off and/or picking up a survey. It is not as easy to turn down someone face-to-face as it is to say "no" over the telephone.

Survey research is a difficult and exacting approach. It requires meticulous attention to detail at every step of the process — questionnaire design, sample selection, survey implementation, data processing and data analysis. A mistake or misjudgment at any point will skew the results, often in ways unknown to the researcher.

To be valid and reliable, survey research must follow strict rules of research. The idea behind survey research is to take a sample from a population, or universe. If we follow good statistical procedures, we should be able to make that sample relatively representative of the universe, although we can never be absolutely sure of our accuracy unless we survey every individual in the population (a census). The total number of individuals surveyed in the population and the way they are selected will determine how accurately the results reflect the universe.

Statistical research on very critical issues, or in close political campaigns, needs to have a high level of confidence and a low margin of error. The confidence level reflects the researcher's percentage of certainty that the results would be the same (within the margin of error) upon replication of the survey. The margin of error reflects the percentage points that the sample results, on any given question, may vary from the population as a whole. Increasing the sample size increases the confidence level and decreases the margin of error. The only way to be 100 percent confident and eliminate the margin of error would be to survey the entire population or take a census. Research regarding an organization's publics generally requires at least a 95 percent confidence level, and a margin of error of five percent or less. Further, the more important or controversial the issue the greater the need for a lower margin of error.

There are two basic kinds of survey sampling: probability and non-probability. Probability sampling is scientifically random; every individ-

> ## > Personal Drop-off

Personally delivering a survey for later pick-up or mailing.

> ## > Confidence Level

The percentage of certainty that the results of a survey would be the same if replicated.

ual in the population has an equal chance of being selected. Nonprobability samples survey whoever is available, for example intercepting students during the lunch hour as they enter the student center or interviewing people at a grocery store on Saturday afternoon.

There are also two kinds of errors: sampling and nonsampling. Sampling errors occur when estimates are derived from a sample rather than a population. A large number of different samples could be complied of the same size and design for a given questionnaire. The variance in the responses from different population samples to the same questionnaire is called sampling error. These differences occur by chance and are measured by the margin of error associated with a particular survey.

Nonsampling errors are mistakes attributed to many sources including response differences, definitional difficulties, differing respondent interpretations and the inability of respondents to recall information. Great care must be taken in selecting the sample and designing and implementing the questionnaire. Questions must be designed to avoid the introduction of bias so that answers accurately reflect the information the researcher needs. Questions cannot be value-laden in such a way as to dictate a response; otherwise, you are not getting an accurate picture of attitudes and opinions. Also avoid questions that request a judgment on two concepts. You may think they are related but the respondent may not, and the information elicited will be inaccurate. "Do you like mustard and mayonnaise on your hamburger?" will not give you an accurate reflection of respondents' preferences for those two condiments. Some people may like one and not the other, and thus be forced into responding "no," leading you to believe they don't like either.

Similarly, you must take great care in the design of answer categories or your data will appear to reflect attitudes it does not. Make sure your answers cover the full range of responses possible. Most questions require a "maybe" or "sometimes" or "other" or even a "don't know" category. Make sure you understand the appropriate uses of semantic differentials and Likert scales. On open-ended questions where interviewers are instructed not to read the answer categories, provide sufficient breadth in those categories for your interviewers to quickly record the

> Sampling Error

Measured as margin of error, it indicates the possible percentage variation of the sample data from the whole population.

> Nonsampling Error

A mistake made in selecting the sample and designing and implementing the questionnaire.

answer given. You should also make sure "other" categories provide room for specific explanations in case you need to create a new category and recode the responses during data tabulation.

Bias can also be introduced in implementing the survey. Ensuring strict confidentiality of responses can lessen courtesy bias. Training interviewers to ask questions without injecting value inflection or personal comments, explanation or other bias is also critical. Further, great care must be taken in coding the surveys and entering the data. Data processing converts the observations and responses into statistics for interpretation. Data analysis manipulates the data to make logical inferences. For the inferences to be reliable, the data must be accurately entered and processed.

> Purposive
Sampling

Identifying and surveying
opinion leaders to
determine attitudes
and behaviors.

Finally, the inferences made must be fully supportable by the data set. A few years ago, a ballot measure in Utah proposed a light rail transportation system to be funded by a small tax increase. When the measure was soundly defeated, many analysts concluded it was a vote against light rail. In reality, it was more probably a vote against the funding method, not the light rail system itself. When we deal with statistics and make inferences from data, we must be very careful that the data support the conclusions. Otherwise, we have established a faulty foundation for decision making.

In addition to the types of survey research discussed above, other variations have specific purposes and benefits. The following short descriptions will provide a basis upon which to investigate the techniques for any given research situation.

> Stratified
Sampling

Selecting the sample to
ensure proportionate
representation of
segments within
the universe.

Purposive sampling. Based on Katz and Lazarsfeld's two-step flow theory, purposive sampling identifies and surveys opinion leaders to determine attitudes and behaviors. The researcher must devise a procedure that selects out the target publics' influentials (or causes them to self-select), and then surveys opinion and behavior. It is also helpful to know a little bit about the influentials, such as where they get their information about certain issues.

Stratified sampling. Truly random sampling should yield a cross section of the population representative of the characteristics within the population (i.e., proportionate numbers of women and men and so on). Whenever we skew the randomness of the sample by using techniques that make it easier for us to complete the research, like surveying every nth number in the local telephone directory, we risk jeopardizing the representativeness of our sample. If obtaining a truly proportionate representation is critical, the research sample should be stratified so that it includes appropriate proportions of the key segments of the overall population.

Internet surveys. A growing area of survey research is conducting surveys over the World Wide Web. While there is inherent bias because of the nature of accessible respondents, this data can be extremely valuable if the purpose is consistent with the population sample. Commercial firms with access to e-mail lists and online survey tools may be the easiest way to accomplish this kind of survey research.

Personal interviews. Very sensitive issues and research that requires deep probing for attitudes and behaviors are best addressed through personal interviews. The personal interview ensures greater control over the sample and the data, but not only is this method costly, it requires a lot of time and well-trained interviewers. Nevertheless, in certain circumstances, it is the only viable method to secure reliable and useful information.

Benchmark surveys. This type of survey is simply a periodic reexamination of attitudes and opinions within the population. An initial survey is done to set a benchmark against which subsequent survey results are compared. Benchmark surveys are good tools for measuring change and evaluating the success of a program.

Panel studies. Sometimes you will want to study attitudes and opinions on a variety of issues over a period of time. Panel studies select respondents who will be available for a follow-up survey, at least once and often several times. For example, a newspaper will select individuals from its readership to follow a specific issue or election and respond to queries at specific points in the campaign. Behavioral studies are also sometimes conducted by panel to assess whether or not a change in behavior is temporary and what motivates permanent change.

> **Panel Study**

Respondents who have agreed to be surveyed repeatedly over time to track opinion and attitude change.

Survey tag-ons. One of the easiest and least expensive methods of obtaining survey data is to add two or three questions to a questionnaire being prepared for another purpose or by someone else. Charitable community organizations often "tag-on" a couple of questions to routine survey research done by corporations in the area. Frequently, the corporation will even pay for the data tabulation as a service or donation to the nonprofit organization. Even if the nonprofit has to pay a fee for tag-on questions, it is still significantly less costly than implementing a stand alone questionnaire.

SUMMARY

To secure a constant flow of the kind of information you need to make decisions, meet challenges and plan strategic action, you must find the right combination of research techniques. The purpose of the research and the kind of information desired drive the selection of methodology. Otherwise your research will sit on the shelf unused because it is inaccurate or because it doesn't provide the information you need to design campaigns that reach the publics you must target within the resources you have to meet the challenges you face.

CHAPTER THREE EXERCISES

1. Volunteer to conduct focus groups for a nonprofit organization. Subsequently, design and implement a short survey to gather opinion, attitudes and demographics on some of its key publics.

2. Using the Internet, search out information that will help you profile an often used target public (like parents or investors). Make sure you access government sources, trade or professional association resources and other documents and studies to fully profile that public, including demographic and psychographic information.

REFERENCES AND ADDITIONAL READINGS

Babbie, E. (1992). *The Practice of Social Research* (6th ed.). Belmont, Calif.: Wadsworth Publishing Company.

Converse, J.M., & Presser, S. (1986). *Survey Questions: Handcrafting the Standardized Questionnaire.* Beverly Hills, Calif.: Sage Publications.

Fink, A. (2002). *The Survey Kit* (2nd ed.). Newbury Park, Calif.: Sage Publications.

Greenbaum, T.L. (1997) *The Handbook for Focus Group Research.* Newbury Park, Calif.: Sage Publications.

Stacks, D.W. (2002). *Primer of Public Relations Research.* New York: Guilford Publications, Inc.

chapter 4

USING RESEARCH FOR EFFECTIVE COMMUNICATIONS PLANNING

"I find that a great part of the information I have was acquired by looking up something and finding something else on the way."
— Franklin P. Adams (1881 – 1960)

American Journalist

LEARNING IMPERATIVES

▸ To understand how to organize research and draw inferences that support strategic planning

▸ To learn how to organize information about publics into profiles to facilitate communication and relationship building

▸ To understand how to use information to determine strengths, weaknesses, opportunities and threats

▸ To learn how to synthesize broad information into a concise situation analysis and core challenge/opportunity

R esearch should be an established and ongoing process in any organization. Successful organizations are always scanning the internal and external environment, gathering data and feedback from key publics and measuring the effectiveness of their communication in moving toward established goals. At some point the key information is pulled together to support planning, but that does not signal an end to research. The savvy professional is always looking for new information that may adjust plans at any point or to reconfirm the validity of current efforts. Measurement that we call "evaluation" may focus on measuring our success rather than gathering information to chart a course. Nevertheless, what we find out from evaluation integrates with the constant flow of other information to become the foundation of new efforts, programs and campaigns.

Research provides the information that helps us find solutions that work. It also demonstrates our credibility to our clients or to management. If the research process can be said to have a beginning, it starts when someone first states a problem or discovers an opportunity. Someone — a client, a customer, a colleague, a supervisor or you — identifies an issue or an opportunity. Then we start to organize what we know around that issue or opportunity. We also reach out to gather what we don't know but need to know.

That's when the real work begins. Facts and information are gathered from all sources and organized to be sorted and evaluated. Figure 4.1 indicates the depth of detail and the breadth of perspective necessary in this process. Although the research checklist in that figure has a commercial product orientation, the same principles apply to the nonprofit industry and to solving corporate issues as well as marketing challenges. When the checklist discusses sales and pricing and profitability, substituting words like participation and cost and success make the checklist applicable to any project or program as well as to products.

If you are designing the first-ever communications effort or strategic communications plan for your client or company, the research section will take a significant amount of time to complete. It will require an exhaustive search. If, however, ongoing communications functions have

figure **4.1**

A Checklist for Communications and Marketing Research

1. The External Environment
- Economic, political and social atmosphere within which the organization operates or the problem or challenge that must be addressed
- Pressures the organization has to respond to and the impact of current events on the operation of the organization and the maintenance of key relationships

2. The Industry
- Companies, dollar sales, strengths, etc.
- Industry growth patterns, primary demand curve, per capita consumption, growth potential
- History, technological advances, trends
- Characteristics, distribution patterns, control and regulation, promotional activity, geographic characteristics, profit patterns, etc.

3. The Client
- History, size, growth, profitability, scope of business, competence, reputation, strengths, weaknesses, structure, etc.

4. The Product, Service or Issue
- The product, service or issue story, development, quality, design, packaging, pricing policies and structure, sales history, trends, distribution, reputation, strengths, weaknesses, etc.
- Product, service or issue sales features (exclusive, non-exclusive, differentiating qualities, competitive position in consumer's mind, etc.)
- Sales force (size, scope, ability, cost/sale)
- Profit history
- Product research and planned improvements

5. Promotions
- Successes and failures of past policy, sales force, advertising, publicity
- Expenditures, budget emphasis, relation to trends
- Ad/PR/marketing strategies, themes, campaigns
- Promotions of competitors and like organizations

6. Market Share
- Sales history industry-wide and share of market in dollars and/or units
- Market potential, industry trends, company trends, demand trends

7. Competition
- Who and where the market is, how it is segmented, future segmentation possibilities, consumer needs, attitudes and characteristics, how, why, when, and where do consumers buy
- Customers past and future, what they have in common, what they like/dislike about product or issue, how they are reached
- Competing ideas and attitudes

8. Resources
- Intervening publics and current relationship, influentials, self-interests
- Attitudes and opinions of benefit and use
- Physical facilities and personnel

9. SWOT Analysis
- Internal and external strengths and weaknesses including publics, resources, attitudes, organization, structure, sales force, ideas, allies and enemies, etc.
- Emergent or possible opportunities
- Threats to the organization and to success

10. Public Profiles
- Demographic and psychographic data
- Situation in relation to product, service or issue
- Current relationship
- Motivating self-interests and influentials
- How they get information on this topic

systematically gathered and organized research data into easily accessible and usable information, your research task will be more of an update. Always take the time to record and file pieces of information you come across in your daily routine. Continually gathering information will make the research task for any given effort or issue much easier.

The next several chapters in this book are designed to take you through the 10-Step Strategic Communications Planning Matrix step by step. The teaching case example at the end of this chapter provides practical application of that process. As we progress through each step of the planning matrix in this and subsequent chapters, the teaching case will illustrate each step as it is discussed in the text.

This chapter is designed to help you pull together information and analysis into a succinct document focused on a specific purpose. That purpose might be a complete strategic plan, a budget request for a new

---

10–STEP STRATEGIC COMMUNICATIONS PLANNING MATRIX

matrix

MATRIX: Research

Steps 1-3 — Background, Situation Analysis, Core Problem/Opportunity

1. *Background*	Planning begins with a synthesis of primary and secondary research providing background information on the industry, external environment, product or program, market situation and current trends in opinions and attitudes. The background section also identifies and profiles potential publics that may be affected by the problem/opportunity or could aid in its resolution/accomplishment. Intervening publics and available resources are also identified.
2. *Situation Analysis*	The situation analysis consists of two paragraphs. The first paragraph is a statement of the current situation and a description of the challenge or opportunity based on research. The second paragraph identifies the potential difficulties and related problems.
3. *Core Problem/ Opportunity*	The core problem/opportunity is a one-sentence statement of the main difficulty or prospect — including potential consequences if not resolved or realized.

communications effort a solution to a problem or challenge, a response to a perceived threat, or a proposal to take advantage of an emergent opportunity. For our purposes here, we call this part of a plan or proposal the research section to facilitate parallelism with the Research, Action Planning, Communication and Evaluation (RACE) model. As depicted in the Strategic Communications Planning Matrix and the teaching case, the research section consists of the background, situation analysis and core problem/opportunity.

Background

The background is a summary of pertinent facts and information drawn from primary and secondary research. It must be comprehensive, but written concisely. It does not contain everything you discovered in research, only the information necessary to establish credibility with your client or manager and build the foundation for your plan. A good background will often depict data and more detailed information in the form of charts and graphs. The checklist in figure 4.1 represents the development of content that may be appropriate for the background.

The background sets the stage for understanding the situation at hand. It contains information about the industry and the client specifically: past efforts and events affecting organizational success and where the client currently stands in the marketplace. Remember that it selects and highlights only those bits of information that build the foundation for the solution or plan you will propose. Although you have not yet fully defined the problem or begun the planning process, some obvious alternatives will have emerged as your team gathered and evaluated the research. The background should organize the information and present it in a way that will lead your client or manager to the solutions you propose.

SWOT Analysis. As you have organized and synthesized your data and information according to the first eight steps of the checklist in figure 4.1, you have probably begun to make some inferences and drawn some conclusions relative to the issue or opportunity you are addressing. At this point, take some time to do a SWOT analysis — Strengths,

Weaknesses, Opportunities, Threats. According to Stacy Collett (1999), a SWOT analysis is:

> A way to analyze a company's or a department's position in the market in relation to its competitors. The goal is to identify all the major factors affecting competitiveness before crafting a business strategy.

Although typically designed to support development of marketing strategy, a SWOT analysis is useful in supporting all the relationships of the organization, not just those developed with customers. It is equally valuable to analyze the internal and external factors affecting issues and the entire environment within which the organization exists. When conducting a SWOT analysis, remember that your organization's relationships with key publics as well as the key publics' opinions and values can also be considered strengths or weaknesses.

This analysis is a great way to sum up your research and focus your knowledge on the opportunity you face and the barriers to be overcome. It tends to take pages of information and focus them into a few key factors that will generate success.

Market and Public Profiles. The last step on the checklist is to use the information you have gathered to profile the publics you may potentially need to reach to solve the difficulty or take advantage of the opportunity. To generate a comprehensive list of potential publics we suggest you conduct a brainstorming session. Carefully follow the rules of brainstorming to ensure no potential publics are left behind and everyone has a chance to contribute. Good group interaction should generate dozens of potential publics. More information on brainstorming is available in chapter seven of this text. We recommend you review figure 7.1, Rules of Brainstorming, to help you develop a solid list of potential publics.

Once the list has been generated, evaluate each public listed for potential contribution to the solution. Some publics will immediately emerge as potentially crucial to the problem/opportunity at hand. These potential key publics should be carefully and extensively profiled using information garnered through previous and ongoing research. Remember that you are not selecting key publics at this point. You cannot select key publics until after you set objectives. But your research will have caused you to identify a number of potential publics that you need to analyze to be familiar enough with the problem to set objectives and select key publics later.

The profiles should contain both demographic and psychographic information (gained through primary and secondary research) as well as any information that will help you reach them (like media preferences and habits). Also include an assessment of your client's or organization's relationship with that public. Remember when you are formulating profiles of publics that you must also identify self-interests and influentials (or opinion leaders). Later you will be using these profiles to help you decide which publics you will need to reach and motivate once you have established your goal and objectives. You will also use the profiles and self-interests to devise the messages that will motivate the individuals within the public. Preparing extensive, thoughtful, in-depth profiles now will make the planning step of the matrix flow more quickly and easily to the best solution.

We call these profiles because when you have completed the task, you should have a portrait in your mind's eye of the John or Jane Q. individual who is a member of that particular public. You should know them intimately, because you may be appealing to them to act in a way that will help you meet your challenge. You should know their ideas, attitudes, values, opinions, behaviors, lifestyles, purchasing preferences, recreation habits, media use and much more. Some of the information in the profile will come from hard data such as census or opinion research. Other information may be from focus groups, secondary research, personal observation and informed stereotypes.

Not all publics on your brainstormed list will need as extensive a profile. As you are assimilating information to profile a public, it may become clear that a particular public will only be needed in an extreme circumstance. As you review the profiles of potential publics in the teaching case at the end of the chapter, you will see senior citizens may have initially emerged as a potentially important group because more than half of those affected by the pesticide spray were seniors. Nevertheless, as you read through the profiles, you will see that addressing those affected by the spray and addressing residents of Goose Creek provides sufficient redundancy that identifying senior citizens as a separate key public is unnecessary.

Similarly, when we came to the profiles of other communities with Spruced Up farms, the solution that had begun to emerge would require targeting that public only if the plan we developed for Goose Creek didn't sufficiently contain the situation. For this reason, the profile for that public was very short.

Some publics on your list will emerge as resources or intervening publics rather than as key publics. Intervening publics — sometimes called third parties or influentials — are essentially opinion leaders. They intervene to assist in getting your message to your key publics, or to motivate key publics to action. In a state immunization campaign for example, health care professionals and the PTA may be two very influential intervening publics.

Intervening publics should be included in the resource portion of the background. They should also be profiled, although not as extensively as the potential publics you identify in step 10 of the research checklist. You do need to know about resource publics though, because you may be requesting their cooperation. You gain their cooperation in the same way you motivate action in key publics: by making it in their self-interest. For this reason, you need to know something about them and to understand their self-interests as they relate to your campaign.

Situation analysis

Although the problem or challenge was identified for us initially as we began the research process, it is important to redefine the situation after we have synthesized all available and pertinent information. The initial perception of the problem or opportunity may be quite unlike the actual situation. Based on the background, assess and describe in one paragraph the situation as it appears after the data has been organized and analyzed.

In a second paragraph, identify any related issues, problems or difficulties. Honestly assess potential barriers to success that must be overcome, but use your research as a confidence builder so your client or manager will be certain that the difficulties can be overcome. Identifying a difficulty and then suggesting a reasonable way to neutralize it may be the best approach.

Core problem or opportunity

Based on the synthesis of research in the background, you have narrowed the issue at hand to a short assessment of the situation and any related difficulties. Now cut to the heart of the problem in one sentence. For example, "Because key publics are not getting adequate and timely information about mobile blood drives, blood donations have declined, threatening the local hospital's immediate access to needed lifesaving units." The statement gets right to the central core of the problem and translates it to a tangible consequence if the problem is not solved. Be careful not to mistake symptoms of a problem for the problem itself. Like an onion, problems are made up of many layers. The layers surrounding the problem often take the form of symptoms and effects. In order to identify the core problem you need to peel back the symptoms and effects to find out what is really causing the difficulty.

SUMMARY

Organizing background research according to the research checklist helps lay the foundation for decision making. The background, SWOT analysis and public profiles help to focus everything we know into a solution or plan. It funnels research into the problem-solving and planning process because it has driven us to think analytically, to evaluate what is known and identify how that will assist in the selection of publics and resources to solve the problem.

The situation analysis likely identifies some key factors not known when the challenge or opportunity was first discovered. Assessing the real situation after we have completed our background analysis helps us focus more clearly on the core challenge/opportunity and to marshal all knowledge, information, skills and resources to succeed.

CHAPTER FOUR EXERCISES

1. Identify an organization with a communications and/or marketing problem. List everything you know about the organization, its environment, the problem and the market. Then list everything you need to know to define the real problem and devise a solution. What research tools and information sources would you use to get that information?

2. Find a nonprofit organization with a communications challenge that you can help solve. Using the research checklist, gather all the information you need to develop a solution to their problem. Using the strategic planning matrix, synthesize the information into the research section of a campaign proposal.

TEACHING CASE: The Case of the Caustic Cloud

This teaching case was developed to help students internalize the 10-step Strategic Communications Planning Matrix. A description of the case problem is given here along with the completed research section (background, situation analysis, and core problem/opportunity). Through this teaching case you will learn how to build a complete campaign, for any marketing or communications problem/opportunity, as you compare each step of the matrix with the example illustrated in the teaching case.

CASE DESCRIPTION

Spruced Up is one of the largest tree farm companies in the United States. The company operates nine farms in Washington, Oregon and California. It had revenues of $950 million in 2003 with $8 million in profits. The company is publicly traded on the New York Stock Exchange (NYSE) under the symbol NYSE:TREE.

Although started in 1952, Spruced Up has experienced rapid growth during the past decade as a result of an explosion in housing construction and landscaping. The company's stock has grown an average of 14 percent annually during the past five years and is actively traded. Part of Spruced Up's appeal to investors has been its proactive environmental policies.

The company had a very favorable reputation in the communities in which it operates until a mysterious cloud appeared over Goose Creek, Ore. While conducting routine aerial pesticide application at the company's largest farm, unexpected wind gusts carried a cloud of pesticide over a portion of the town. The incident occurred in the early afternoon on Wednesday, May 5, 2004, and has the town's residents in a fevered pitch. Roughly 40 people, mostly elderly and school children, reported respiratory distress the day of and several days following the incident. The Goose Creek Town Council has called an emergency meeting for May 10 and has summoned the company's CEO to respond to community outrage.

Goose Creek, a community of 60,000 residents, is also home to an extension campus of the state agricultural university with 3,500 students, many of whom are involved in pest control research. Spruced Up's Goose Creek farm employs approximately 4,000 people from the town and surrounding communities.

The company follows strict procedures for aerial insecticide spraying. Spruced Up is particularly careful that the insecticide used and the method of application does not pose a threat to employees or residents. Weather conditions are closely monitored — particularly wind velocity and direction — to contain insecticide application to Spruced Up properties. Community exposure to insecticide from any of the farms is rare. Only one other incident has been reported in the past 10 years. The other incident occurred in 1993 when a pilot inadvertently dropped spray on a small community in Northern California.

Although aerial spraying is routinely used on all Spruced Up farms, the company fears local outrage may affect its operations throughout Oregon and California. Spruced Up believes aerial insecticide application to be not only the most thorough but also the most cost effective way to protect its trees from deadly infestations.

MATRIX: Research
   Steps 1-3 — Background, Situation Analysis, Core Problem/Opportunity

SAMPLE CAMPAIGN

Note: This background example is abbreviated for space. Background research should not be unduly limited. Nevertheless, only directly relevant information should be included in the background text of your strategic plan. Additional charts, graphs and other information should be included. Profiles of potential publics should contain relevant demographics and psychographics such as opinions, attitudes, beliefs, behaviors, lifestyles and information sources.

BACKGROUND

Spruced Up is a significant employer in Goose Creek, Ore. The company employs roughly 15 percent of the town's adult working population. Spruced Up has also been active in the community supporting activities such as Little League baseball, the women's shelter and the state's agricultural college. In addition, the company has donated all of the shrubs and trees for Goose Creek's new Tucker Memorial Park sports complex completed in late April 2004.

Spruced Up is a vibrant, fast-growing company with headquarters in Eugene, Ore. The company has recorded a profit every year since it went public in 1998. Spruced Up stock is traded on the New York Stock Exchange under the symbol NYSE: TREE. The company recorded profits of $8 million on revenue of $950 million in 2003. Annual share growth has averaged 14 percent. The stock is currently trading at $32 per share and does not appear to have been affected by the May 5 incident. One of the factors contributing to the company's fast growth has been a strong demand for landscape and reforestation as a result of a healthy new home construction market in the United States. Low mortgage rates continue to brace the construction industry against a four-year economic downturn.

Spruced Up is viewed favorably by most environmental groups active in the area. The company has won praise for its low-impact approach to the environment. Its use of organic fertilizers has been the focus of several industry articles and even highlighted in a 2001 Wall Street Journal cover story. The company is the largest supplier of reforestation seedlings in the Northwest. Spruced Up stock is held in several "green," environmentally conscious, mutual funds.

The insecticide used by Spruced Up on May 5 is a mildly toxic preventative agent that is relatively new in the industry. Warning labels indicate the possibility of respiratory distress and caution against human exposure. Nevertheless, extensive testing has shown the active ingredients to be relatively harmless to humans in their diluted state. Spruced Up's procedures for aerial spraying require all employees to remain indoors during application. An official notification of aerial spraying dates is routinely posted in the local newspaper 10 days prior to spraying. It is also placed in the monthly city newsletter sent to all Goose Creek households.

Agricultural scientists on the extension campus are divided with regard to the safety of the insecticide in question when used in aerial application. Not much conclusive research has been done on this particular product. While no one believes it to be dangerous to the majority, some suspect that exposure by those with weaker immune systems may cause long-term health concerns.

Nonetheless, Spruced Up's internal scientists and agricultural specialists believe aerial spraying of this insecticide to be the least toxic, most cost-effective way to prevent infestation that could cause the loss of entire crops during the next several years.

Three physicians in Goose Creek treated 40 individuals who had respiratory difficulties subsequent to the incident. None of the cases posed long-term health concerns. All but two of those affected were released without need for medication or follow-up care. An elderly gentleman and an eight-year-old girl were treated for asthma-like symptoms. Both now appear to be symptom-free.

A short article about the May 5 incident has appeared in the local newspapers in two other communities where Spruced Up has farm operations. Neither of the stories received front-page coverage. The incident was mentioned briefly on the local Dan Barber radio talk show on Thursday morning, but not much detail was given and no calls were taken on the subject because not enough was known and Barber didn't think is was fair to delve into commentary on the story with so few facts. The story in the Goose Creek Squawker, the local paper with a circulation of 8,000, was on the front page of the Thursday morning edition without comment from Spruced Up because the story occurred right on deadline. A follow-up story is set to run on Friday morning with information on the pesticide and comment from Spruced Up, and with updated information on the medical condition of those affected. The derogatory comments of a member of the town council regarding Spruced Up's careless pursuit of profits will also be in the story. By Thursday afternoon, the Squawker had received an unprecedented 35 letters-to-the-editor complaining about Spruced Up's disregard for their employees and local residents. Three of the letters are set to run in the Friday morning edition.

Profiles of potential publics

Local media

Goose Creek has one daily newspaper, the Goose Creek Squawker, which ran a front page story without Spruced Up's comment on Thursday morning. They have a follow-up story scheduled for Friday morning's edition that is more balanced as it reports the innocuous nature of the pesticide and Spruced Up's comments as well as an update on the medical conditions of the 40 victims. The story does quote a town councilwoman criticizing Spruced Up for a "profits over people" mentality. The 8,000 circulation hits over half the households and most of the businesses in Goose Creek.

There are three local radio stations that receive good listenership from Goose Creek and surrounding areas. One is a news/talk format that captures the attention of most of the local business and professional people, community leaders, senior citizens and the academics. A second station is a teen music format and the third is a 60s and 70s music station that draws from Goose Creek residents, parents and blue collar workers (including Spruced Up's employees) who don't listen to talk radio. This station has a very short local news show every hour from 6–9 a.m., at noon and from 4–7 p.m. It didn't have the story on Wednesday, and didn't get it on the air for the morning or noon broadcasts Thursday. It may or may not hit the evening broadcasts on Thursday, but will probably be on the air by Friday.

A talk show host on the talk radio station, Dan Barber, deals with local community and political issues including the environment on his morning show. While the news of the aerial spraying incident hit too late for him to pull together intelligent commentary for a Thursday program, he did mention the incident. We can assume that as a result most of the community leaders, business and professional people, senior citizens (some of whom were affected) and college professors know about the incident either from the newspaper or from radio.

The three television stations that cover the Goose Creek area are from a significant population center (200,000 people) about 80 miles away. Goose Creek gets little local news coverage from two of them, but most people tune into the nightly news on one of the three stations. The one station that does provide some news coverage of Goose Creek picked up the aerial spraying story and will have a reporter at the town council meeting on Monday night.

Other media are in the form of newsletters. One is from the City of Goose Creek and goes monthly to all households in the city limits. Another goes monthly to members of the local chamber of commerce. The third significant newsletter is a small weekly publication that goes to employees at the agricultural college.

With the exception of television media, other media outlets are typically cooperative because they are always looking for content. They have provided positive coverage of Spruced Up's community involvement. Nevertheless, people with news typically have to come to them because they are short staffed and don't have a lot of time to dig it out or investigate a story.

Current relationship:

- Cooperative

Influentials:

- For the mass media, their audiences

- For newsletters, their gatekeepers (publishers) and audiences/members

Self-interests:

- Scooping other media
- Being financially viable by getting news that their viewers, listeners and subscribers want and need
- Doing as little work as possible to get information

Financial and trade media

Financial and trade media are simply interested in Spruced Up as a company and in its products. The aerial spraying incident would make news only if it was thought to threaten revenue, profits or stock price. These are the media Spruced Up deals with most and their relationships are based on trust. Spruced Up is always open about its financial picture and its niche is in a pretty stable industry. These media would have no reason to pick up the story or even want it unless it had created a problem that could have financial or business ramifications. If the incident is smoothed over quickly and completely, no disclosure to these media would be expected.

Current relationship:

- Cooperative business relationship, mutual respect

Influentials:

- Their audience, industry analysts, fund managers

Self-interests:

- Getting the story first and right
- Being financially viable by getting news that their subscribers want and need
- Being independent of the source
- Being considered the best source for financial and trade news

Industry analysts/fund managers

As with the financial media, this story would not be of much interest to the industry analysts and fund managers unless the situation got out of hand and threatened the company's financial stability or ability to do business. This public is interested in the financial picture and profitability. They are concerned with the validity of the stock price and the growth of profits. Currently this situation shows no potential of threatening either.

Current relationship:
- They know Spruced Up and respect its stability

Influentials:
- Professional colleagues and financial media

Self-interests:
- Getting the analysis right, choosing the right stocks
- For fund managers, making profit for clients
- Professional stature

Spruced Up shareholders

Shareholders come in a few varieties. The shares held in mutual funds (the so-called "green" funds) are controlled by the fund managers discussed previously. About 22 percent of Spruced Up stock is held in these funds. There will be no need for any advisory or communication with this public unless the situation becomes litigious.

Another category of shareholder is the individual investor. Some in this category have purchased the stock for their portfolio because they either know the company well and trust its track record, or because they know how to do research and diversify their portfolio by selecting sound investments in many industries. Either type of investor knows the company well and will not be unduly alarmed by the aerial spraying incident, although they will monitor the outcome closely if they hear about it. They are a steady kind of investor rather than a nervous investor. They will watch the company's response if they have picked up on the news, but would not be concerned unless the incident got out of hand. Although some may live in the area, most are probably from other communities and have not received any news about the incident. Only 7 percent of the stock is spread among this kind of small individual investor.

In this group you also have the large investors, those who control large blocks of the stock and who are personally known to and cultivated by the management of Spruced Up because they are major investors. The senior management of Spruced Up at the headquarters in Eugene maintain frequent contact with these individuals and many are also professional colleagues. Approximately 23 percent of the stock of Spruced Up is controlled by four such large investors. These large investors would typically view the aerial spraying incident with little interest, understanding that it will be successfully handled locally because the company's reputation for environmental care is exceptional, and the nature of the pesticide and incident are so innocuous there really shouldn't be a problem.

The senior management of Spruced Up, including the chairman of the board who started the company and the current CEO, his son, owns 27 percent of the stock. Because they are corporate executives, they will be concerned, but they were also immediately notified of the incident, all relevant information and the actions proposed to contain and resolve the challenge presented. They elected not to send any of their corporate communications staff to assist the local staff, demonstrating complete trust in the ability of local staff and management to handle the situation.

The final group of stockholders is employees and retired employees who have purchased stock through employee stock purchase opportunities as part of their retirement plan. They own 21 percent of the stock. This group of stockholders might be a bit more concerned than the other stockholders and any rush to sell would result in a fall in the stock price. This is definitely a group that needs some information from the company. Most would be considered routinely within the employee public, but those who are retired would not receive information targeted just at employees. Rash decisions to sell on their part may cause the company broader problems in the financial community. The employees' analysis will describe them in more detail and provide the necessary analysis on information sources, influentials, current relationship and self-interests. The retirees would fall into the category of senior citizens, but may need to be targeted separately because their concerns would go beyond being affected by the spray. They would have more poignant financial concerns.

In general, shareholders would be a significant public for Spruced Up to target if concern from other publics and the spraying incident in general are not effectively addressed and resolved. However, if Spruced Up can handle the crisis in a professional manner, it is probably not necessary to target this public initially.

Current relationship:
- They know and like us because we make money for them

Influentials:
- Fund managers discussed above
- Individual investors are influenced by industry analysts and financial media as well as by fellow investors and Spruced Up management
- Large investors are influenced by Spruced Up corporate executives, financial analysts,

fellow investors and colleagues
- Employee investors are influenced by corporate executives, fellow employees and employee investors
- Retired employee investors are influenced by corporate executives, fellow retirees and current employees

Self-interests:
- Making a profit
- A viable, secure, moderate growth investment for retirement

Spruced Up employees

The local farm employees about 4,100 people from Goose Creek and surrounding rural areas. Of that, 1,000 are seasonal employees, mostly students working in the summer. Of the permanent employees, 25 percent are shareholders through the employee stock purchase plan. Spruced Up pays decent wages for farm work. It doesn't pay as well as logging or the mills, but the work is not nearly as grueling and is much safer than the other industries. Among the permanent employees, overall job satisfaction (which includes wages) was at 75 percent in an employee survey done last year. The seasonal employees rated job satisfaction at 82 percent. In the same survey, 92 percent of Spruced Up employees considered the company to be a "good" or "very good" community citizen.

That survey also measured the level of trust of employees for local management and it was a 4.2 on a scale of one to five with five being absolute trust in all matters. The trust comes from more than just working at the company. Most of the managers at this farm have been promoted from within the ranks. Even the chief operating officer (COO) is a local boy who began working at this farm to put himself through a forestry degree at the local college. The company later sent him to Eugene to work in the headquarters office while he completed an MBA (which the company paid for) at the University of Oregon. He came back three years later as a senior manager and worked his way up to COO. He is well respected and well liked. Many consider him a friend.

Most of the permanent employees are raising families in Goose Creek. They have the same concerns and networks as residents and parents, but they have the added benefit of being tied into the company grapevine. Because they love their jobs and love their company, they are good representatives for Spruced Up in the community.

Employees are fully aware of the policy that all employees must remain indoors during aerial spraying of the crops. They understand that the pesticide is not toxic, but that it could cause some problems if directly exposed. Nevertheless, many fudge a bit on the policy, waiting until the last possible moment with the plane overhead before dashing indoors. Many have breathed the spray and consider it harmless. Nevertheless, they are concerned that the company needs to do right by the people who were affected by the spray so that they can continue to be proud employees. As blue-collar workers, most get their information from the oldies radio station and the local newspaper. More importantly, they get information about Spruced Up from work and information about how the community feels from friends and neighbors who are anxious to talk to them because they are Spruced Up employees.

Current relationship:

- Cordial, both parties satisfied with regular transactions

Influentials:

- Government contracting and regulators, their own stockholders, their own clients
- Local direct purchasers influenced like other Goose Creek residents

Self-interests:

- Getting the best price for quality seedlings and plantings
- Maintaining the source of supply

Goose Creek residents affected by spray

The residents affected by the spray include the elderly and young children, both of whom are more susceptible to respiratory distress. The public of concern regarding the young children is their parents. Only 15 of those affected were children, 12 elementary school age and three in junior high school. The other 25 were elderly residents. There is no clear evidence that the asthma-like symptoms were caused by the spray, but it is assumed that the short-term rise in respiratory emergencies and the aerial spraying accident are linked.

All but two of those affected were released without medication or necessary follow-up care. The other two were kept under observation for a couple of hours and provided with an inhaler to use as needed to reduce the irritation of nasal passages and lungs. Both patients appear to be fine. In spite of the minimal side effects, the parents of the children affected and the elderly residents affected are extremely concerned. They were assured by physicians there would probably be no side effects, but they are still a bit frightened from the experience of not being able to breathe well for several minutes. They fear that a more serious incident would cause more debilitating effects. They understand that this was an accident, but they don't think Spruced Up should be using any kind of chemicals that would cause any ill effects if an accident occurs. They don't want Spruced Up's business to be affected by this because they know people who depend on their jobs there. But they are also afraid. They want some assurances and they don't think it's fair that they had to pay medical expenses (even if some were just insurance co-pays) and emergency room charges because of Spruced Up's mistake. They are not inclined to sue, but do think some compensation is in order. Some had to actually leave work and are out sick/family time off because of it.

The elderly residents and parents are typical members of the Goose Creek community. They get their information in the same way as other residents. Influentials for this public are their family members, their family doctors and their community leaders. Most of the members of this public are personally acquainted with one or more members of the town council. They trust their community leaders to do the best for the residents of Goose Creek, but they will be at the town meeting and closely watching the outcome. They want some answers and assurances of their own.

Current relationship:
- Tentative
- Have viewed Spruced Up as a good community resident but are now concerned, afraid and need some answers

Influentials:
- Physicians, community leaders, family members and close friends

Self-interests:
- Being healthy and safe
- Not being afraid to go outside or to let children go outside
- Getting their medical bills paid

Goose Creek doctors and EMTs

There are 35 general practice physicians and 10 licensed EMTs in Goose Creek. This number includes emergency room physicians. Further, the Goose Creek Fire Department has three stations in the city. Only one of the three responded to emergency calls following the incident. The medical community in town is led by a handful of older doctors who have practiced in

Goose Creek for 25–30 years, some of whom were actually reared there. A few are younger doctors who came to Goose Creek because it was an area that needed doctors but had a hard time keeping them. The small town atmosphere may be a great place to raise kids, but no doctor will ever get rich here. Nevertheless, the doctors are among the highest socioeconomic group in Goose Creek. Just over 50 percent of this group has lived in Goose Creek less than five years. Nearly 40 percent do not intend to stay for an extended period of time. By nature, the local doctors tend not to panic, and the three who treated people after the aerial spraying incident assured their patients there would be no adverse effects. Two of the three who treated people are emergency room physicians. Six of those affected were either treated on site or taken to the emergency room by EMTs connected with the local fire department.

Doctors obviously have a higher level of education than the norm, having attended both college and medical school. They typically keep up on the medical literature, particularly that provided by pharmaceutical sales representatives and others like them who bring specific information directly to the doctor. They will investigate an ailment if they are uncertain of its ramifications and that investigation typically begins by calling a colleague who might know the answer. They will respond well to any responsible information provided by Spruced Up about the pesticide used and the potential adverse effects and proper treatments.

As a group, the general practice physicians are completely unconcerned with the incident. The emergency room doctors and the EMTs are more concerned, but primarily they just want to be prepared to treat patients in any similar incident in the future. They are radio news listeners (primarily the local news/talk station) and read the newspaper. They are typically uninvolved in community affairs or events because of limited time. Their opinion leaders are their spouses and professional colleagues.

Current relationship:
- Good, but a bit strained because of some lack of information

Influentials:
- For the doctors, each other and scientific studies/experts
- For EMTs, their supervisors and professional colleagues

Self-interests:
- Knowing whether or not the pesticide is harmful
- Knowing what to do if it happens again
- Being seen as competent

Goose Creek Town Council

The town council has five members elected for rotating terms of five years each. Two members — one a banker and one a plumber — are from leading families in town and are well-known and well-respected. They have both been re-elected to the council several times and have the longest history of service in this capacity. Another council member is a botany professor at the college who applied for the faculty position so he could raise his kids in a small town with traditional values. He is perhaps the least-known member of the council because he has no family ties in town beyond his immediate family.

The newest member of the council is a mother and housewife who has been active in the PTA and in community volunteerism and was encouraged by friends and neighbors to run for the council. She was a popular candidate and won by a wide margin. The remaining member of the council owns a local lumber mill. He worked in the mill part-time to put himself through school in forest engineering at the local college. He saved his money since he was a kid and purchased some property at a low price while he was in college. A few years later he sold the timber on the property and made a handsome profit, which allowed him to make a substantial down payment on the mill.

The council members are elected officials who serve in their spare time for a modest stipend. They officially direct the full-time city manager and city employees. They are sincerely interested in the best interests of the community and are truly community servants. Nevertheless, all enjoy their status as respected community leaders to greater or lesser degrees. They are often in the public eye and rather enjoy the acclaim they get from friends and neighbors from that status. They are particularly supportive of local business because they recognize the necessity of the tax base to support local schools and employers to keep unemployment down and the economy functioning. But, they also want a safe community free from the social problems experienced in the cities.

The banker and the plumber always vote as a block on the council, and they are always pro-business. The botany professor is relatively new to the council but also tends to vote quite conservatively. The former PTA leader is conservative on most issues but is an ardent defender of the children and disadvantaged in the community. She is the one who made the derogatory comments to be published Friday morning in the Goose Creek Squawker.

The mill owner is a "pull yourself up by your bootstraps" kind of guy who likes low taxes. He supports a strong educational system, but he believes parents have the lion's share of the responsibility to make sure their kids get a good education. He and the PTA leader often disagree; he thinks she is a "bleeding heart liberal." Their influentials include the city manager (because he is an information source and has the institutional memory), their constituents (friends and neighbors) and local business leaders. They read the local newspaper, listen to local radio and are consumers of national media, but they also stay connected to local information through the city newsletter, the Chamber of Commerce newsletter and the college employee newsletter. They are tied into various local grapevines and generally are the first to know of local happenings and local opinion.

Current relationship:
- Basically cooperative, but now a bit tentative
- Willing to cooperate, but need to see evidence of responsible action

Influentials:
- City manager, constituents, business leaders, academics

Self-interests:
- Solving the problem amicably with all parties feeling satisfied
- Appearing to be competent and working for the constituents' best interest
- Keeping Spruced Up open and profitable as part of the tax base

Goose Creek voters/residents

Goose Creek is the kind of a small town with traditional values where people are long-time residents; they are born, work and retire in Goose Creek or the surrounding communities. Goose Creek voters are residents who are very active in the community and frequently attend city council meetings and most town events. They feel a sense of pride in their community and want the town to remain safe and prosperous. They make extra efforts to ensure they are informed of what's going on in the community so they can vote appropriately and get involved whenever possible. Few people are new to Goose Creek, although some have moved in for employment at the Spruced Up farm and the agricultural college. That means many of the residents are related to each other either immediately or by extension. The elderly residents that were affected by the spray may not only be concerned for their own welfare; they may also be concerned that their grandchildren may be affected by subsequent accidents. It is the kind of town where every one knows everyone else in their neighborhoods and church groups because they all grew up together or went to school together or played on sports teams with or against each other. A few family names have dominated local activities and local politics. The Tuckers, Brooks, Bakers, Huddlestons, Martins, Gowens and Pynes have family members throughout the community. They have family members who work for Spruced Up, who own their own small businesses, who work in the local financial industry and at the college. And Joe Baker, a local banker, and Wilson Pyne, a local plumber, are on the town council.

Goose Creek is a blue-collar town. Nevertheless, it is also a very conservative, non-union community, rare for Oregon metropolitan areas but typical of its more rural locales. Most of the residents work at the Spruced Up farm or in the lumber industry in some way. Some are loggers and some are mill workers. A few of the rural residents are farmers who understand the need for the application of pesticides and are familiar with the safety of the pesticide used by Spruced Up. The majority of Goose Creek residents are in the lower ranges of middle income families ($40,000 to $60,000 a year per household). While the university employs about 500 workers, only 280 are academics. The remaining 220 are in the middle income range and relate well to the blue-collar logging and farming community; in fact, most have spouses or relatives working in those other industries. Nearly 75 percent of Goose Creek adults consider themselves Republican (whether or not registered). The remainder lean Democratic, primarily the more liberal academics and those employed in nonprofit and social service sectors. Of the 60,000 residents, about 40 percent are children under the age of 18. Goose Creek has two small high schools, three junior high schools and several elementary schools.

Most residents appreciate the community involvement and support from Spruced Up. They recognize it as a stable and valued employer and community resident. Some vaguely recall the incident in 1993, but don't remember any details because it didn't happen in this community and there was no real fallout from the incident. It really didn't cause much controversy. In a survey conducted last year, 85 percent of Goose Creek residents thought Spruced Up was a "good" to "very good" community resident.

Most Goose Creek adults read the local newspaper and listen to local radio. Other community information sources include networks through church groups, neighborhoods, families and workplaces. Again, the key work places include the logging companies, lumber mills, the Spruced Up farm and the college. The local chamber of commerce is a key information source for local business people.

The incident has the residents and voters concerned and a bit frightened. They are concerned that they may become victims of caustic pesticide in the future, but they are willing to give Spruced Up a chance to respond to community concerns. They will be listening and watching carefully to see what Spruced Up has to say and what they do to make things right by those affected by the accident.

Current relationship:

- Good, but they have some questions to be answered

Influentials:

- Community leaders, family members, fellow workers and friends who are Spruced Up employees

Self-interests:

- Health and safety
- Economic security
- A good community to raise families

Goose Creek parents

Goose Creek parents are profiled well by the profile of voters and residents. The 60,000 population of Goose Creek represents 12,000 households and 9,000 of those include at least one parent and one child. Of those, 77 percent have two parents in the home. Average number of children under the age of 18 in a home is three. The vast majority of the parents work. In nearly 80 percent of households with two parents, both work either full or part time.

Parents are more than a little concerned for the vulnerability of their children to respiratory distress resulting from exposure to Spruced Up's pesticide applications, and fear long-term consequences. Nevertheless, most have mixed emotions because fully 80 percent of households are partially or entirely supported by employment in the timber industry either by direct employment or employment in support industries such as at the Spruced Up farm. They don't want to lose their jobs, but they want their kids to be safe. They may be skeptical, but they are willing to give Spruced Up an opportunity to correct the situation. Parent's ranking of Spruced Up on last year's community resident survey was identical to overall residents. In fact, parents are nearly identical in all ways to residents except the level of concern is a bit elevated.

Current relationship:
- Tentative
- They fear for the safety of their children

Influentials:
- Community leaders, family members, fellow workers and friends who are Spruced Up employees

Self-interests:
- Health and safety of their children
- Economic security
- A good community to raise families

Goose Creek academics

The small community of academics (280 teachers and professors) actually poses little threat to Spruced Up farms. A small, but vocal, group are environmentalists and "tree huggers" that have continually attacked the local logging industry with the result that the majority of townspeople ignore their rants. They have not targeted Spruced Up in the past because they provide seedlings for replanting, although they don't really support it either because it feeds the timber industry. They are not counted among more mainstream environmentalists who have praised Spruced Up's environmental consciousness.

Far more credible in Goose Creek and in the majority on the faculty of the college are the academics who specialize in the agricultural industry. They are perceived as more down to earth and reasonable. They are trusted by the townspeople and could be considered opinion leaders for this particular issue. The survey a year ago found 60 percent of the academics believed Spruced Up to be a "good" to "very good" community resident. A professor of botany at the college is on the town council. Spruced Up has actually contributed a couple of million dollars to support faculty research in agriculture, particularly forestry and botany, and for student scholarships.

By nature, the academics in the last category are not eloquent or even vocal. They typically stay out of political issues and are more interested in their kids' high school football or basketball season. The typical academic in this category is male (age 35-55) and married with an average of three children, at least one approaching or in high school. They earn approximately 15 percent more than the average Goose Creek resident, but invest their earnings back into their homes and families rather than on luxury items. Many have a family history in Goose Creek, having been raised here and returned to work at the university after receiving academic credentials. They get their local information from the newspaper and radio, and through the grapevine. The television stations available locally are from the larger population center (a city of 200,000) 80 miles away from Goose Creek. The stations rarely carry Goose Creek news, although one did cover the aerial spraying accident and will have a reporter at the town meeting on Monday, May 10.

The environmentalist academics are typically young (age 28-35) and teach in the liberal arts and humanities. Most are unmarried or married to another environmentalist academic and have few if any children. They are typically new to Goose Creek (within the last five years) and have chosen this community because of its woodland setting. These individuals have set themselves apart from the local residents, considering most to be uneducated "hicks." These individuals are the source of many of the letters to the local newspaper, but they are also key consumers of the paper. They do not listen to local radio, preferring an NPR station. They are heavy consumers of national media, both newspapers and cable news channels.

Current relationship:

- Strong because Spruced Up supports the university

Influentials:

- University officials, colleagues, family members, community leaders

Self-interests:

- Professional stature
- A good community to raise families, as well as health and safety of children
- Economic security

Senior citizens

Seniors in Goose Creek have typically spent their lives here. They are shirt-tail relatives to almost everyone in the community in one way or another. Nearly all have children and grandchildren who live here as well. They are also connected throughout the community and know each other well because they've spent a lifetime with these same friends and neighbors in Goose Creek. Because of their history here, they are strongly connected to the traditional logging and lumber industries, and nearly 30 percent are retired or have a spouse that retired from the local Spruced Up farm and hold its stock as part of their retirement funds.

The senior citizens value Spruced Up's community-mindedness. They are aware of their modest contribution to help build the local senior center and are reminded of it every time they go to play Bingo in the Spruce Activity Hall at the center. In last year's survey 89 percent of seniors considered Spruced Up a "good" or "very good" community resident. Nevertheless, this public is seriously distressed from this incident. It isn't so much anger at Spruced Up as it is a fear of their vulnerability. Word has passed quickly through the grapevine at the senior center, through church groups, families and neighborhoods that the majority of those affected were seniors. Even though they know the pesticide isn't deadly because they've been around long enough to know Spruced Up couldn't and wouldn't use it if it were, they also realize that older people often die from ailments that have little or no effect on younger people. They fear for their lives. They know the spraying must continue if Spruced Up's farm is to be productive. They fear there is nothing that can be done to prevent them from being sickened or possibly killed by it.

While most of this public reads the newspaper, their most credible sources are talk radio and the senior grapevine that stretches through the senior center, churches and neighborhoods. They aren't going to oppose Spruced Up, but they see the spraying as just one more thing in the air that causes them respiratory difficulty. And most seniors recognize that respiratory difficulty is the bane of old age, and the ultimate cause of most deaths among seniors.

Current relationship:
- Fatalistic, they support us, but fear our practices

Influentials:
- Each other, family members, the two town council members who are from local families (Baker and Pyne)

Self-interests:
- Health and safety, as well as a safe place for their children and grandchildren
- Economic security
- Meaningful golden years

Other communities with Spruced Up farms

Although no two communities are completely alike, seven of Spruced Up's nine farms are in towns very similar to Goose Creek. The other two farms are in more populated areas. If the aerial spraying incident is handled quickly and effectively, the company's other farms will experience no difficulties from it. If the situation gets out of hand, then each of these communities will need to be considered individually. Most likely, media relations will be the extent of the effort needed. Nevertheless, if more in-depth efforts are needed to regain the loyalty of these communities, many of the strategies for publics and supporting tactics could be borrowed from Goose Creek, as could some of the collateral material.

SITUATION ANALYSIS

Spruced Up is a vibrant, fast-growing company that enjoys a positive reputation in the communities within which it operates. It also has a solid reputation as an industry leader and pioneer in safety and environmental practices. To maintain this strong financial position and reputation, the company must quickly and responsibly respond to those affected by the May 5 incident. The problem occurred when a cloud of pesticide intended for Spruced Up's nearby tree farm was inadvertently blown over a portion of Goose Creek. This is the first aerial spraying accident the company has experienced in 10 years and did not result in any lasting heath concerns. However, the local community is worried about the company's potential to inflict future harm on local residents.

Failure to adequately diffuse the situation could result in a reversal of public support and a weakening of Spruced Up's financial position. If the company fails to be perceived as concerned about Goose Creek residents and does not act to prevent future incidents, then it may lose support from its employees and public support in all of the communities in which it operates. Related difficulties could include hiring challenges, employee dissatisfaction, loss of investor confidence, customer concerns, increased costs, lawsuits and diminished revenues.

CORE PROBLEM/OPPORTUNITY

To maintain its growth and financial strength, Spruced Up must quickly address community concerns in Goose Creek about the safety of its operations and communicate its ongoing commitment to its employees and the communities where it operates.

REFERENCES AND ADDITIONAL READINGS

Collett, S. (1999). "SWOT Analysis: Quickstudy." *Computerworld.*
July 19.

Stacks, D.W. (2002). *Primer of Public Relations Research.* New York:
Guilford Publications, Inc.

chapter **5**

SETTING GOALS AND OBJECTIVES

"If you fail to plan, plan to fail."

— Unknown

LEARNING IMPERATIVES

▶ To be able to turn problem statements into appropriate goals

▶ To understand the characteristics of good objectives

▶ To learn how to write specific objectives to support the accomplishment of a goal

The second step of the RACE model is action planning. Planning and the programming it generates is how we get from here to there. "Here" is where we are now. It is our current situation as we have described it after synthesizing our research and redefining the challenge or opportunity we face. "There" is where we need to be, having overcome the challenges and taken advantage of the opportunities. Planning helps us look ahead, to chart our course to ensure we get there. Like sailing a boat, planning must be flexible and open to alteration and correction as we receive feedback or obtain new information. Nevertheless, unless we know where we are going and have some idea of an appropriate course to get there, our arrival at the destination will be left to chance. The more complete our planning of the best course (based on good research), the better our chances of arriving at success.

The matrix approach to planning

> Planning

The process of using research to chart the step-by-step course to solve a problem, take advantage of an opportunity or meet a challenge.

The heart of the Strategic Communications Planning Matrix is the action planning section. The research process, the subsequent organization and analysis of data and the redefinition of the situation and the core challenge, all lay the foundation for the action planning process. Cutlip, Center and Broom (2000) call this a "searching look backward," a "wide look around," a "deep look inside" and a "long look ahead."

The next three parts of the process — action planning, communication and evaluation — are separate and distinct in practice, although the process may require revisiting a prior step while in the midst of implementation of the plan. The Strategic Communications Planning Matrix addresses each of the remaining three steps as discrete functions. Nevertheless, this is a planning matrix; the emphasis is on planning each step in the process before implementing. Thus, the resulting plan, although dynamic, becomes a document to drive both the communication and evaluation steps in the process.

Planning occurs at two distinct levels within any organization. Long-term planning looks at the entirety of the organization and its mission. It identifies goals and objectives and publics and messages that address the long-term accomplishment of that mission. Planning at this level becomes a guide for planning more specific short-term campaigns or communication efforts. They are the second level of planning. Managing a crisis, launching a new product line and repairing a damaged reputation are all more specific efforts within the overall long-term plan. Although they are focused on a more specific challenge, they always reinforce key messages to organizational publics and support the goals and objectives of the long-term plan. Nevertheless, by their nature, they may also address publics that may not be long-term key publics to the organization but that are crucial to the accomplishment of the short-term effort.

Research helps us define the challenge and the current environment within which the opportunity has occurred or will occur. Matrix planning identifies what specifically needs to be accomplished (goal and objectives) to overcome the challenge, who (key publics) we need to reach and/or motivate to accomplish the goals and objectives, what we need to convey (messages) to those publics to stimulate action and help us achieve our objectives, and how (strategies and tactics) to get those messages to those publics so they both receive and act upon them.

The process is analytical, with the decisions made and actions planned in each step driving the decisions made and actions planned in each subsequent step. Further, the steps must be taken each in turn. For example, the key publics for a particular problem-solving effort cannot be selected until we have determined the goal and the objectives necessary to achieve that goal. Only then can we select the publics that are key to accomplishing those objectives. Similarly, we can only design effective messages after we have analyzed a key public and determined its self-interest. The decisions we make about the information a public needs, what will motivate it to act and what opinion leaders can influence it are prerequisite to designing that public's message.

Effective informational and motivational messages cannot be designed for a given public without a thorough analysis of its research profile, examination of the status of the current relationship with that public and knowledge of its self-interests as they pertain to the problem at hand and related issues. Strategies and tactics appropriate to send the designed messages to the selected publics cannot be determined until we know what those messages are. Quite simply, the matrix approach requires us to decide what we want to do, who we need to reach to do it, what messages we need to send to obtain cooperation and how we can most effectively send those messages. The steps must be taken in order or our planning is left to chance and will most likely be flawed and off-track.

We have all seen campaigns that had good research but somehow misconnected in the planning process. One poignant example is Salt Lake City's campaign to win the bid for the 1998 (and subsequently the 2002) Olympic Winter Games. Previously, the Denver organizing committee had to withdraw its candidacy as the United States' representative in a previous Olympic games bid because of opposing public opinion in the Denver area. Consequently, the Salt Lake City organizers decided it was important to have a public referendum on the issue to demonstrate to the United States Olympic Committee (USOC) and to the International Olympic Committee (IOC) that the Utah public was fully supportive of Salt Lake's candidacy. With support running high in the state (upwards of 80 percent), the organizing committee expected the referendum would send a strong message from the Utah public in support of the effort. Nevertheless, their own polling showed they had weak support and even opposition among senior citizens, environmentalists and ultra-conservative segments of the population. While these groups actually comprised only a small percentage of the Utah publics, the organizing committee worried that, in an off-year election, those three segments of the population were the most likely to vote. Given that information, their goal and objectives were to get out the supportive vote.

The strategy was to air clever, creative and visually appealing television spots (tactics) that gave people a good feeling about Utah hosting the Olympic games. At the end of the spots they showed a box with a check mark in it to indicate a vote supportive of the Olympic bid. But the ads were essentially still seeking intrinsic public support of the games. The ads didn't ask people to get out of their chairs and go vote. The bid already had a high public approval rating. What the committee really needed was to motivate those who approved to get to the polls and cast their support-ive vote. But the committee (through its ads) never asked the approving public to actually go vote. So they didn't. The referendum ultimately passed by a very slim majority, and the organizing committee was plagued with explaining the low margin of public support to the IOC in almost every subsequent interaction.

Once the city won the opportunity to host the 2002 Olympic Winter Games, the organizing committee no longer had to address the issue of citizen support to the IOC. Nevertheless, the low voter support of the ref-erendum was continual fodder for the active (albeit minority) opposition to the games in Utah. No public opinion poll could ever entirely dispel the results of the actual vote.

The Salt Lake City Olympic Organizing Committee had good research data and analysis. They knew what they had to do (get out the supportive publics who don't typically vote in an off-year election). They knew specif-ically the profiles of the publics they had to reach. Yet they designed a mes-sage that did not ask those publics to do what the committee needed done, and they sent it in a broadly targeted tactic through a mass medium ill-suited to the purpose at hand (reaching and motivating highly segmented publics). Each step of the matrix planning process must build on the pre-vious step. The logic must flow consistently and coherently. Disregarding the information accumulated, the decisions made and actions planned in one step will almost always ensure that the decisions made and actions planned in the next step are off-target and headed for failure.

With this important lesson in mind, the next few chapters address the action planning steps of the Strategic Communications Planning Matrix. This chapter begins that discussion with identifying what needs to be done to meet the challenge or seize the opportunity at hand.

Establishing the goal

Once the core problem or opportunity is accurately established, set-ting the goal is a simple task with the planning matrix. The goal is actual-ly a positive restatement of the core problem. If your challenge is declin-

> **Goal**

The result or desired outcome that solves a problem, takes advantage of an opportunity or meets a challenge.

10-STEP STRATEGIC COMMUNICATIONS PLANNING MATRIX

matrix

MATRIX: Action Planning

Step 4 — Goal and Objectives

Goal   The goal is a one-sentence statement of the end to be achieved to resolve the core problem or seize a significant opportunity. The goal does not have to be stated in quantifiable terms.

Objectives Objectives are numbered or bulleted statements of specific results that will lead to the achievement of the goal. Objectives must be: specific, measurable, attainable, time-bound and mission-driven.

ing confidence among investors leading to a decline in stock price, your goal is to re-establish confidence so stock price will increase. If your problem is a lack of accurate information regarding the process of organ donation causing a shortage of available organs for transplant, your goal is to convey appropriate information in such a way as to increase the number of organs donated. The goal should be broader and more general than the objectives that follow. A goal also does not have to be specifically measurable. The measured achievement of strategic objectives should ensure that the overall goal is obtained.

Nevertheless, setting the goal may not be as simple as it appears. Too often, organizational communications and marketing personnel act unilaterally to set goals to solve problems. But those functions are not isolated tasks within an organization; they should all be integral parts of the management function and team. Setting campaign goals in isolation, or without consideration of the organization's overall goals, is dangerous and can lead to a lack of support at critical junctures.

Two precautions can aid the practitioner in avoiding this problem. First, if the daily communication function has been approached strategically, or planned in accordance with the organization's mission and goals (including the goals of various other departments such as public relations, advertising and marketing), then communications is guided by the organization's mission. In other words, communications and marketing practitioners should always set and follow goals and objectives that support the overall organizational mission.

A second precaution is simply to verify the campaign goal's compliance with organizational goals and objectives. After setting the goal, take a moment to ask yourself if it supports the overall organizational mission. Does it mesh with marketing and communication goals and objectives? Does it cooperate to create an environment in which the organization progresses toward achievement of its goals? It is typically not enough to "not conflict" with the organization's communication and marketing missions and goals. Truly sound and defensible goals and objectives will enhance and support the overall organizational mission and goals. Figure 5.1 identifies some examples of possible organizational goals. Remember that effective communication with key publics is necessary to create the environment in which the organization can reach its goals. Any single campaign, whether designed to solve a problem or to proactively position the organization, must be planned within the framework of the organization's goals.

figure **5.1**

Examples of Typical Organizational Goals

Business Sector
- Maintain profitability
- Maintain and gradually improve stock rating
- Achieve a positive trust ranking
- Maintain an operating environment with minimal government regulation

Public Sector
- Increase use of funded social programs
- Cut overhead and increase flow of funds to programs
- Decrease fraudulent use of social programs
- Improve citizen access to and use of information
- Increase government funding

Nonprofit Sector
- Expand research efforts
- Expand program reach
- Secure private financial support of programs

Identifying objectives to accomplish the goal

Once the goal is set, the challenge is to break down what you want to accomplish into smaller, more specific tasks. If your company's goal is to expand a research program, your communications campaign may need to set objectives that involve securing funding, attracting personnel and building community support for the renovation of facilities. Objectives are specific, measurable statements of what needs to be accomplished for the goal to be reached. Whereas a goal may be somewhat ambiguous (i.e., not defining how much is enough funding or profit), objectives must be absolutely free from ambiguity.

In the communications literature, approximately eight characteristics emerge to guide the formulation of good objectives. They should be:

> Objective

Specific, measurable statements of what needs to be accomplished to reach the goal.

1. **Written**. This characteristic may appear to be obvious, but too often we begin planning by assuming everyone understands our purpose and objectives. Unless they are written, they have probably not been well considered, and there may be differing perceptions of what the objectives really are. One member of the team may be working toward something entirely different than the other members because his/her perception of the task is different than the rest of the team's. Putting the objectives in writing helps to avoid differing perceptions of what needs to be accomplished.

   Further, when objectives are written, they serve as reference points throughout the planning process. When you come to a point of disagreement on any element of the planning process or when you run out of ideas somewhere in the process, it often helps to go back and review exactly what it is you are trying to accomplish. Finally, written objectives serve as tangible guides for evaluation and evidence of success, not only for the program or project but also for you as a professional.

2. **Specific and clearly defined**. To be free from ambiguity, the task must be specific and clear. It often helps to quantify the objective, and each objective should address only one task. You shouldn't write a single objective to increase awareness of both an issue and an organ-

ization. Moreover, sometimes simple name recognition is enough, but the majority of the time you need to be specific about what kind of awareness you are seeking. Do you want to increase awareness of an organization's existence or of a specific product line? Are you specifically targeting HIV awareness, or of the effect of its transmission to newborns? And what levels of awareness are you seeking based on current levels of public knowledge? Having task-specific objectives helps you more clearly understand what publics you need to reach and what you need each public to do. Those tasks actually become part of the strategies for key publics later in the planning process.

3. **Measurable and improvement-oriented**. It is a given that an objective should be improvement oriented. It must specify a task that works with other tasks to achieve the goal or meet the challenge. In order for an objective to truly guide the program and demonstrate its ultimate success, it must also be measurable. Measurement can be in percentages or in actual figures (a dollar amount of funds needed, sales targets, total number of volunteer hours sought, number of votes necessary). Oftentimes, it is helpful to indicate the measurable target in terms of improvement (sales increased 20 percent from $5 million to $6 million or inoculations increased 10 percent annually from 500,000 to 550,000).

When you work with percentages, remember to carefully state the percent increase or decrease and use clarifying phrases. Otherwise, you might set yourself up to disappoint management's expectations created by your own objectives. If you want to decrease the percentage of high school students who have experimented with drugs by 50 percentage points, you should follow up that number by specifically stating the decrease (from 75 percent to 25 percent). If you really had in mind a 50 percent decrease (rather than a 50 percentage point decrease), you would have reduced the percentage from 75 percent to 37.5 percent (or 50 percent of 75). Similarly, a 20 percent increase in participation among a total population of 100 is not 20 people. The percent increase depends on the current level of participation, not the total population. If 50 of 100 people are currently participating, a 20 percent increase would be ten people (20 percent of 50), from 50 to 60 participants, or a ten percentage point improvement. Be very precise when you state your measurement.

Statistics on opinion or action may not always be readily available. If you absolutely know the level of knowledge or participation is minimal, just state the level you want to take it to. If you don't have statistical measures for something, find another way to count the improvement. Remember that circulation data (readership/viewership) is not a reliable measure of receipt and retention of a message. Just because someone subscribes to the newspaper doesn't mean he/she paid attention to your story.

4. **Credible**. Being credible simply means that the accomplishment can be directly attributed to your efforts. For example, if the advertising or public relations teams set an objective to obtain a 5 percent increase in product sales and then attempt to claim sole credit for that accomplishment, they will not only incur the disapproval of their marketing counterparts but also of top executives who recognize they are claiming credit for improvement for which they are not alone responsible. Set objectives and then design programs which are directly attributable to the success you claim. If your task is public relations, focus on creating the environment within which other organizational entities can succeed.

5. **Acceptable**. This characteristic refers to the acceptability of the objective to the organization and its management. To be acceptable, an objective must be in line with and support the organizational mission, goals and objectives. It must address issues, problems and improvements that management perceives as valuable.

6. **Realistic and attainable**. Can you really achieve what your objective specifies you will achieve? Keeping objectives specific and clear will also help to keep them realistic. But you still need to set your sights on significant improvement. Top management will scorn objectives that are too easily attainable. Executives have little respect for employees and managers who are unwilling to reach a bit, to take

some risks and to challenge themselves. Nevertheless, if you shoot for the moon and just hit the stars, you may be branded as having fallen short, even if the stars were all you really needed to reach.

7. **Time-bound**. The duration of a communications or marketing campaign is determined by the problem or opportunity being addressed. Some may require short, quick efforts (a few weeks or months) while others may necessitate longer-range efforts. Some campaigns have built-in deadlines (i.e., special event for a product launch). Other efforts want to change perceptions and attitudes, which change very slowly. Good objectives must identify the time frame within which the program must be completed and benchmarks for the measurement of long-range campaigns.

8. **Budget-bound**. Although you don't always know the budget available for a specific program when you are at this preliminary stage of planning, you don't want budget considerations to curtail your creativity, innovation and imagination (you might come up with a program the organization believes it can't afford not to fund). Good objectives take into consideration the probable budgetary range. While you must set objectives to solve the problem and reach the goal, the objectives you set also shape the organization's expectations of you and your communications and marketing team. Budgetary limitations may necessitate objectives that create more modest expectations. They may also force greater creativity in your planning. Although larger budgets will lay the groundwork for a more ambitious program, the reality of today's business environment is that there is limited funding.

In addition to the characteristics of good objectives, it is important to recognize the two basic kinds of objectives, each serving a different purpose but both integral to the overall accomplishment of any campaign. The first kind of objective lays a foundation of information and awareness necessary for any kind of persuasive effort. It addresses the dissemination of information and the increase in awareness necessary among publics before they can develop attitudes to drive the behavior you are seeking.

Informational objectives are usually easy to accomplish because you are just spreading information, not attempting to change anything. In fact, much of today's corporate communications practice is heavily engaged in information dissemination and awareness- or consciousness-raising. Nevertheless, Wilcox, Ault and Agee (2002) contend that it is difficult to measure the accomplishment of such an objective because you are trying to measure a cognitive function (increase in information or understanding) on a sliding scale (how much information or understanding).

Motivational objectives, on the other hand, are more easily measured and harder to achieve according to Wilcox, et al (2002). It is a relatively simple matter to measure a desired behavior. People voted for your candidate or they didn't; consumers bought the product or they didn't; children were inoculated or they weren't. Nevertheless, changing attitudes and opinions and creating the triggering event to move the public from attitude to behavior is much more difficult than just disseminating information and raising awareness of an issue or problem.

Use awareness objectives to lay the foundation for persuasive efforts or motivational objectives. People can't vote the way you want them to on an issue if they are not aware of the issue and its effect on their lives. Consumers cannot buy a new product that will make life easier or more pleasant if they are not aware of its existence. Set awareness and information objectives (with all the characteristics of good objectives) that will lay the foundation to accomplish your motivational objectives. Keep in mind that disseminating information is easy but motivating behavior is more difficult. You will typically be able to reach a far higher level of awareness than you will behavior. You may be able to inform upwards of 90 percent of your target population on a particular issue. (You'll probably never reach 100 percent awareness; there is always some small percentage of people who travel through life oblivious to just about everything). Nevertheless, 90 percent awareness does not translate to 90 percent motivated to act. The achievable percentage of behavior will always lag behind the level of awareness. On some issues it may be only slightly lower; on other issues there may be a dramatic difference.

SUMMARY

The Strategic Communications Planning Matrix guides the planning process in communication and problem solving. It is the analytical tool that ensures research data and information are applied to solving the problem at hand. This matrix requires that good information, sound reasoning and clear logic drive decisions regarding what objectives you need to accomplish to solve the problem, what publics you need to reach, what messages you need to send to motivate those publics to act and what communication tools (tactics) will ensure key publics select and act on your messages.

The matrix transforms each step of the RACE model into strategic functions. It ensures that the communication process is not just a succession of steps to be completed, but that it is an interactive, integrated methodology for finding the best and most timely solution for the most appropriate cost. The process must be guided by mission-oriented goals and clear, measurable objectives. Remember that a campaign goal is a positive restatement of the core problem identified in the research section of the matrix.

Objectives lay the foundation for the successful selection of key publics, their messages and the strategies and tactics that will deliver the messages and motivate action. Well crafted objectives are: written, specific and clearly defined, measurable and improvement oriented, credible, acceptable, realistic and attainable, time-bound and budget-bound.

CHAPTER FIVE EXERCISES

1. Based on your research, create goals and objectives for the nonprofit organization you identified in the previous chapter's exercises. Make sure you set a goal that overcomes the problem you identified, and set objectives to attain the goal that follow the eight characteristics of good objectives.

2. Select a local company and request a copy of its mission statement and goals. Then brainstorm the objectives necessary to reach the goals. Make sure your objectives meet all the criteria of good objectives.

TEACHING CASE: The Case of the Caustic Cloud

MATRIX: Action Planning

Step 4 — Goal and Objectives

SAMPLE CAMPAIGN

Goal

Spruced Up's goal is to maintain its positive reputation in Goose Creek and its growth and financial strength by quickly addressing community and employee concerns related to the safety of its operations.

Objectives

1. Ensure that all Goose Creek residents affected by the insecticide have been properly cared for by Friday, May 7.
2. Ensure that 95 percent of Goose Creek residents affected by the insecticide (or their parents) are content with the company's actions to resolve the incident by Friday, May 14.
3. Regain 85 percent level of perception that Spruced Up is a "good" or "very good" community resident by May 31 and again by October 31.
4. Distribute short-term treatment instructions and background information about the spray to the 45 general physicians, emergency room doctors and EMTs in the Goose Creek area by Friday, May 21.
5. Obtain a 75 percent level of perception that Spruced Up operates "safely" and "responsibly" regarding employees and the community by May 31 and again by October 31.
6. Mitigate negative effects to Spruced Up's financial position by keeping overall dips in the company's stock price to less than 5 percent for at least 30 days following the incident (stock was trading at $32 at the market close on May 4).

REFERENCES AND ADDITIONAL READINGS

Cutlip, S., Center, A., & Broom, G. (2000). *Effective Public Relations* (8th ed.). Englewood Cliffs, N.J.: Prentice-Hall, Inc.

Drucker, P. (1974). *Management Tasks, Responsibilities, Practices*. New York: Harper and Row.

Hainsworth, B.E., & Wilson, L.J. (1992). "Strategic Program Planning." *Public Relations Review*, 18:1, 9-15.

Koestler, F.A. (1977). *Planning and setting objectives*. New York: Foundation for Public Relations Research and Education.

Newsom, D., Turk J.V. & Kruckeberg D. (2004). *This Is PR: The Realities of Public Relations* (8th ed.). Belmont, Calif.: Wadsworth Publishing Company.

Norris, J.S. (1984). *Public Relations*. Englewood Cliffs, N.J.: Prentice-Hall, Inc.

Wilcox, D. L., Ault, P. H., & Agee, W. K. (2002). *Public Relations: Strategies and Tactics* (7th ed.). New York: Harper and Row.

chapter **6**

KEY PUBLICS AND MESSAGE DESIGN

"An audience is not a demographic.
Demographics are the boundaries, psychographics fill in the boundaries."

— Linda Hadley

Director of Research, Porter Novelli
2002 PRSA International Conference

LEARNING IMPERATIVES

▸ To learn how to select effective key publics

▸ To learn how to be able to determine each key public's relevant self-
interests and key opinion leaders, and to assess the status of the
relationship between the organization and each key public

▸ To learn how to design effective messages for each key public that
incorporate relevant self-interests

I n the last chapter, we discussed setting the objectives to be accomplished to meet the challenge of the core problem. Having done so, we can identify the key publics or audiences whose cooperation will be essential to achieving those objectives and design the messages that will motivate those publics to act, or to allow the organization to act.

Although the terms "public" and "audience" are often used interchangeably, public is actually a more accurate concept. "Target audience" may imply an inanimate one-dimensional group of identical individuals just waiting to receive and absorb your message. "Public" is more descriptive of a multidimensional active and interactive group of individuals with a few common characteristics that allow us to group them for the purpose of building relationships through communication and cooperation.

For some communicators, it has become habit to select key publics before setting objectives. As a result, they often set objectives that are public-specific. Frequently, the publics are assumed to be only those the organization has previously targeted for strategic relationship building. While it is important for an organization to identify and build relationships with specific publics upon which its long-term success depends, it is equally important to recognize that any given communications effort may need to encompass publics other than those previously identified as organizationally key.

To assume all organizational challenges can be met through communication with that set group of publics is a prescription for failure. If you select publics before you have determined specifically what you need to do to meet the challenge/opportunity, you are setting the objectives based on who you want to reach rather than what you need to accomplish. You may be successful at reaching the organization's existing key publics, but you risk missing other publics necessary to solve or seize the particular problem or opportunity at hand.

A good example is a campaign to increase the number of organ donors on the campus of a large private university. Publics were selected for the campaign before objectives were set. It was determined that student Reserve Officer's Training Corps (ROTC) members would be a good target because they were predisposed to the public service represented by organ donation. That is a logical conclusion, but the public was not a practical choice in a campaign for which an objective was set to motivate 10,000 students to sign organ donor cards. Why? Research showed that although the student ROTC members would be easy to motivate, most were already designated organ donors. Further, there were fewer than 200 ROTC members on the campus. With a need to motivate 10,000 students that necessitates reaching more than 10,000 students — spending time and money on a public of only 200 does not make sense.

Further, as you reanalyze your problem/opportunity and the goal (most often in the evaluation process when it is too late to correct your error before top management notices it), you may find you needed to accomplish a task (or objective) you hadn't anticipated when you selected your publics. If you select publics and set objectives for those publics, you are likely failing to identify some tasks that will be necessary to accomplish the goal. You will probably do a great job of reaching your designated target publics, but there is a real chance those publics will not be key publics, or the ones you needed to reach to complete the tasks that would accomplish your purpose. Don't waste time and money informing and motivating publics that don't need informing or motivating. Success among them will not significantly contribute to improved percentages of participation because they are already participating.

You are much more certain to accomplish your goal if you determine the specific tasks (objectives and benchmarks) necessary to achieve it and then decide which publics you must reach and motivate to complete those tasks. Your strategies for a public then become the specific tasks you must accomplish with that public to achieve your objectives. If you must persuade one-third of the students in a student body of 30,000 to designate themselves as potential organ donors, you choose publics that are, among other considerations, of sufficient mass to contribute significantly to the accomplishment of that task.

> **Key Public/ Audience**

Segmented groups of people whose support and cooperation are essential to the long-term survival of an organization or the short-term accomplishment of its objectives.

DETERMINING KEY PUBLICS

By this time in your study and practice of marketing communications and public relations, you are well aware that there is no "general public." Targeting a general public is useless because no one will pay attention to a message that isn't specifically targeted. Yet our function as a communication profession and our use of so-called mass media seem to perpetuate our tendency to generalize publics. In fact, communicators will often segment publics and then devise a single message to reach all of their segmented publics through one of the mass media. The segmentation was a waste of time and resources, and the message sent even more so a waste. We would do well to remember that just because a medium is designated mass does not mean that the publics consuming the information provided therein are mass.

Just as people read a newspaper by selecting out what they want to perceive based on headlines and leads, they choose to perceive our message only when we design it specifically to appeal to them. It is clear that

---

10–STEP STRATEGIC COMMUNICATIONS PLANNING MATRIX

matrix

MATRIX: Action Planning

Step 5 — Key Publics and Messages

Key Publics   Key publics include a description of each audience that must be reached to achieve the goal and objectives. Four elements should be identified for each public or audience:
1. Demographic and psychographic profile
2. Motivating self-interests
3. Status of current relationship with the organization and issue
4. Third party influentials and other opinion leaders

Messages   Messages are public-specific and appeal to the public's self-interests. They are designed to be primary or secondary. Primary messages are one or two sentence summary statements similar to sound bites. Secondary messages are bulleted details that add credibility to and support the primary messages with facts, testimonials, examples, etc.

for a message to be selected, perceived and retained from the mass media, it must be carefully and specifically targeted to a segmented public included within the readership or listenership. If its appeal is general, no public will consider it for perception and retention. It may get sent, but if it doesn't obviously and openly address the self-interests of specific target publics, it will never be received.

There are lots of ways to segment publics. The way you choose to segment publics for a particular campaign must depend upon the issue and your purpose. If you are addressing the quality of education in the community, public segmentation would include parents, teachers, administrators and future employers. If the issue is zoning regulations within that very same community, your segmentation would recategorize the community members as non-property owners, residential property owners, commercial property owners or business people and civic and government leaders. They are the same people, but how you segment or group and describe them for the purpose of reaching and motivating is based upon the issue at hand and their particular self-interest in that issue.

Understanding the need to target publics that help us fulfill our objectives, how do we actually go about selecting those publics key to meeting our challenge? In the background step of the research section, you brainstormed a list of publics or audiences that might be involved in the solution to the problem or issue facing the organization. Then you used the primary and secondary data gathered to profile those publics — their demographics as well as their opinions, attitudes, values, beliefs and lifestyles. Because you have completed that analysis, you know the status of each of those potential publics regarding your current challenge. Now, review your objectives and determine which of those publics can help you accomplish the tasks described.

Remember that more than one public may need to be reached to accomplish each objective or task, and also that a key public may help you achieve more than one objective. It may be helpful to identify which objectives a particular public can aid in achieving so the strategies you write for that public fully contribute to fulfilling those objectives.

Bear in mind that there may be several different combinations of key publics that can help you accomplish the goal. As described in figure 6.1, your task is to discover the combination that: first, does the best job of combining to solve the problem; second, is most logical in terms of ongoing organizational efforts to build relationships; and third, provides the most benefit for the cost in terms of resources (time, money and effort). Consider, for example, a presidential election campaign. Political campaigns are probably one of the best examples of using thorough research to guide decision making. The research consultant to a presidential candidate has access to thousands of pieces of information from a variety of research techniques that include, at a minimum, focus groups, panel studies and opinion polls. The consultant has divided the voting population into dozens of different segments and has an in-depth, research-based profile of each. The research profiles the attitudes, behaviors and voting preferences of every demographically segmented public by age, income, education, gender, religion, geography, job and any other descriptor you can imagine. Further, the consultant has included in the profiles lifestyles, consumer preferences, habits and other psychographic and value-based characteristics.

With all those segments, there are literally hundreds of combinations of publics that could accomplish the task — election of a president. A strategist might, for example, choose a combination that includes, among others, 24-32 year-olds, Catholics, blue collar workers and Northeastern voters. The job of the strategist in a political campaign is to select, from the dozens of profiled segments, the combination of voter publics that will best assure victory in the election (priority one in figure 6.1). In selecting

---

figure 6.1

Priorities in Selecting the Best Combination of Key Publics

1. Which publics working together will produce the best overall solution?
2. Which publics make the most sense for long-term organizational relationships?
3. Which combination of publics will get the desired result for the least amount of additional time, money and other resources?

publics to bring victory, the strategist should also consider those publics whose cooperation will be most crucial to the long-term success of the newly elected president (priority two). Finally, the strategist should consider the combination of publics that will bring the most benefit for the least cost (priority three).

Too often in the past, business has operated with that third priority as the first consideration. Leading our decisions with only cost considerations has landed us in the current crisis of trust among those publics most essential to survival of organizations in our society. The key publics selected to meet any challenge we face should be those best combined to facilitate proper resolution and long-term success. If cost considerations become a concern, they should be addressed in more creative use of resources rather than jeopardizing the long-term health of the organization.

> **Intervening Public**

An individual or public used as a message channel to reach and influence a key public.

It is appropriate here to mention and define intervening publics. An intervening public is one that carries our message to the publics we ultimately need to reach and influence. Media and opinion leaders or influentials are intervening publics that are often used in communications and persuasion. Teachers or PTA volunteers in school are sometimes good channels to get a message to a parental public. Intervening publics are not typically designated as key publics unless you need to persuade them to help you. If you need to develop or strengthen a relationship with an intervening public to ensure its cooperation, then you might designate it as key. For example, if you've had a problem with media being hostile, unresponsive or inaccurate, you may need to identify them as a key public and develop strategies and tactics that will improve your relationship with them. Otherwise, media are typically an intervening public or channel we often use to reach our key publics.

Because writing objectives and then determining and integrating the efforts with the appropriate publics to reach those objectives can be confusing to those not accustomed to viewing a program holistically, figure 6.2 has been created to clarify the relationship of objectives, key publics and strategies. A key public will often be helpful in accomplishing more than one of your objectives. Strategies for those publics should be planned with a complete view of all you need to accomplish with them. Otherwise strategies for separate objectives will be isolated from each other and may result in tactics that don't integrate well into the overall campaign plan, and in some cases even conflict with each other.

If a key public is viewed in terms of all the interrelated tasks necessary for that public to help you accomplish your goal, the strategies

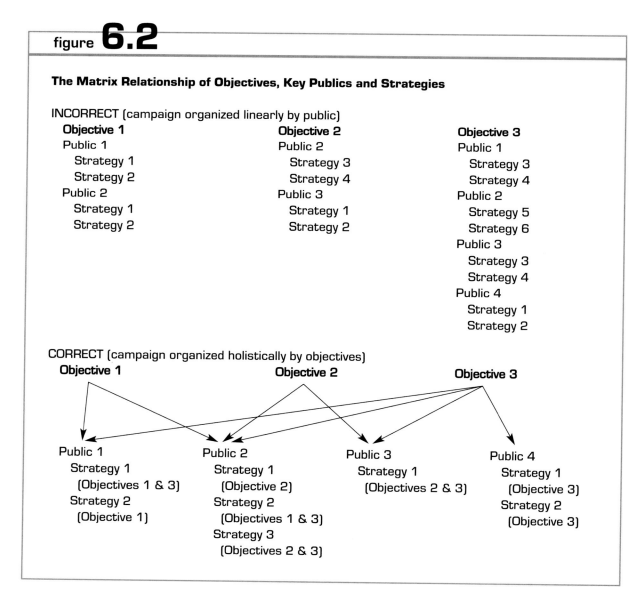

figure 6.2

The Matrix Relationship of Objectives, Key Publics and Strategies

INCORRECT (campaign organized linearly by public)

Objective 1	**Objective 2**	**Objective 3**
Public 1	Public 2	Public 1
Strategy 1	Strategy 3	Strategy 3
Strategy 2	Strategy 4	Strategy 4
Public 2	Public 3	Public 2
Strategy 1	Strategy 1	Strategy 5
Strategy 2	Strategy 2	Strategy 6
		Public 3
		Strategy 3
		Strategy 4
		Public 4
		Strategy 1
		Strategy 2

CORRECT (campaign organized holistically by objectives)

Objective 1   **Objective 2**   **Objective 3**

Public 1	Public 2	Public 3	Public 4
Strategy 1	Strategy 1	Strategy 1	Strategy 1
(Objectives 1 & 3)	(Objective 2)	(Objectives 2 & 3)	(Objective 3)
Strategy 2	Strategy 2		Strategy 2
(Objective 1)	(Objectives 1 & 3)		(Objective 3)
	Strategy 3		
	(Objectives 2 & 3)		

designed for that public will be interrelated and mutually reinforcing. Such an approach increases your ability to repeat and reinforce messages, to use economies of scale and to coordinate strategies to enhance their contribution to the overall campaign. Separating publics and strategies by specific tasks or objectives tends to fragment your efforts and loose the advantage of overlap and reinforcement.

As depicted in figure 6.2, fulfilling objective one may require communication with, and action on the part of, publics one and two; objective two may need the support of publics two and three; and objective three may need action from all four publics to be accomplished. Similarly, a strategy written for public three may help to fulfill both objectives two and three, or at least not conflict with other efforts to fulfill those objectives. To succeed here, we must suspend our tendency to think linearly and try to be more holistic in our approach to what actions we need from our publics. If we view objectives and actions as separate from each other, we not only loose the advantage of reinforcing messages and action, but we also run the risk of creating misunderstanding by fragmentation and conflicting messages and actions.

As you select the key publics necessary to accomplish your objectives, you should refer to the profiles created based on your research. Your profiles should have specifically identified the relevant self-interests of each public, that public's influentials or opinion leaders (who are potential intervening publics) and your current relationship with that public both as an organization and as it regards the particular issue with which you are dealing.

Identifying self-interests

Once you have selected key publics, review and focus their profiles on the tasks you want the publics to complete or the roles you need them to play. As you focus the public profiles, honestly and candidly assess the self-interests that will motivate those publics to do what you need done. Remember that people don't do what you want them to do just because you want them to do it. They act in their own self-interest, and unless you can plainly identify those self-interests and appeal to them, the public will not act as you would like them to. Do not, however, confuse self-interest with selfishness. The measure of success in our society has very much become position (power and fame) and money (and the material goods money buys). Yet human resource literature in the business field and studies of persuasive communication show that people are more often motivated to act from intrinsic values like care and concern, community improvement, quality of life, needs of family and friends and because it is the "right thing to do."

Clearly, it is in our self-interest to feel good about ourselves, to take care of our families and friends, to improve the quality of our community and living situation. That doesn't mean money and power are not motivators, but relying upon them as the primary or overriding self-interests for our publics will probably limit our success. Refer back to Chapter One's discussion of the critical values underlying trust and relationships in the theory of strategic cooperative communities. You will note that material property is only one of those values and its place in the priority is much lower than the people-oriented values.

As you will see in the next chapter, appealing to the self-interest of a public is necessary at two levels. You already know you must use a self-interest appeal to move a public to action. But with the clutter of messages and information bombarding everyone today, we must also appeal to self-interest just to get a public to pay attention to our message. Think again of the newspaper analogy. People choose to perceive a message only when they believe it is in their self-interest to do so. Regardless of the channel used, you have to get over the perception hurdle before you can complete your primary task of informing or motivating.

Identifying opinion leaders and influentials

At this same point in our analysis of publics necessary to accomplish our objectives, we should again rely on our public profiles to consider who influences our key publics. Who are their opinion leaders regarding the particular issue or campaign we are addressing? A public's influentials or opinion leaders are individuals (either by personal acquaintance or reputation) who have the credibility to effectively give advice, affect opinion or call for action. Influentials are typically heavy consumers of media and possess significant information and expertise.

Influentials and opinion leaders may be formal or informal. A formal opinion leader is one whose influence results from status or position, either elected or appointed in some way. Political officials, public figures, civic and religious leaders, and teachers are good examples of formal opinion leaders. Informal or personal influentials may include family and friends, co-workers and peers. If the issue is health-related, influentials may include the family doctor. If it regards the maintenance of your car, you may be influenced by the mechanic across the street. You would probably not ask the doctor how to fix your car or the mechanic about maintaining your child's health.

Influentials do not have to be personally known to us to be opinion leaders, and formal opinion leaders are seldom personally known. Role models often become opinion leaders. If children idolize a professional sports figure, they are likely to take the advice of that figure regarding certain behaviors. You may not personally know the governor of your state, but you would probably accept his/her judgment on certain issues of importance to the state.

In today's ever-changing media society, media figures may sometimes take the role of an opinion leader. Theoretically, we understand that media typically do not have the power to change opinion (McCombs and Shaw, 1972). Media tell us not what to think, but set the agenda for what we think about. They further reinforce decisions we have already made. Combining that theory with the theory of selective perception (Klapper, 1960), it becomes apparent that people choose the media — particularly the news genre — they pay attention to based on what they already believe. The vast number of listeners and viewers who select to perceive talk show hosts like Rush Limbaugh and Sean Hannity already agree with what they expect will be the positions of those hosts. They select the media that will strengthen and reinforce their beliefs.

Nevertheless, as people have become more isolated and insular in their personal lives, certain media personalities have become influential. It cannot be denied that some media figures like Oprah Winfrey, Dan Rather and Diane Sawyer clearly have influence on opinion and behavior. Their respectability and their ubiquitous presence have truly given them the status of opinion leaders on certain issues.

At this point you are probably wondering how to figure out who a public's opinion leaders are. Formal opinion leaders are relatively easy to determine. We see them every day (like political officials) or know who they are by the issue or influence involved (like religious leaders). Nevertheless, just because someone may hold a position of authority does not guarantee he/she can actually sway the opinion of our key public. Further, informal opinion leaders are more difficult to determine. How do we find out who influences a key public? The answer is deceptively simple: we ask them. Part of research is asking people who influences their opinions and who they trust to help them make decisions. Focus groups and surveys are particularly useful in this process.

In using opinion leaders and influentials as a channel in communication efforts with key publics, keep in mind they are best used to persuade and motivate. You would not typically use an opinion leader to disseminate information because that would be wasting their influence unless it was particularly difficult to draw attention to the specific information you are trying to disseminate. It is usually fairly easy to disseminate information. It is more difficult to persuade or to move a public to action. Opinion leaders and influentials are particularly valuable in the motivation effort.

We all have a diverse circle of influentials and opinion leaders. We trust their judgment. We take their advice. They are typically better informed on the particular topic and trusted because of past performance. They have great influence on our attitudes and behaviors. Nevertheless, their credibility is based upon our assessment of their character and judgment. Influentials lose influence if they are perceived to be manipulated or manipulative. Using them in that manner is unethical and will ultimately lead to a decline in their influence.

Assessing relationships

It is also important to assess the current state of the relationship the organization has with each identified key public. This assessment should also have been a part of the public's profile, but may be refined at this point in your planning.

Assessment of a relationship with a key public may use a formal methodology like establishing a scale of strength indicators of the relationship, or the assessment may be more informal. Nevertheless, research has shown the key factors or dimensions to be considered include the levels of loyalty, trust, openness, involvement, community investment and commitment (Ledingham and Bruning, 1998; Bruning and Ledingham, 1999; Bruning and Ledingham, 2000).

Significant research has been conducted within the relationship building and the relationship management schools of thought in public relations. While that discipline has been advocating a relationship building approach to dealing with all organizational publics since the mid-1980s, it is only recently that research has led to the methodology to measure the strength of those relationships. The six factors identified above are those most often identified and measured. Loyalty and trust are arguably two-way factors, the strength of which is measured both from the perspectives of the organization and the publics. The other four primarily measure the key public's perception of the organization's performance. The openness, involvement, community investment and commitment of the organization to key publics are typically seen as responsibilities only on the part of the organization.

The purpose of your communication, particularly long term, is to strengthen the relationships with key publics and move them to mutually beneficial action. Communication that highlights the organization's performance on these six factors will help you do that.

DESIGNING MESSAGE STRATEGIES

Now that you know what you need to do to resolve your problem and whom you need to reach to accomplish that, you are ready to design the messages to be sent to motivate your key publics to do what you want them to do. Remember that messages are public-specific. You cannot successfully incorporate a public's self-interest into a message generalized to all publics. Each public will need a different appeal based on its particular overriding self-interest.

The message strategy is in two parts. The first is primary messages that resemble sound bites. The primary messages encompass what you are trying to motivate the public to do and include a short self-interest appeal. For example, in a campaign regarding children's nutrition, one primary message might be: "Healthy adults come from healthy children. Ensure your child's future with a healthy diet today."

> Primary Messages

Sound bite statements that encompass what you need the public to do and an appeal to the public's self-interest to act.

The number of primary messages for a key public will depend upon the number of tasks (objectives) you have set for that particular public. If you need this public's help and support in only one task, you may have only one primary message. Several tasks or desired actions will require more primary messages. Typically, a key public will have two to four primary messages.

The second part of message strategy is secondary messages. These messages contain all the facts, statistics, case studies, examples and other information to support the primary messages. The secondary message to support the primary message example above may include studies on childhood obesity and other statistics, and the components of a healthy diet recommended by the Food and Drug Administration (FDA). It may also include case studies or examples with emotional appeal and use the credibility of opinion leaders or celebrities.

Here, it is important to note that good motivational messages always tap into a public's self-interests. Never forget that people don't do what you want them to do just because you want them to do it. Individuals act in what they perceive to be their self-interests. You must determine and appeal to the shared and relevant self-interests of the public you are trying to motivate. We mentioned above that message strategies are typically public-specific. The exceptions to this rule are campaign themes and slogans or advertising tag lines. A theme or slogan is a short, compelling, attention-getting phrase that reminds a public of the specific messages you have sent them in other channels. You are already aware of some of the pervasive slogans that have high retention value. The "Just Say No" anti-drug slogan or Nike's "Just Do It" are both good examples.

Advertising tag lines are similar to slogans. They summarize and add emphasis to the advertising message and almost always come at the end of a television or radio ad or appear at the bottom of a print ad. Developed in 1992 by the market research firm Wirthlin Worldwide, the tag line "Plastics Make it Possible," and the campaign built around this theme redefined the debate about plastics. The message of the campaign, summarized in the tag line, focuses key publics on the positive associations they have with plastic such as keeping food fresh, keeping people safe and making possible many of today's lifesaving medical technologies. Instead of directly taking on the environmental concerns people have about plastic, the campaign works to generate appreciation for the material's unique properties. "Plastics Make it Possible" has been so successful the American Plastics Council continues to use the tag line and theme to drive its advertising — more than 10 years after its conception.

Notwithstanding their usefulness in summarizing key messages, slogans and advertising tag lines cannot stand alone as messages to your publics. They are useful in creating synergy among publics in a campaign and can dramatically affect recall of public-specific messages sent in other channels. A slogan like "Working Toward a More Healthy Community" will bring to mind public-specific messages regarding economic well-being to a business public, messages of physical and mental health to the health care public, and messages of combating drug and alcohol abuse to a parental public. The slogan in and of itself is not an effective message. It is only as good as the public-specific messages it supports.

Staged events often — but not always — use the same kind of appeal to several key publics as do slogans or themes. For example, a campaign to increase awareness of cancer prevention techniques and raise money

> ### Secondary Messages

Bulleted details that include facts, testimonials, examples, etc. that support a primary message.

> ### Tag Line

A slogan or summarizing theme that appears at the end of an advertisement.

for cancer research may target all of its publics with a staged event at a local hospital or cancer treatment center that includes blood screening, free mammograms for women, nutritional workshops, informational booths, family activities, food, children's games, a fund raising home crafts bazaar and a five-kilometer fund raising run. Its slogan may be something like "Cancer Prevention in Cleveland: A Community Affair."

Nevertheless, promotion of the event would still be reliant on public-specific messages, strategies and tactics, because every public will have a slightly different motivation for attending the event. And the slogan, delivered to all publics through the event strategy, becomes a "big idea," but is only one of the messages (and one of the strategies) for reaching your key publics and accomplishing your objectives. You will need to separately and sufficiently plan other informational and motivational strategies for each public to fully accomplish your objectives and goal.

At the heart of the planning process are the decisions we make about key publics, messages and the best way to get those messages to those publics. It is in this central part of the process that we need most to be guided by our research and information. Yet, we are most tempted to rely on instinct alone. Not that instinct is necessarily bad. It is often a subconscious process of integrating bits and pieces of knowledge and information, and charting an appropriate course given the data. But, it can also be an unwillingness to believe information and data because it conflicts with limited personal observation. In the latter case, instinct usually leads us to follow courses that fail to solve, and often exacerbate, the problem. To avoid that error, we would be wise to always test our instinct against the information and data gathered through research.

If you identify a public is motivated on a particular issue by its self-interest in quality of life for their children, your message must convey the importance of that result. Parents concerned about their children's safety from gang violence are motivated by messages and arguments that promise or affect preservation of safety, not by arguments of taxpayer cost. ("Can we place a monetary value on a child's life?") On the other hand, taxpayers concerned about growing demands on their income to solve social problems are motivated by messages that seek to moderate the cost

> Slogan or Theme

Short, catchy phrase that integrates primary messages and appeals to the broad interests of many key publics.

as they propose solutions. ("Lock them up; we can't keep spending money on expensive programs for the socially deviant!")

How you segment publics to achieve your objectives and the self-interests you identify dictate the messages to be sent. The message strategy then contains two essential factors: 1) your purpose or what you need to accomplish and 2) your appeal to the self-interest of those you need to motivate to accomplish your purpose. Messages will essentially be both informational and motivational. Designing primary and secondary messages in this way provides you an in-depth treatment of messages for those communication tactics that allow for length (like newspapers and brochures) while also creating short, memorable messages for time- and space-limited media.

SUMMARY

Once objectives are set, we can select the most effective combination of publics to accomplish them. To be holistic in accomplishing the goal, we need to remember that more than one key public may be needed to reach an objective and that a key public may help satisfy multiple objectives. At this point, we may also select intervening publics to help us get our messages to the key publics.

To develop effective messages for each of our key publics, we review and refine the public profiles assimilated in the research. We particularly need to identify each public's overriding self-interest regarding the issue or effort at hand. We also need to know who influences each public and assess our current relationship with each public. This analysis leads to the design of primary and secondary messages to provide information and motivate our publics to action. Effective messages depend upon solid analysis of the publics selected to accomplish the objectives.

CHAPTER SIX EXERCISES

1. Select a local small business and do a brief analysis of its function and the issues routinely faced. Then identify the organization's key publics, the key public's self-interests, the key public's influentials and the organization's current relationship with each key public.

2. Conduct some focus groups to discover the formal and informal opinion leaders and influentials of a couple of segmented publics on an issue of your choosing.

3. Identify a nonprofit organization and analyze the messages it sends to different publics. Identify primary messages and their supporting secondary messages and make recommendations for alterations or additions that would make the messages more effective.

TEACHING CASE: The Case of the Caustic Cloud

MATRIX: Action Planning
   Step 5 — Key Publics and Messages

SAMPLE CAMPAIGN

Goose Creek residents affected by the spray

This public needs to be satisfied that they are not at personal risk from this incident and the company's ongoing operations. We need their satisfaction to maintain the high perception ratings we have received from the community. If they believe they have been dealt with fairly, they will become advocates for Spruced Up, rather than opponents.

Primary message:
- Spruced Up is committed to the safety and well being of our employees and our community.

Secondary message:
- The procedures in place for safety have worked well at this farm since it was established.
- Industry studies show the pesticide to be safe. Tests have shown this pesticide to have less toxicity than any other pesticide on the market.
- We will research why our weather information was not sufficient in this case and evaluate alternative sources of information.
- We encourage you to watch the monthly newsletter for advanced notifications of routine aerial spraying.
- As a courtesy and to minimize the risk of human exposure, we are making a commitment to conduct aerial spraying only between sunrise and 7:30 a.m.

Primary message:
- Spruced Up regrets any discomfort you've experienced.

Secondary message:

- We have created a procedure to reimburse you for your medical costs.
- Submit the forms we are leaving with you and the company will send you a check within a few days.
- Call the company executive who visited you directly if you have additional questions or problems resulting from this incident.
- EMTs and physicians in the area are being sent information on how to provide short-term treatment in the unlikely event this would ever happen again.
- We recognize that the spray incident may have inconvenienced you and want to give you something for your trouble. We are leaving you a gift certificate for a live tree or cut Christmas tree from the Spruced Up farm.

Goose Creek EMTs and physicians

It needs to be reinforced to this public that Spruced up is committed to its employees and the community and would not do anything that would cause harm. This public needs to be assured that the spray poses little medical danger. They also need to feel prepared to deal with the situation and to provide short-term treatment if the incident were to be repeated or if residents were to be exposed to the spray from other agricultural operations in the area. If they feel they have all the information they need to handle the current and possible future situations, they will continue to be supportive of Spruced Up.

Primary message:

- Spruced Up is committed to the safety and well being of our employees and our community.

Secondary message:

- Spruced Up will share with you research showing the pesticide to be safe.
- Although it is unlikely something like this will happen again, we want you to feel prepared to treat patients that might be exposed to the insecticide through any number of agricultural operations in the area. We are therefore sending you short-term treatment recommendations as well as background on the spray.
- Resources are available to you, including a 24-hour phone line, should you have further questions about the insecticide or any of the company's activities.

Goose Creek voters

This public is familiar with Spruced Up as a significant employer and contributor to the economy. They are interested in the company's response and expect them to effectively manage the situation. If their concerns regarding future incidents can be addressed, they will maintain favorable views of the organization and recognize its many positive contributions to Goose Creek.

Primary message:
- Spruced Up is committed to the safety and well being of our employees and our community.

Secondary message:
- Spruced Up has a proven safety record — only one other very minor spraying accident has occurred in the past 10 years.
- Spruced Up uses the safest chemicals available. The pesticide used is the least toxic of any solution available on the market.
- Spruced Up carefully examined insecticide research — some of which was conducted at the local college — to ensure there would not be any detrimental affects to anyone exposed to the pesticide.
- We encourage you to monitor the routine notifications of future sprayings in the town newsletter and on the company's Internet site.
- We are investigating weather information systems to see if alternative systems would give us more accurate readings of wind conditions.
- As a courtesy and to minimize the risk of human exposure, we are making a commitment to conduct aerial spraying only between sunrise and 7:30 a.m.
- We are also adding a 24-hour helpline to answer questions and provide basic company information.

Primary message:
- Spruced Up is proud to be an active part of Goose Creek and its future.

Secondary message:
- We love being a part of this community.
- Spruced Up is a significant employer in Goose Creek. The company employs roughly 15 percent of the town's adult working population.

- Spruced Up continues to be an active supporter of community activities such as Little League baseball, the women's shelter and the state's agricultural college.
- We're looking forward to the grand opening of Tucker Memorial Park and will be there to help you celebrate on July Fourth.

Goose Creek Town Council

This public wants to see Spruced Up successful and profitable because of its contribution to the community in terms of tax dollars, jobs and charitable involvement. They need to be reminded of those contributions now more than ever. They do, however, feel a strong responsibility to their constituents and want to see Spruced Up act in a responsible manner to those affected by the incident. They want Goose Creek to be a safe place and will need to see evidence that Spruced Up is taking measures to ensure this end. If the council is convinced Spruced Up is taking responsibility for its actions and that affected constituents are being treated, support from the group towards Spruced Up will continue.

Primary message:

- Spruced Up is committed to the safety and well being of our employees and our community.

Secondary message:

- Spruced Up has a proven safety record — only one other very minor spraying accident has occurred in the past 10 years.
- Spruced Up uses the safest chemicals available. The pesticide used is the least toxic of any solution available on the market.
- Spruced Up carefully examined insecticide research — some of which was conducted at the local college — to ensure there would not be any detrimental affects to anyone exposed to the pesticide.
- We encourage you to monitor the routine notifications of future sprayings in the town newsletter and on the company's Internet site.
- We are investigating weather information systems to see if alternative systems would give us more accurate readings of wind conditions.
- As a courtesy and to minimize the risk of human exposure, we are making a commitment to conduct aerial spraying only between sunrise and 7:30 a.m.

- We are also adding a 24-hour helpline to answer questions and provide basic company information.
- Spruced Up continues to be an active supporter of community activities such as Little League baseball, the women's shelter and the state's agricultural college.
- We're looking forward to the grand opening of Tucker Memorial Park. We're excited to be there with you on July 4.

Primary message:

- We are proactively responding to the spray incident.

Secondary message:

- Company officials have personally visited each of the 40 people affected by the spray.
- We are reimbursing individuals affected by the spray for their medical expenses and any lost work time in the two days following the incident.
- We are also providing the families of those treated for respiratory distress with a Spruced Up gift certificates for the inconvenience the incident may have caused.
- Spruced Up is sending physicians and EMTs short-term medical treatment and background information on the insecticide.
- We have established a 24-hour helpline for anyone with questions related to the spray incident or the company's general operations.
- We are working with the local media to provide information concerning the pesticide and our commitment to the safety of our employees and our community.
- A company scientist is visiting personally with the EMTs and physicians who treated people exposed to the spray to make sure they have all the information they need to follow up patients and to prepare for an unlikely future event of this kind.

Primary message:

- Spruced Up's business success is a major factor in the economic prosperity of Goose Creek.

Secondary message:

- Spruced Up is the single largest tax-payer in Goose Creek.
- The company employs approximately 4,000 people from Goose Creek and the surrounding communities.
- Roughly 20 percent of all money circulating through Goose Creek businesses originates with Spruced Up and its employees.

Spruced Up employees

Employees trust the company and value their jobs. They know the company is strong on safety and sometimes goes to the extreme to protect them. They are likely to get questions from friends and neighbors in Goose Creek about the insecticide incident. They want Spruced Up to resolve the situation and maintain a high-level of trust from residents so they can continue to feel proud about where they work. If this public sees the positive evidence of Spruced Up's efforts, they will maintain their high level of support and trust in their employer.

Primary message:

- Spruced Up is committed to the safety and well being of our employees and our community.

Secondary message:

- Spruced Up has a proven safety record — only one other very minor spraying accident has occurred in the past 10 years.
- Spruced Up uses the safest chemicals available. The pesticide used is the least toxic of any solution available on the market.
- Before choosing a new insecticide last year, the company researched all products available and determined that the product used on May 5 was the safest to humans and one of the most effective against harmful insects.
- We do not fault any company employee for the May 5 incident. It was an accident caused by unreliable weather data.
- We will research why our weather information was not sufficient in this case and evaluate alternative sources of information.
- As a courtesy and to minimize the risk of human exposure, we are making a commitment to conduct aerial spraying only between sunrise and 7:30 a.m.
- Please use the 24-hour helpline to report any problems or submit your ideas for company improvements.

Primary message:

- We're meeting with and making sure anyone exposed to the insecticide is taken care of quickly.

Secondary message:

- Individuals experiencing any kind of problems from exposure to the spray have been visited personally by a member of Spruced Up's executive team.

- The insecticide does not pose any serious long-term health risks — independent research supports this claim.
- EMTs and physicians in the area will be sent medical treatment information detailing active ingredients and short-term treatment suggestions for patients exposed to the insecticide.

Primary message:

- Spruced Up is proud to be an active part of Goose Creek and its future.

Secondary message:

- We love being a part of this community.
- You make up approximately 15 percent of the town's adult working population.
- We continue to be an active supporter of community activities such as Little League baseball, the women's shelter and the state's agricultural college.
- We hope you and your families will join company and community officials at the grand opening of Tucker Memorial Park on the Fourth of July.

REFERENCES AND ADDITIONAL READINGS

Bruning, S. and Ledingham, J. (1999). "Relationships between organizations and publics: Development of a multi-dimensional organization-public relationship scale." *Public Relations Review*, 25(2):157-170.

Bruning, S. and Ledingham, J. (2000). "Organization and key public relationships: Testing the influence of the relationship dimensions in a business-to-business context." In Ledingham and Bruning (eds.) *Public relations As Relationship Management: A Relational Approach to The Study and Practice of Public Relations.* Mahwah, N.J.: Lawrence Erlbaum Associates, Publishers.

Klapper, J.T. (1960). *The Effects of Mass Communication.* New York: Free Press.

Ledingham, J. and Bruning, S. (1998). "Relationship management and public relations: Dimensions of an organization-public relationship." *Public Relations Review*, 24:55-65.

McCombs, M.E. and D.L. Shaw (1972). "The agenda-setting function of mass media." *Public Opinion Quarterly*, 36:176-187.

Wirthlin Worldwide (1997). "The American Plastics Council Campaign." *A Case Study of Award Winning Advertising Research and Strategy.*

chapter 7

DESIGNING STRATEGIES AND TACTICS TO SEND MESSAGES

"The roots of successful decisions often lie in obscure places. ... The truly great decisions happen. They arise from spur-of-the-moment phone calls and from crazy ideas you try when you're desperate."

— Stuart Crainer

Author of "The 75 Greatest Management Decisions Ever Made"

LEARNING IMPERATIVES

▸ To design strategies that reach a public with a message to motivate a desired action or behavior

▸ To creatively select the best channels to deliver the tactics that support strategies

▸ To design creative and effective tactics delivered through specific channels

▸ To brainstorm creative strategies and tactics

▸ To use copy outlines to channel creative ideas into strategic communication tools

N ow that we have established what needs to be accomplished, who we need to reach to accomplish that and what messages will motivate action, we can design our strategies and tactics to send those messages. Strategies and tactics are public-specific — they are designed with one public in mind. They are the best way to give a key public its own message to motivate desired behavior.

We can draw a simple analogy to military strategy. In an overall challenge to win a battle one objective might be to secure a certain piece of ground or a particular town. The strategy would then be devised to coordinate the effort to achieve that objective. The strategy may be to weaken the town's defenses and attack through a particularly vulnerable spot in the wall. The tactics supporting the strategy may be an artillery barrage, aerial bombing, a Special Forces patrol to plant explosives to create a breech, and a ground assault through the wall into the town. The strategy provides the overall approach to a particular objective answering what and, very generally, how. Tactics are the specific plans to achieve the strategy step-by-step.

In communicating with an organization's publics, the strategies are the approaches to reaching a designated public for a particular purpose with the message that will inform or motivate that public. Almost like mini-objectives for that public, strategies determine what purpose you are trying to accomplish in reaching the public with the message (i.e., to inform, to increase awareness, to persuade or to motivate to do something) and what channel you are going to use to send that message (i.e., influentials, mass media or workplace communication). Because strategies are designed to reach a specific public with a specific message you created to appeal to the public's self-interests, strategies must be public-specific.

The tactics that support the strategies identify in more detail how you will send the message within the strategy (i.e., employee meetings, newsletter articles, bulletin boards, payroll envelope stuffers and letters from the company president in a workplace campaign). Tactics are strategy-specific because they support a single strategy targeted at a particular public.

A word on creativity

Because of the importance of creativity, we'll take a short detour here to help you enhance your creative efforts. Step six in the matrix requires high levels of creativity to devise strategies and tactics that break through all the other information and persuasion clutter with which your publics are bombarded. You must design creative strategies and tactics that will cause the target public to choose to perceive your messages, choose to retain them and choose to act upon them. The matrix process provides the framework or strategic structure to focus your creativity, ensuring it is on target in terms of meeting your challenge. Once you have focused efforts on a particular public, and you know what messages you need to send to motivate the desired action within that public, you must draw on creativity to deliver those messages. Channel your creativity to determine the best strategy for getting your message to your public. Then, let your creativity loose again on detailing the tactics to accomplish the strategy.

Only by channeling your creativity within the analytical process will you avoid a common mistake: allowing a creative tactic to drive your campaign. Just because you have a great opportunity to use a celebrity in a campaign doesn't mean that approach will serve your public, purpose and message. Great creative ideas not founded in logical reasoning and analysis of public, purpose and message result in lots of money wasted on campaigns that accomplish nothing. Remember the lesson of the Salt Lake City Olympic bid committee. Their television spots were extremely creative and visually appealing. But the issue passed by only two or three percentage points, denying them the public referendum of overwhelming support they sought. If you get a creative idea that doesn't work for a specific purpose, public and message, put it on the shelf to be adapted and used in a later communication effort. The idea isn't wasted if you can use it appropriately at a later time. It will be wasted, and perhaps even harmful, if used inappropriately now.

French naturalist Jean-Henri Fabre writes of the processionary caterpillar. Processionary caterpillars feed on pine needles as they move through the forest in a long procession, with one head fitted snugly

> **Creativity**

The process of looking outside ourselves and our routine to discover new ideas and innovative solutions.

against the behind of the caterpillar before. In his experiments, Fabre enticed a group of these caterpillars onto the rim of a flower pot where he got the first one connected with the last so they were moving in unending procession around the top of the pot.

Fabre expected the caterpillars would catch on to their useless march and move off in a new direction, especially since he had placed food nearby. Not so. The force of habit caused them to continue moving in their unending circle, round and round the rim of the flower pot. Even though food was visible nearby, the caterpillars continued their march for seven days and nights, and probably would have continued longer had they not collapsed from sheer exhaustion and ultimate starvation. The food was outside the range of the circle, off the beaten path. They followed instinct, habit, custom, tradition, precedent and past experience. They confused activity with accomplishment. They were in constant motion, but they made no progress.

> **Brainstorming**

A structured group creative exercise to generate as many ideas as possible in a specified amount of time.

Creativity is the process of looking outside ourselves, our habit, our custom and tradition to find new solutions and innovative ideas. The strategic program planning process is designed to analytically drive our planning and decisions. But it should not limit our creativity in searching for new ideas, channels and tactics to get our messages to key publics. In fact, unless we develop creative strategies and tactics, our publics are not likely to perceive the messages we have designed to motivate them.

Most of us think that creativity is inborn, you either have it or you don't. But the greatest scientific discoveries and inventions came out of years of experimentation, trial and error. The Royal Bank of Canada tells its employees that innovation is like playing hockey: the best players miss more shots than they make. But they also try more often. The more you shoot, the more you score. That's why one of the rules of brainstorming (see figure 7.1) is not to evaluate or criticize while in the brainstorming process. The object is to get as many ideas on the table as possible, no matter how ridiculous they might initially appear. Those ridiculous ideas, re-evaluated, rearranged and combined, frequently become the innovative solutions that are praised, awarded and used as examples of phenomenal creativity.

figure **7.1**

Rules for Brainstorming

1. Assemble a diverse group of people (at least three).
2. Set a time limit for the brainstorming session. Plan no less than five minutes but no more than 20 minutes to ensure urgency and, hence, a rapid flow of ideas.
3. Record the session for later transcription.
4. Do not evaluate ideas while in the session. Even laughter can be an act of evaluation that may stifle the flow of ideas (although in a truly free flowing session, it is difficult not to laugh).
5. Engage in freewheeling. Verbalize any idea that comes into your mind. Otherwise you are silently evaluating your own ideas and perhaps censuring the most creative ones.
6. Reserve the details for the post-session evaluation. Use your time to generate as many ideas as possible, not to explain your ideas in any detail.
7. Piggyback on ideas. For example, if someone mentions a tactic like bumper stickers, try to spiral off with similar transportation-related ideas like bus boards or sun visor wraparounds.
8. Take some time as a group after the session to evaluate each idea for its merits. Try to find ways that each might work. Try modifying, combining and rearranging before discarding an idea.

Thomas Edison said that creativity is "10 percent inspiration and 90 percent perspiration." It may well begin when you realize that there is no particular benefit in doing things as they have always been done. It also does not require complete originality. Creativity often means borrowing and adapting ideas. Modify and rearrange, make them bigger or smaller. Brainstorm ways to change and adapt an idea. In fact, practice brainstorming on a topic just to see how many different ideas you can come up with. Try free-association. Piggyback on ideas. Practice saying whatever idea comes into your head.

These are all good exercises, but to be creative, you must first allow that you can be. Break the barriers to creative thinking identified in figure 7.2. Explore your imagination. Think. Create fantasies and play with ideas. And then cultivate the habit. The more you challenge yourself to think creatively, the better you will become.

In her book, Teaching Creative Behavior, Doris Shallcross (1981) provides a number of exercises that require you to challenge the parameters

---

figure **7.2**

Roger von Oech's Mental Locks to Creativity (1983)

Be Practical
Don't disregard impossible suggestions, rather use them as stepping stones to workable solutions.

That's not my area
Specializing causes us to miss out on a lot. Interdisciplinary answers are better solutions.

DON'T BE FOOLISH
Poking fun at proposals provides feedback that prevents group think.

I'm not creative
Self-fulfilling prophecy. Allow yourself to be creative.

To err is wrong
Get over the stigma that being wrong is all bad. Use mistakes to learn.

THE RIGHT ANSWER
Looking for the one right answer keeps us from realizing that there may be many possibilities.

FOLLOW THE RULES
Creativity is often enhanced by breaking the rules, going outside the normal parameters.

THAT'S NOT LOGICAL
Don't disregard thinking outside the boundaries because it doesn't fit the analytical approach.

Play is frivolous
Fun environments are productive creative environments.

Avoid ambiguity
Introducing ambiguity into a creative session can help generate answers. Also use humor and paradoxes.

---

of your thinking. For example, how many squares do you see in the figure below? The expected answer would be 16, but count all the squares. Assuming this figure is on a flat plane, there are 30 of them, all different sizes. One is the outside square. You will also see two-by-two squares and

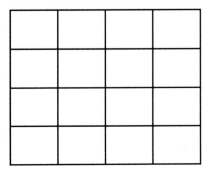

three-by-three squares. A door is opened to our creative brain when we obtain permission, indeed are given direction, to look outside the traditional boundaries and expected perception!

The next test from Shallcross is one you may have seen before, but that powerfully illustrates the need to go outside the boundaries we set for ourselves. Connect all nine dots with four straight lines. Go through each dot only once and do not lift your pencil from the paper. Take a few minutes to take this test before reading on. (The solution is located at the end of the chapter.)

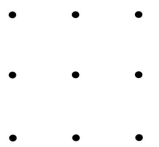

This test is specifically designed to show us that we set our own artificial boundaries. There was no instruction indicating the connecting lines had to be kept within the invisible boundary set by the dots in the diagram. Yet we are accustomed to setting those boundaries ourselves. One of the greatest marketing ploys of all time was to print a margin line an inch in from the edge of notebook paper. Most of us automatically observe that margin and leave the space on the left side of the line blank. Most notebook paper is used for taking notes no one else will ever see. What does it matter if we observe the margin? But much more notebook paper is sold to students in any given year because of that artificial boundary.

Where did we learn to set these kinds of invisible boundaries? Remember when you began coloring? What are some of the first lessons — or rules — you were taught? One was to always color inside the lines. That rule was so ingrained that we even traced the lines with the crayon before coloring to make sure we didn't accidentally breach the boundary. We were also taught to choose the appropriate colors. Frogs are green, not purple or blue. So we always had to choose the right color for the item pictured, so much so that fights erupted in grade school over color crayons. Now grade school kids buy their own set of crayons so they don't have to fight with anyone to get the green crayon for their frog. But in a graphic design, wouldn't a purple frog get more second glances than a green one?

Creative ideas and solutions are, by nature, out of our typical range of experience. Problems with obvious, traditional solutions seldom require much time. To find truly innovative solutions to challenges we face, we must reach outside our comfort zone, those boundaries we have created for ourselves.

Fear is probably the single greatest barrier to creative behavior. Author John Holt has said that the real test of intelligence is "not how much we know how to do, but how we behave when we don't know what to do." What do we fear? We fear failure and rejection. No one likes their ideas to be rejected, laughed at or ridiculed. We often fail to contribute our ideas for fear we will look silly or stupid. We think that people who fail do not get promoted. They do not get raises. So we believe. But if we never take a risk we will also never succeed.

Remember the hockey player and work to create an environment friendly to creativity. Accept that mistakes will be made, but praise the effort to find new ideas and solutions, even if you frequently miss the mark. Companies that foster this kind of environment are typically known for their creative products and solutions. Some even give annual awards for the most spectacular failure because management recognizes that if employees are afraid to be creative, the company will lose its competitive edge in the marketplace.

While you may not be working for an organization with such policies, you can still create that kind of environment within your work area. Make your workplace safe for creativity. Praise the creative effort even if the ideas don't or won't work. Celebrate new ideas and ways of doing things. Color a few frogs purple.

DESIGNING STRATEGIES AND CHOOSING
APPROPRIATE CHANNELS

As we said earlier, your strategy for message delivery to a particular public is public-specific. In other words, you don't determine how you are going to send a message until you know who you are trying to reach and what you are trying to tell them. The strategy inherently identifies the public, and then addresses what you are trying to do in support of your objectives and the channel you propose to use to send the appeal.

As has been mentioned, strategies are like mini-objectives for each public. They identify what action or behavior is desired. Just like objectives, the action part of a strategy may be informational or motivational. Informational strategies (also known as awareness or educational strategies) lay a significant foundation of information for the motivational strategies that ask the key public to act in some way.

As with objectives, it may not be necessary to have a separate informational strategy. If a public is already sufficiently educated and is latently ready to act, necessary information can be carried by the motivational strategy to avoid the risk of fragmenting your strategies and messages. All motivational strategies will contain some information messages either in separate tactics or within each tactic. A tactic that appeals for a citizen's vote will almost always include some information to justify the action. Your job is to determine whether a separate informational strategy is necessary for that public. If there is a significant lack of knowledge and understanding, you probably need an informational strategy to lay a foundation before you can implement strategies to motivate behavior. If the information is already pervasive and people just need to be reminded, the informational tactics within a motivational strategy will be sufficient.

As you know, objectives always require a metric of some kind. Each objective must specify improvement that can be measured. The action identified in a public-specific strategy may also be stated in measurable terms. While not all strategies will detail the action this specifically, it may be necessary for some to do so. If a campaign supporting a local municipal bond requires 55 percent of the vote to pass, public-specific

> Strategies

Public-specific approaches to achieve objectives.

strategies may break that overall percentage down into manageable pieces for each public. A 55 percent overall vote may translate to 85 percent of business leaders, 65 percent of white-collar workers, 45 percent of blue-collar workers and 58 percent of stay-at-home parents. The strategies for each public may include the measurements to support the overall objective.

Determining the right channel to send the message in a strategy is dependent upon both the message itself and the public being targeted. Take a look around. Some marketing and communications strategies have become so pervasive in our society that we don't give them a second thought. What has become the almost exclusive strategy to market beer to the age-segmented male audience? The primary strategy is to use sporting events as the channel to deliver beer-drinking messages to that target public. And, that channel has literally hundreds of potential tactics, many of which employ humor, to carry the message within the channel. What is the predominant fund-raising strategy of your local United Way? It is the workplace campaign. The strategy provides the channel within which messages are focused at a specific public with the ability to give using tactics that overlap and reinforce one another to accomplish the purpose.

A more specific example is an objective to raise participation in edu-

10-STEP STRATEGIC COMMUNICATIONS PLANNING MATRIX

matrix

MATRIX: Action Planning
Step 6 — Strategies and Tactics

Strategies   Strategies identify approaches to send messages to each public through specific channels in order to motivate action. Multiple strategies may be required for each public.

Tactics   Tactics are communications tools and tasks required to support each strategy. Each strategy is supported by a number of tactics designed to convey key messages to a specific public through the communications channel outlined in the strategy.

cational programs for handicapped children. Parents of handicapped children would be a key public (the who) needing an informational message regarding the resources available and a motivational appeal to use them. One strategy for that public would be to raise participation in available programs (the what) using the Parent-Teacher Association (PTA) network in schools (the channel). Tactics would necessarily include printed collateral materials explaining the programs available. Other tactics may involve using the personal influence of PTA leaders in a meeting, presentation, or home visit to introduce parents to the literature and encourage them to take advantage of the resources available. As is clear from the last chapter, opinion leader influence is best exerted by people the parents perceive to be operating credibly in a relevant issue environment. The PTA would have credibility in the area of educational programs for children. The individuals functioning in those leadership roles will probably also be known to the parents, perhaps as friends and neighbors, perhaps as community leaders.

> Channel

The conduit or medium through which messages are sent to a specific public to accomplish a specific purpose.

The channel stipulated in the strategy should be the best way to get the message to the public for the outlined purpose (i.e., staged events, workplace communication or opinion leaders). In order to be sufficiently planned, each strategy requires the development of specific tactics within the channel (communication tools like signage and t-shirts at staged events, newsletters and e-mail in the workplace and meetings or personal visits with collateral material for opinion leaders). In the previous example, we decided it was necessary to use opinion leaders or personal influence and printed collaterals to reach the key public with the message. The tactics specify the communication tools within the channel more clearly, perhaps a brochure on available programs and an application to participate. Other possible tactics might be a booklet explaining the learning techniques most successful with handicapped children, a fact sheet on local programs and funding, a listing of support groups and a contact sheet for more information. The written tactics would be introduced and/or distributed through personal contact with PTA leaders, like a phone call or a personal visit. Perhaps a follow-up tactic or some other kind of supportive tactic will also be necessary. By focusing tactics within a specific channel, you ensure the members of the key public will receive the message at least once, but likely more than once. Such focused overlap makes it more certain the message will be selected to be perceived, retained and acted upon.

The point is that you must carefully consider your public in determining the best ways to reach them. How this particular public best receives this type of message for this purpose is the relevant question. You must also carefully consider the message being sent to ensure the channels and media selected are appropriate for the message.

Brainstorming alternative channels and related tactics

It is critically important here to recognize that our effective and extensive use of the mass media to communicate with target audiences may belong to past decades. While mass media are highly effective in generating name recognition, even their information-disseminating utility is not as great as before because of declining trust. In the Golin/Harris 2002 Trust Index, the communications business sectors all had negative trust scores (Golin, p. 240). Of them all, public relations had the least negative score (-31), followed by journalism (-38) and then advertising/marketing (-41). While mass media channels have their place, in an environment where media are not trusted, it is unwise to rely on them too heavily.

We are accustomed to segmenting publics for the purpose of persuasion. We have long recognized that identifying a group of people who share common interests and lifestyles (and who may interact with one another) is the best way to devise an appeal that will motivate them. Now, segmentation is required not just to persuade, but to reach our desired publics. Readership of that traditionally broad print communication medium, the newspaper, is declining. Among those who still read a newspaper, their selectivity in what they read has increased. Broad audience magazines are also disappearing, replaced by highly segmented special-interest and professional or trade publications. The explosion in cable and satellite television technology is already creating highly segmented viewership, which will continue to increase. And radio has long been segmented by the preferences of listeners for differing formats and music.

The lesson to be learned is that the mass media (which arguably never did reach a mass public) are declining in their ability to reach our publics with the messages we need sent. The good news is that as a medium becomes more specific and segmented, it becomes a better buy in terms of reaching the public segments we need to target. So while our jobs may be a bit more difficult in that we need to exercise a greater range of creativity and expertise in using differentiated communication tools, we are promised higher rates of success because of the narrowing of mass and multimedia audiences.

Similarly, with the widespread use of technologies that make production of communication materials easy and inexpensive (like desktop publishing), the range of diversified and alternative media has burgeoned. Even the smallest of business operations can afford a desktop publishing system that enables them to produce sophisticated and impressive communication materials for very little cost. Local faxing improved immediacy and almost eliminated some mailing costs. But even the fax machine is being abandoned in favor of electronic mail with all its iterations and attachments. New technology has eliminated or significantly reduced the cost of long-distance telephoning nationally and internationally, and it has provided immediacy in written communication with a personal touch. The range of Internet capabilities helps us creatively reach a highly segmented public at an incredibly low cost.

As readership of newspapers declined — some newspapers have been driven out of business — the readership and number of newsletters has exploded, and the percentage of newsletters delivered electronically is steadily increasing. Hardly an organization can be found that doesn't produce at least one newsletter and many produce a separate newsletter for a number of publics. Local United Way organizations have separate newsletters for their volunteers, corporate contributors, organizations wanting to participate in volunteer opportunities and for their funded agencies. Corporations have newsletters for employees, for shareholders and investors, for stakeholders and for customers. Professional societies and trade associations also publish newsletters. Special interest groups

> ## > Segmentation

Defining and separating publics by demographics and psychographics to ensure more effective communication.

produce newsletters. Sports fans have hundreds of newsletters and magazines to which they can subscribe, some of which address only the performance of their favorite college or professional teams. The opportunities provided by specific channels of communication for segmented publics are endless. And all of those publications to very specifically segmented publics are constantly looking for copy that is relevant to their readership.

The opportunities now provided by the Internet include a growing range of options to creatively communicate a message. As in the early days of radio, advertisers now create online programming, similar to soaps and sitcoms, to secure vehicles for product promotion. Audio, video and online conferencing has been made relatively inexpensive through the Internet. Affinity portals, web sites visited often by a particular group of especially interested individuals, are an excellent way to reach some targeted publics. Chat rooms, listserves, online forums and many other Internet features are effective tactics to be considered. Smart use of search engines and web site links can also provide opportunities to communicate a message to publics already predisposed to be receptive.

As with any technology, the Internet brings both possibilities and problems. While making it easier, faster and less expensive to send messages to certain publics, the Internet also makes it easier for opposing publics, or just someone with a grudge, to attack your organization or products online. It is virtually impossible to block or even monitor everything anyone wants to post regarding your organization. And there is no filter or screen for lies and misrepresentations. No one asks whether or not the attack is credible — sometimes not even the media whose responsibility it is to ask. It is tremendously difficult to deal with false information that can be published so broadly, freely and anonymously. This dilemma underscores the importance of continual trust building efforts among all key publics.

Even with all the drawbacks, new technology has indeed provided us myriad channels to reach our publics. The key in writing creative strategies is to break out of our traditional mode of using broadly based mass media and find communication channels and tools that reach segmented publics. Our publics are far more likely to read a newsletter that comes to them for a particular interest or reason than a direct mail piece that goes to every postal customer. They are far more likely to respond to advice given through a segmented channel from an organization to which they choose to belong than to counsel given broadly in the mass media. They will be even more responsive to messages delivered by a special interest cable channel than through the major television networks. Break the barriers that cause you to choose the traditional media channels for all your communication. Take off the blinders and use some creativity in devising strategies and tactics to reach your publics with messages to which they will pay attention and respond. Try something different, something never before done.

There are literally dozens of channels we might use to reach a key public. Put yourself in the place of one of your publics and see through your mind's eye how they receive information throughout the day. What communication channels do they encounter and pay attention to as part of their daily routine? Figure 7.3 on the next page may help you begin to see how numerous and differentiated those channels can be.

Choose channels that will cause a key public to perceive a specific message about a particular issue. Remember that communication in most channels is supplemented with printed collateral materials (as in the above example regarding parents of handicapped children and the PTA). Nevertheless, collateral materials are seldom used alone as a channel. Focus several tactics in the chosen channel to reinforce the message. This way, the message is delivered in several rifle shots, rather than scattered by multiple shotgun blasts. The next section should help you get started on designing channel-specific tactics to deliver the message.

TACTICS FOR COMMUNICATION AND ACTION

Designing communication tactics is perhaps what most communicators do best ... and do worst. Most of us seem to be fairly adept at inventing catchy slogans and creative visual events and displays. The problem is

---

figure **7.3**

Examples of Possible Channels for Some Potential Key Publics

Possible Key Publics	Some Possible Channels *
Business Executives	Political and Community Opinion Leaders Community Business and Service Clubs Professional Associations Professional/Trade Media Commuter/Transportation Media Long Distance Travel Media Country Clubs and Golf Courses
Teachers	Parents School Districts/Government Professional Associations/Unions School Supply/Services Retailers Textbook/Classroom Resource Wholesalers Educational Travel Providers Alma Mater Colleges
Mothers of Elementary School Children	Medical Professionals and Facilities Children's Retail Stores Schools and Teachers Parent-Teacher Associations Religious Organizations Food and Household Retailers Homemaking/Women's Media
College Students	Campus Media and Collaterals Alumni College Sporting/Entertainment Events National Preprofessional Associations Fitness and Recreation Facilities/Retailers Financial Institutions On- and Off-campus Housing Units

* These represent only a very few of the possible channels for these publics. Literally dozens of channels exist for those creative enough to discover them.

not typically too little creativity in tactics, it is rather too little channeling of that creativity to ensure that our tactics are those best suited to deliver predetermined messages to specific publics. It is not usually our creativity that fails; it is our ability to strategically use that creativity that has been problematic.

Another problem has been the tendency to rely on the same tactics or communication tools over and over. Although there is nothing wrong with reusing tactics that work well with particular publics, communicators should be careful not to fall into the routine of the processionary caterpillars described earlier. Using a tactic repeatedly sometimes causes us to select that tactic without thinking about its appropriateness to get a particular message to a particular public for a particular purpose. We fall into a pattern of selecting tactics because we've always used them, or because the tactic has always worked before.

> Tactics

Strategy-specific communication products that carry the message to key publics.

Remember to review the analytical process to select communication tools each time you design messages and strategies for publics. Change is one of the only constants in business and marketing. Publics change, circumstances change, purposes change, messages change and communication channels change. If communicators stay with the same plan for the same publics without recognizing the constantly changing environment, communication efforts will miss their targets. A practitioner will be left (possibly without a job) wondering why it didn't work this time since it had always worked before.

The other inherent danger in using the same tools continually is stifling creativity. With such a broad array of tactics in the communications tool kit, communicators may ignore other creative and innovative ways to get messages to publics. But in a society flooded with messages in the typical media channels, creative and innovative delivery of messages is necessary to cut through the message clutter to reach our targets. Remember your challenge is two fold: You must motivate the members of your key public to choose to perceive the message (and retain it), and to choose to act upon it. Both require an appeal to the public's self-interests, but self-interest appeals alone will not get you over the perception hurdle. We may not find a solution to our specific need in the textbooks that teach us how to design communication tactics. We must be able to create innovative delivery systems and then follow the principles of good communication to send our messages in creative ways that command attention.

The diversity of tactics available is limited only by the imagination. Nevertheless, there are abundant numbers of books, articles and other references that identify a variety of some of the standard communication tools and their appropriate uses. We refer you to a broad range of easily available literature (some of which is identified in this chapter's references) that suggests dozens of tactics and instructions on their preparation and use. Because of the vast resources which give specific direction on preparing and using communication tools, it is not our purpose here to review specific tactics. Rather, it is more important to provide a process to assist communication professionals in determining how to select the tactics most appropriate for a specific public, purpose and message.

Most popular introductory textbooks in communication segment tools and tactics into written, spoken and visual categories. But true communication professionals focused on key publics and messages recognize that such divisions are artificial, especially considering that the most effective tactics combine at least two, and often all three, of those senses. Further, that type of categorization puts undue emphasis on the medium or channel, with less thought of the purpose, the target audience and the message itself. Such categorization may be partially responsible for communications practice that is excessively tactic-driven rather than strategic. It perhaps encourages creativity focusing on media, developing award-winning pieces for print, broadcast and now the Internet, rather than on using media as tools to get messages to the publics you need to reach for your campaign.

It might be more reasonable to address tactics in a grid (see figure 7.4) with one axis ranging from personal communication to mass-produced messages, and the other measuring the level of interaction (two-way communication) from highly interactive to noninteractive. The grid visually depicts how we design tactics for a specific public. When we need a highly interactive approach, we also make the tactic highly personal — increasing the likelihood of selection and retention. The other end of the grid forms a megaphone which depicts a wide distribution of a message with little or no interactivity. For example, if the public and the specific message to be delivered requires a personal or peer influence, the tactics will be designed to invoke personal interaction and may include phone calls or handwritten notes or invitations. If, however, a breadth of coverage rather than personal influence is needed, a medium with a broader reach to publics (remember there is no general public) may be more appropriate, including tactics such as public service announcements, radio actualities or Internet broadcasts. In the middle of the grid would be highly segmented media like newsletters or special interest magazines, annual reports and speeches with moderate opportunity for interaction.

Identifying communication tactics in this fashion helps us select the best communication tools for the public, purpose and message. Otherwise, the medium (print/broadcast) and budget tend to determine

> Interactivity

The degree to which the tactic provides interaction between the sender of the message and the receiver.

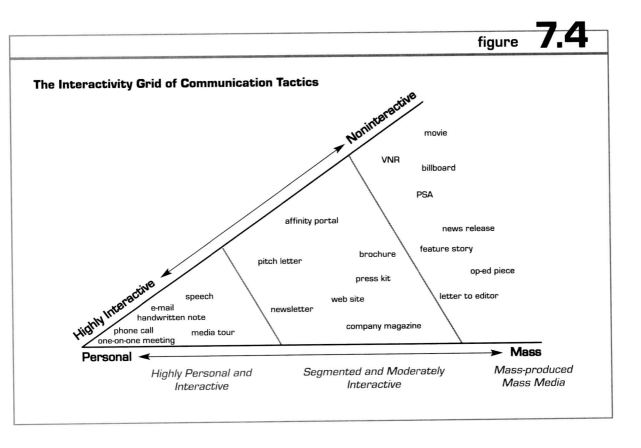

figure **7.4**

The Interactivity Grid of Communication Tactics

what tactics we use rather than which tool would best accomplish our purpose. Using the grid, tactics fall into three categories: highly personal and interactive, segmented and moderately interactive and mass-produced mass media.

Highly personal and interactive

The basis of the relational or cooperative community approach to public relations is the overwhelming power of personal and interactive communication. The personal influence of opinion leaders and peers is particularly important in a persuasion campaign. It is in this area of tactics that creativity and innovation are most needed. This type of tactic is very specifically tailored to the public (usually made up of identifiable individuals) and personalized in its delivery. It is typically direct human-to-human communication, often handwritten, spoken one-on-one and/or delivered in person by an influential.

A personal delivery system engenders interactivity. Interactivity is important in several ways. First, interaction is a basis of strong relationships and cooperation. Second, as discussed in the chapter on persuasion, it is a key to the crystallization of opinion. Third, interactivity provides a personal commitment and stimulus for action. For these reasons, this kind of tactic is highly effective. Nevertheless, it is also time consuming and often expensive. The advantages must be weighed carefully against the costs (time and money) to determine the best circumstances in which to use personal communication channels and tools.

In some situations, it's possible to create the one-on-one communication hierarchically. A good example is the United Way's workplace giving campaign. Companies that support the United Way in their community by running workplace campaigns identify a company representative who is trained by local volunteers to hold an employee information meeting and to subsequently personally ask each person in the company to support local community social service efforts through monthly payroll deductions. In larger organizations, the company representative trains a representative in each department to make the personal ask. This hierarchical system uses opinion leadership, personal influentials and one-on-one communication supported by collateral materials to reach hundreds of thousands of people within a community. Nevertheless, it is highly labor intensive, even though the laborers are volunteers.

Segmented and moderately interactive

This kind of tactic combines the best of both worlds. Although not nearly as personal, it still provides a highly targeted message to a larger target audience than personal communication typically can. This category of tactic uses, or sometimes establishes, a channel that is specifically designed for an already segmented public. Good examples include newsletters and special interest magazines that have analyzed and been designed to meet the needs of a very specific group. Another example might be a stockholder meeting for all stockholders which, in some companies, can be thousands of people. The segmentation of cable channels also allows for the effective use of this kind of tactic.

These types of tactics are also typically more interactive than the mass media. Because the target audience is an interest group, it tends to be more responsive in publication surveys, and more active in initiating feedback letters, phone calls and faxes. This environment is perfect for communicators to build in response mechanisms that provide the interactivity necessary for symmetry in communication with the organization's key publics.

Further, because the segmented channel has already identified the needs of its audience, it is a fairly simple matter for the public relations practitioner to tap into and help satisfy those needs. Such channels are often shorter on funding than traditional media channels, and are therefore hungry for material that honestly meets the needs of their audiences. It is to the practitioner's advantage to identify such channels that target the organization's typical key publics, and to include them within the plan to build strong, mutually beneficial relationships.

Internet tactics will often fall into the segmented and moderately interactive category. As of 2003, more than 110 million American adults are online (Lenhart et al, 2003). Tactics using the Internet have proliferated such that the primary question is not whether we can use one to reach our publics but how and when it is appropriate to do so. Penetrating ethical questions surround the use of pop-up ads and other online tactics. Some just irritate, but others verge on the unethical. We must always remember that the fundamental basis of a relationship with a key public is trust. In our zeal to communicate and motivate, anything we do that erodes trust comes at too high a price.

In 1997, a Middleberg/Ross Media in Cyberspace Study reported that 91 percent of surveyed journalists were online to some degree. Now, almost all journalists prefer this method of communication. In fact, the most common method of pitching a story to a journalist now is by e-mail. The credibility of online communication has risen as well. Journalists search the Web for verifiable facts and for the opportunity to interact with a source. The Media in Cyberspace Study also reported that journalists were more interested in the interactivity of a company web site than with the audiovisual bells and whistles we spend so much money to create.

More recently, web sites have become the first organizational point of contact for all key publics. Web sites must be carefully planned to communicate the organization's messages to its key publics. The elements of the web site should be mapped out like separate tactics with particular publics, purposes and messages in mind. From Frequently Asked Questions (FAQs) to corporate histories and product information pages, the needs and self-interests of various key publics should drive the messages and their delivery. It is important for communicators to include Internet habits in the profiles of their key publics to know what kind of online tactics will be effective.

Mass-produced mass media

This type of tactic is perhaps the most familiar to communicators. The use of electronic media (which with today's technology includes print as well as broadcast media) to broadly disseminate messages will undoubtedly characterize communication for years to come. The technolɔgy facilitates broad coverage of publics that probably would not be reached any other way. Nevertheless, it is important to remember the advantages and disadvantages of specific mass media channels and to use them appropriately (see figure 7.5). Further, just because we use mass media does not mean we are targeting a mass audience. It is just as important to segment publics and design public-specific messages for mass media as it is for segmented media.

Mass media provide immediacy, credibility and a strong impact. Nevertheless, practitioners often take a passive approach to mass media placement. While we don't directly control news placements, there are communication tools available that will help us be more active in building relationships with media. Satellite media tours, syndicated columns or programs, radio actualities as part of news releases, B-roll accompanying video news releases and other techniques can help get a message used more readily than it might otherwise have been. We have the ability now to send photos over the Internet and even to stream video. Such tactics can be quite effective if we will remember a few important guidelines.

- Become acquainted with your media contacts and work to meet their needs as they meet the needs of their audiences. Be familiar with their past work and what kind of material they prefer. You should make their jobs easier.

- Know the media market or audiences and adapt your material to meet their needs. Don't expect media to accept copy or programming that is blatantly self-serving. You must provide solid news.

- Localize your material. Whether it is a video news release, a feature story or a public service announcement, unless it specifically targets the local community it will not be used.

- Provide quality media products. Use their writing style and make sure to provide error-free copy well in advance of deadline. Provide a consistent point of contact and train people for interviews. Select interviewees who are knowledgeable and personable.

- Don't call a news conference unless you have a story that legitimately requires one. If it can be handled in a news release, use a news release.

figure **7.5**

Advantages and Disadvantages of Primary Mass Media Channels

	Advantages	*Disadvantages*
Television	High impact because it combines sight, sound and motion. Immediacy and credibility of message. Popular medium with large audiences. Worldwide coverage. Access to segmented special interest channels.	Time limits message content. High production costs. Expensive for advertising. Sometimes difficult to access and provides little feedback.
Radio	Good saturation of local markets and geographical selectivity. Relatively low cost and easy to change copy. Well targeted by listener profiles. Daily use by large numbers of people. Local endorsement. Fast and flexible placement.	Short time segments place limitations on message. Limited opportunity for feedback restricted primarily to talk format. No visual appeal.
Newspapers	Geographical targeting. Broad reach of income groups at low cost. Immediacy if newsworthy and timely features. Highly accessible and credible.	High cost for national advertising. Short message life. Primarily black/white, but with some color opportunity especially with photos. Newsprint is a low quality, dirty medium.
Magazines	Highly segmented audience, typically more affluent. High quality, visual with color and credibility. Lengthy messages. Pass-along readership. Issues often retained.	Usually not dominant in a local market. No immediacy, early deadlines. Duplicate circulation. High production costs.
Internet	Expanding use and savvy users increase credibility of legitimate messages. Broad usage and easy to post information quickly. Comparatively inexpensive as a channel. Fast and flexible. Visual medium that can combine sight, sound, motion and interactivity. Public seeks information. Usage easily tracked.	Some public segments still not online. Potentially high technology and start up costs. Can also be expensive to establish and maintain a prominent Internet presence.

Note: Many analyses include "wasted coverage" as a disadvantage for all mass media. Nevertheless, if you use the strategic planning matrix approach, you will budget to reach those specific publics identified. Any overlap in the message is not wasting resources since you planned the resources necessary to reach those specific publics. It doesn't usually matter if the message is received by members of untargeted publics.

Communicators will continue using mass media extensively for message dissemination. Make sure to establish strong media relationships based on honesty, trust and ethical practice to enhance your ability to use mass media to target key organizational publics.

Other considerations in selecting communication tools and devising tactics

Although tactic selection should depend primarily on the public and the best way to reach them to accomplish your purpose, the content of the message will also be a determinant. For example, detailed messages with lots of information usually require a printed medium that allows a receiver the luxury of rereading or studying. Similarly, broadcast messages must typically be simple and highly memorable because they cannot be reviewed at will. In both of these cases, the content and length or difficulty of the message are factors in media selection.

Further, the practitioner should consider the degree to which he/she controls the medium selected. Heitpas discusses two types of media channels: controlled and uncontrolled. Controlled channels allow the practitioner to dictate the content, timing and placement or distribution. Examples are paid advertising, trade shows and brochures. Such tactics are entirely designed and written by the communicator. No intervening gatekeepers affect the final product and its placement. Nevertheless, that advantage is tempered by a typically higher cost and lower credibility. Publics are well aware that controlled tactics convey exactly what the organization paying for the space wants said. There is no doubt in the consumer's mind that when he/she is reading paid advertising that the advertiser is telling only one side of the story to motivate consumer purchase.

On the other hand, uncontrolled channels are typically more credible because of the intervention of a third party, most often a reporter. They are usually less costly because much of the work is done by the "objective" third party. But the practitioner is unable to dictate the exact copy or message, placement or timing. The risk that the message may be buried or distorted is the price paid for credibility gained through perceived third party objectivity.

Finally, you should remember that combinations of tactics are often preferable to tactics used individually or in isolation. If you determine that a critical company policy statement included in a press kit may not be fully appreciated by key opinion leaders unless you use a more personally interactive tactic, mail it to them separately with a handwritten note from an organizational executive or some other influential indicating key points that may specifically interest them. If you think your key investors need more personal attention regarding the latest stock jump, send them a copy of the news clipping with an "FYI" (for your information) corner notation from the president of the company. There are a number of ways to "personalize" a mass media (or even a segmented media) message.

On the other hand, some personal and interactive messages may be made mass through media coverage and editorial comments. However, use care when deciding whether or not to turn a personal message into a mass message. It may not only dilute the appeal, it may alienate those originally touched by the personal message.

Some communication tools lend themselves to all three categories of tactics. A special event, for example, may be designed to be personal and interactive (like a private dinner for a major donor), segmented and moderately interactive (like a media tour of facilities or an award ceremony), or mass-produced mass media (like the Democratic or Republican national conventions). Turning a special event into a media event requires that care be taken to stage the event with messaging for the immediate attendees, but package it in such a way that the messages will appeal over the airwaves to listeners and viewers. Just remember that even though a special event is organized as a celebration or some other routine commemoration, you've wasted the organization's opportunities and resources if you don't also use it to convey primary messages to key organizational publics.

Further, combining tactics stimulates greater care in assuring our full array of tactics are integrated to support and enhance each other. Even using name tags at a staged event can be planned to strategically support other tactics. You might color code the tags to identify separate key publics and prepare separate packets of supporting materials to be distributed based on name tag color. All tactics should be developed to magnify the effect of other tactics. They should be timed to support and enhance each other. The whole of the tactics supporting any strategy should be greater than the sum of the parts. They are like pieces to a puzzle that must interlock and intertwine for the complete picture to appear.

For example, at a United Way campaign kickoff luncheon for the company representatives described earlier, the new theme was "Helping the Dream Come True." Literature at the place settings provided a written explanation of the theme selection and its focus on people and agencies working together to realize the dreams of the community to eliminate illiteracy, domestic violence and other social problems. The table centerpieces reinforced the theme which was printed on a ribbon woven through the piece. Sparkling confetti around the centerpiece provided twinkling stars associated with dreaming. The entertainment was a group of handicapped children singing a song about dreams. And the dessert was served with fortune cookies whose fortunes had been replaced with the goals of the local United Way-supported social service agencies worded as community "dreams" for the coming year. The "dream" theme was carried throughout the year (and into the next year) in all communication efforts. Each member of the United Way team and the directors of supported agencies were trained to include the community's "dreams" in specific terms in every communication opportunity. The communication tools were all designed to reinforce each other and to send the message "resonating" throughout the key publics in the community.

DEVELOPING INDIVIDUAL TACTICS

As was mentioned at the beginning of the chapter, the process of developing communication strategies and tactics must employ creativity and innovation. The Strategic Communications Planning Matrix provides the analytical framework necessary to channel creativity in the planning process. But it is also necessary to channel creativity at the tactical level. Otherwise, the creator may lose the proper focus on public, purpose and message.

Copy outlines

The secret to maintaining focus in the creative process at the tactical level is to employ an analytical tool to plan the necessary content of a tactic or communication tool before actually writing or designing it. Copy outlines have been devised for this purpose (see figure 7.6) to supplement and extend the strategic planning matrix. The copy outline plans the specific details of the communication piece to make sure it is consistent with the overall plan, and to ensure that all important details are included in the copy. Similar to an outline used to organize and detail a paper or presentation, the copy outline is an analytical piece that joins the public, purpose and message in logical persuasive fashion.

> ### > Copy Outline

An analytical tool that extends strategic planning to creation of effective tactics.

The copy outline begins by identifying the targeted public, which must be one of the publics identified in the campaign plan and the public for which the strategy supported by the specific tactic was designed. It also states the desired action and identifies the public's self-interest as part of the appeal.

Then the copy outline gets specific in terms of details. Keeping in mind the public and purpose identified in the copy outline, what are the primary and secondary messages that public needs to receive to understand and perform the desired action? These become the copy for your tactic and, in effect, become the first draft of the communication tool. The messages should be specific enough that another member of your campaign team, your firm or your department in an organization can edit and produce the communication tool without much other information. The messages contain each piece of information necessary to inform the public and motivate them to act. That means, for example, that you must be specific and accurate about dates and times of events you are publicizing, provide contact information for individuals to request more information, and include statistics when supporting logical arguments for a brochure.

figure **7.6**

Sample Copy Outline: Brochure

Key public (audience) including current level of understanding of product/service:

Secondary publics (audiences), if any:

Action desired from public(s):

How that action ties to the primary public's self-interest:

Primary messages: (usually 2-5, short statements/selling points to be conveyed)
Secondary messages: (bulleted supporting data, facts, cases, testimonials, etc.)

1. Primary Message:

Secondary:
-
-

2. Primary Message:

Secondary:
-
-

3. Primary Message:

Secondary:
-
-
-

Influentials (third-party opinion leaders who may influence the key public):

How they will be used to influence the key public (testimonials, examples, etc.):

Proposed cover title and cover copy:

Proposed cover photos/graphics (if any):

Method and timing of distribution (self-mailer, point of purchase display, etc.):

Brochure size and paper (weight, finish, etc.):

Print quantity and number of colors:

Other graphics to be used (other than cover):

Timeline/deadline:

After identifying the messages, the copy outline requires you to list third party influentials and how they are used either as part of the messages or in distributing the tactic. For example, in a brochure on personal hygiene for low-income parents, you might use testimonials or information from a recognized health care provider. You may also use nurses at free clinics to distribute the brochure. Both methods use third-party influentials or opinion leaders to strengthen the appeal.

Make sure to include specific details in the copy outline. When the brain is in the analytical mode, you can determine exactly what information must be included to accomplish your purpose. But when the brain shifts to the creative mode, you may fail to include critical information in the process of creating great copy. You must channel your creativity by knowing the public, purpose and message, and then you must check the resultant creation against the copy outline your analytical mind created for effectiveness. The most frequently omitted detail in primary and secondary messages (or copy) is the information that provides a way for the public to do what you have asked them to do. Nothing is more frustrating to people than to be persuaded to act but not be given the information necessary to do so. Provide a phone number to call, a web site to get more information or specific instructions on what to do.

Next, the copy outline details your planning for distribution. If it is a media product, designate each specific media channel (broadcasting station, newspaper or other publication) that will receive the communication product. Indicate the delivery method and if any follow-up is required. If it is a brochure or flyer, indicate how it will be distributed. If it is a billboard, indicate size and location, as well as describing any visual appeal or art.

Appendix B contains copy outlines for a variety of communication products; each has been appropriately altered to request the specific information that must be determined in the analytical process to help drive the creative process and to check its resultant accuracy and completeness. Although the copy outlines provided herein will help you when designing communication tools, you will use a vast array of tools for which copy outlines are not provided. Make sure you understand each communication tool or product well enough to custom design your own copy outlines for other kinds of communication tools. That shouldn't be a difficult task. For each tactic you use, you should plan the key public or target audience and secondary audiences, the action desired and the self-interest appeal to motivate that action, and then the primary and secondary messages that carry that appeal. Identify third party influentials and how they will be used. Some tactics will include art or photos. Describe what they should be and how they support your messages. Some tactics require distribution. Indicate how that will be accomplished. For each communication tool identify specific production needs like print colors and quantity. Always include a deadline to keep you on task.

Remember that the copy outline is the analytical tool to make sure your creative products follow your strategic plan and stay on target with your public, purpose and message. It contains the specific detail you determined was necessary to inform, persuade and motivate the public to action. It is important to shift your thinking to an emphasis on the process of analytically creating the copy outline. The majority of your time spent on tactic creation should be in developing the copy outline. It is the most important task in the creation of tactics and should receive the bulk of the time expended. A good copy outline actually becomes the first draft of your product. You will find that, if you plan your copy outlines carefully and completely, your communication tools will always be on target and will take less time to create.

Product pages

Once a communication product is completed, convert the copy outline to a product page (see figure 7.7). Your clients or managers do not need to see the entire planning process for a proposed product. That's really a trade secret you might want to keep to yourself. But the product should have a cover sheet to explain its purpose and proposed use. The product page in itself is impressive as it demonstrates the quality of your planning and the strategic thought behind the development of the piece. It convinces your clients or managers that the product was the result of systematic planning and thought. They will be more assured of the wisdom of committing resources to production because the product has been designed to achieve the purpose identified in the planning to reach goals and objectives already established.

The product page is simply a shortened copy outline. It identifies the product, its public, the action desired and the primary messages to be conveyed. It also includes detail on distribution and use in the overall

---

figure 7.7

Sample Product Page

Product:

Key public (audience) including current level of understanding of product/service:

　Secondary publics (audiences), if any:

Action desired from public(s):

　How that action ties to the primary public's self-interest:

Influentials (third-party opinion leaders who may influence the key public):

　How they will be used to influence the key public (testimonials, examples, etc.):

Overriding message and tone:

Primary messages: (usually 2-5, short statements/selling points to be conveyed)

　1. Primary Message:

　2. Primary Message:

　3. Primary Message:

Method and timing of distribution:

Timeline/deadline:

communications effort. It provides enough information to set the stage for your client to understand what he/she is reviewing. Using copy outlines and product pages will ensure that your research-based planning carries into product development. These two tools will help to keep your efforts strategic and on target.

> Product Page

A cover page to introduce the communication product to the client, demonstrating its strategic design and use.

SUMMARY

Carefully planned strategies and tactics will ensure not only that your messages reach your target publics but also that they motivate a desired action or behavior. Strategies determine which channels are most appropriate to reach key publics. Tactics detail the creative tools designed to convey our messages and solicit action from our publics. They are the tasks that must be done to implement the campaign or project. Copy outlines are used to create communications pieces that are consistent with our overall strategy and plans. They also make sure important details are included in the copy and the desired action from key publics is clearly stated.

Because many practitioners often find themselves choosing and implementing the same strategies and tactics over and over, it is important to remember the need for creativity. Use brainstorming and other techniques to look outside yourself, your habits, your customs and your traditions to discover new solutions and innovative ideas. Experiment through trial and error. Creativity is often the result of borrowing ideas from others and reshaping them into your own new ideas. Strategic communication requires creative thinking and implementation particularly in the planning of strategies and tactics.

CHAPTER SEVEN EXERCISES

1. Watch local media to discover a local organization running a campaign to solve a problem or meet a challenge. Try to identify all the strategies and tactics being used to send messages to the publics. Evaluate the effectiveness of the strategies and tactics, and think about how you might have designed them differently or sent them through different channels to make them more effective.

2. Using the non-profit organization you analyzed in the chapter six exercises, design new strategies and tactics to send the messages of the organization.

3. Using a local or national organization with which you are familiar, identify two or three publics of that organization. Then brainstorm for each a list of six to eight unique channels within which to send messages. Then brainstorm a list of at least 10 different tactics for each channel.

Solution to Shallcross test

How easy the answer appears when we give ourselves the permission to breach the perceived boundaries.

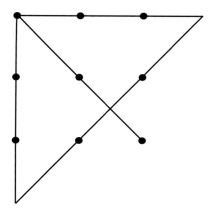

TEACHING CASE: The Case of the Caustic Cloud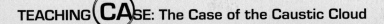

MATRIX: Action Planning

Step 6 — Strategies and Tactics

SAMPLE CAMPAIGN

Goose Creek residents affected by the spray

Strategy one:
- Ensure that each person affected by the spray is being properly cared for through personal contact with a company representative.

Tactics:
1. On Thursday (or Friday) send a senior company official to meet with those affected by the spray to extend regrets and see if they need additional help. Provide a direct home and office phone number for the company official in case additional questions arise.
2. Explain the incident more fully and communicate the company's safety record and procedures. Also explain the company's new commitment to further minimize public exposure by not spraying after 7:30 a.m.
3. Ask each executive/manager who meets with affected residents to submit a report by the end of the day May 7 giving the condition and care of each individual.
4. Send follow-up information about the insecticide not previously available to the doctors including any symptoms that could indicate a reaction and immediate care instructions. Also provide the approximate schedule of aerial spraying and a 24-hour phone number to call for information or to talk to a company official. (This toll-free phone line should be established at headquarters and manned at all times by communications staffers in the first full week after the incident. After that, it could be staffed in off hours by an answering service that would take a message for a response the following business day.)

5. Send medical reimbursement forms with company officials to leave with those affected by the spray. Explain how they can recoup medical exam, short-term treatment and lost work costs directly related to the spray incident.
6. Make sure company representatives take a gift certificate for a live tree or cut Christmas tree to each family of those affected by the spray incident.
7. Have company officials follow-up by phone on Friday, May 14 with each person to see if any issues are unresolved and if those affected by the spray are content with the company's response (evaluation tool).

Strategy two:
- Maintain the high level of esteem for Spruced Up by full disclosure of the incident through local mass media:

Tactics:
1. Place the COO as a guest on Dan Barber's Friday morning talk show to discuss the aerial spraying incident and take questions and give answers regarding the incident, the company's safety record and procedures, and the harmlessness of the pesticide. Also explain the commitment not to spray after 7:30 a.m.
2. Purchase a full-page ad in the Sunday Squawker for an open letter to Goose Creek residents that explains the incident, provides full information on the pesticide and re-emphasizes Spruced Up's commitment to the community and its employees. Provide information about the 24-hour helpline.

Goose Creek medical professionals

Strategy one:
- Provide detailed information on the pesticide used by Spruced Up and industry-recommended procedures for emergency and short-term care through personal contact and collateral material.

Tactics:
1. Within one week of the incident, send a company scientist and a communications staff member to meet with the EMTs and three physicians that treated residents exposed to the insecticide.
2. Mail information about the pesticide along with a letter from the company, informa-

tion on the company's aerial spraying procedures and medical treatment suggestions to the 45 EMTs and physicians in the area on Tuesday, May 18 to ensure its arrival by May 21 (evaluation tool).

3. Remind medical personnel in the letter that the aerial spraying schedule is printed in the local community newsletter and published on the company's web site. Also provide them with the 24-hour helpline number.

Goose Creek voters

Strategy one:
- Ensure residents that the incident was an accident because of an unexpected wind gust, but that their safety and the welfare of the community are of paramount concern to Spruced Up through local mass media.

Tactics:
1. Place the COO as a guest on Dan Barber's Friday morning talk show to discuss the aerial spraying incident and take questions and give answers regarding the incident, the company's safety record and procedures, and the harmlessness of the pesticide. Also explain the commitment not to spray after 7:30 a.m.
2. Buy a full-page ad in the Sunday Squawker for an open letter to Goose Creek residents that explains the incident, provides full information on the pesticide and re-emphasizes Spruced Up's commitment to the community and its employees. Provide information about the 24-hour helpline.

Strategy two:
- Maintain the high level of public approval of Spruced Up through full disclosure, incident management and open Q&A at the town council meeting.

Tactics:
1. The COO and two local senior executives (one a communications executive) will be present and will respond openly and honestly to all questions and concerns.
2. Explain Spruced Up's efforts to take care of the 40 residents that reported short-term respiratory problems associated with the pesticide.
3. Provide information about the new 24-hour helpline.
4. Communicate the company's efforts to research and select a safe pesticide. Reiterate

the fact that the incident was an accident caused by very strong, unexpected winds.

5. Provide a calendar of approximate dates and times of aerial spraying and remind council members and residents attending that this information is printed in the Goose Creek community newsletter as well as published on Spruced Up's web site.

6. Announce the change in spraying procedures that will limit spraying to the hours between sunrise and 7:30 a.m.

7. Provide a summary of facts about Spruced Up's operations including its contributions to the community, impact on jobs and the local economy and charitable work. Reiterate the company's commitment to employees and the communities in which it operates.

8. Hire a local research firm to conduct a survey of residents/voters on May 31 to determine the level of perception that Spruced Up is a "good" or "very good" community resident (evaluation tool).

9. Include question(s) on the May 31 survey to measure level of perception that Spruced Up operates "safely" and "responsibly" regarding employees and the community (evaluation tool).

10. Conduct a follow-up survey on October 31 to measure level of perception that Spruced Up is a "good" or "very good" community resident and that it operates "safely" and "responsibly" regarding employees and the community (evaluation tool).

Goose Creek Town Council

Strategy one:
- Ensure that the majority of council members feel Spruced Up has responded appropriately to the pesticide incident through influentials and personal contact with council members.

Tactics:
1. Respond quickly to the city council's request to attend the next council meeting and answer any preliminary questions over the phone.

2. Have a Spruced Up executive meet with the city manager in advance of the council meeting to gain his/her support of the company's actions to handle the incident.

3. Provide the city manager with early information about the pesticide, the aerial spray-

ing, the company's response to those affected, change in spraying hours, the 24-hour helpline and a list of company executives who will attend the meeting.

4. Have the company COO appear at the council meeting to explain the company's actions in person and to respond, along with other company experts, to questions from the council and residents.

5. Ask one of the agricultural professors who worked on pesticide research at the local college to attend the council meeting and comment on the pesticide's safety.

6. Have the COO follow up with a phone call to each council member within a week of the town meeting to address any additional questions or concerns members may have.

Spruced Up employees at Goose Creek

Strategy one:
- Have the well-respected COO provide accurate information and complete disclosure about the pesticide cloud to Spruced Up employees, and thereby maintain their support and trust, through company meetings.

Tactics:
1. Announce to employees that two company meetings will be held — one in the morning and one in the afternoon — on Friday, May 7 for all full-time and part-time employees to explain what caused the pesticide cloud and the company's response.

2. Have company management greet employees as they arrive for the meeting.

3. Have the COO explain the situation and open up the meeting for questions to be answered by the COO and Spruced Up management involved with the situation.

4. Announce the new 24-hour helpline and the restricted spraying hours.

5. Invite all employees to attend the town council meeting.

6. Ask a communications staff member to track Spruced Up's stock price through June 5 or obtain a 30-day stock history report from the company's investor relations department (evaluation tool).

REFERENCES AND ADDITIONAL READINGS

Benn, A. (1982). *Twenty-Three Most Common Mistakes in Public Relations*. New York: AMACOM.

Cutlip, S., Center, A., & Broom, G. (2000). *Effective Public Relations* (8th ed.). Englewood Cliffs, N.J.: Prentice-Hall, Inc.

Golin, A. (2004). *Trust or Consequences: Build Trust Today or Lose Your Market Tomorrow*. New York: AMACOM.

Hainsworth, B.E., & Wilson, L.J. (1992). "Strategic program planning." *Public Relations Review*, 18:1, 9-15.

Howard, C. & Mathews, W. (2000). *On Deadline: Managing Media Relations* (3rd ed.) Prospect Heights, Ill.: Waveland Press.

Lenhart, A. et al (2003). "The evershifting Internet population: A new look at Internet access and the digital divide," *Pew Internet and American Life Project*. www.pewinternet.org.

Newsom, D., Turk J.V. & Kruckeberg, D. (2004). *This Is PR: The Realities of Public Relations* (8th ed.). Belmont, Calif.: Wadsworth Publishing Company.

Norris, J.S. (1984). *Public Relations*. Englewood Cliffs, N.J.: Prentice-Hall, Inc.

Shallcross, D.J. (1981). *Teaching Creative Behavior*. Englewood Cliffs, N.J.:Prentice-Hall, Inc.

Tucker, K., Derelian, D., & Rouner, D. (1994). *Public Relations Writing: An Issue-Driven Behavioral Approach* (2nd ed.). Englewood Cliffs, N.J.: Prentice-Hall, Inc.

von Oech, R. (1990). *A Whack on The Side of The Head: How to Be Creative*. New York: Warner Books.

von Oech, R. (1983). *A Whack on The side of The Head: How to Unlock Your Mind for Innovation*. New York: Warner Books.

Wilcox, D. L., Ault, P. H., & Agee, W. K. (2002). *Public Relations: Strategies and Tactics* (7th ed.). New York: Harper and Row.

chapter 8

CALENDARING AND BUDGETING

"Do not squander time, for that is
the stuff that life is made of."
— Benjamin Franklin (1706–1790)

American Inventor, Journalist and Statesman

LEARNING IMPERATIVES

▸ To learn a format for calendars and budgets that supports strategic planning

▸ To understand the importance of calendaring interactivity among tactics

▸ To learn the value of creativity in the calendaring and budgeting processes

F ailing to act at the right time can be detrimental to any organization whether responding to a crisis or pursuing an opportunity. Timing can indeed be everything. Thus, the timing of events plays a crucial role in the strategic planning process.

The next two steps in the strategic planning matrix deal with the timing or calendaring of activities and budgeting for the cost of those activities. Both require very specific detail. Although much information is available in the communications and business literature about calendaring and budgeting, a few important points need to be emphasized here for you to understand these steps in the matrix.

Primarily, it is important to remember that a calendar and a budget are part of the strategic planning process. They should be considered carefully so that timing and cost are addressed within the overall framework of the organization's goals as well as the plan's objectives. Electronic tools for calendaring and budgeting abound. One of the best formats for a calendar is a Gantt chart (see figure 8.1) that allows you to view the schedule for each public by strategy and by day, week, or month. Both the calendar and budget should detail tactics by public and strategy. Organizing your calendar and budget in this way allows your client or corporate executive to quickly determine when tactics will target a specific public and how much each will cost. It also provides an easy "line item veto" when your client or executive wants to eliminate a public or strategy for any reason. It is a simple matter to delete that section of your plan and subtract the cost from the total. You will quickly have the revised budgetary figures, without having to return to your office to figure out how much of the budget was allocated for the deleted plans. Following this process also makes you much more aware of the cost of information and persuasion efforts among each of your key publics, and you are conversant in the interactive scheduling of the campaign by public.

Calendaring

We cannot overemphasize that a calendar is strategic. When you calendar a plan, you are not just picking dates; you are finding the premier

figure **8.1**

What is a Gantt chart?

A Gantt chart is a horizontal chart (usually a bar chart) developed as a production control tool in 1917 by Henry L. Gantt, an American engineer and social scientist. Frequently used in project management, a Gantt chart provides a graphical illustration of a schedule that helps to plan, coordinate, and track specific tasks in a project. Gantt charts may be simple versions created on graph paper or more complex automated versions created using project management applications such as Microsoft Project or Excel. Dozens of other software packages are also available to help build quick effective Gantt charts.

Sample Gantt Chart

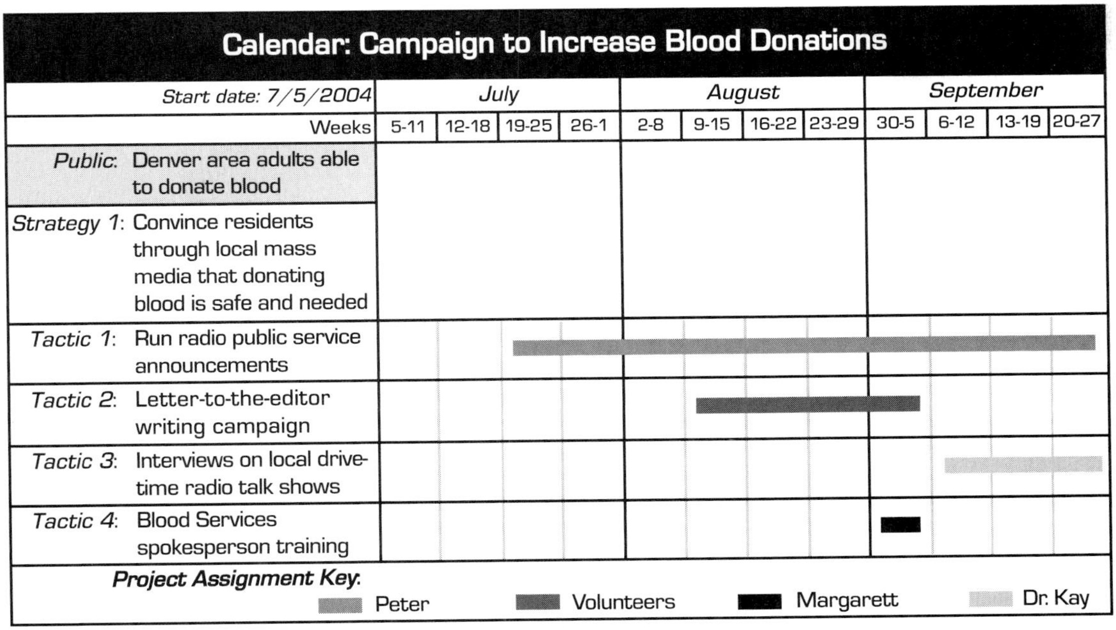
Calendar: Campaign to Increase Blood Donations
Start date: 7/5/2004
July
August
September
Weeks
5-11
12-18
19-25
26-1
2-8
9-15
16-22
23-29
30-5
6-12
13-19
20-27
Public: Denver area adults able to donate blood
Strategy 1: Convince residents through local mass media that donating blood is safe and needed
Tactic 1: Run radio public service announcements
Tactic 2: Letter-to-the-editor writing campaign
Tactic 3: Interviews on local drive-time radio talk shows
Tactic 4: Blood Services spokesperson training
Project Assignment Key:
Peter
Volunteers
Margarett
Dr. Kay

moment for an event to be held, a mailing to be sent, an ad campaign to launch. Timing is critical to success. A few important guidelines can help make sure your calendaring is effective.

1. **Interactivity is key**. The timing of tactics should be such that you magnify, reinforce and build on other tactics within publics and across publics. Schedule the grade school poster contest to conclude

in time to use the winning posters in your efforts to solicit sponsorships from local businesses.

2. **Check for conflicts seasonally and within communities**. It is difficult to compete with traditional events and efforts. The annual Oktoberfest is probably not the time to schedule an unrelated event.

3. **Build on tradition and other regularly scheduled events**. The beginning of a new school year might be a great time to launch an effort to change a habit or routine. Perhaps when the kids go off to school is the best time to market a "read-a-book-a-month" book club to women.

4. **Always provide enough lead time for production and other arrangements**. Plan for collateral material to be complete far in advance of the time it is needed. Make all reservations and invitations to key participants well in advance of the event. Doing so will leave time to reprint if needed or even to reschedule.

5. **Plan backward from the implementation date**. If the launch is in July, when should the media pieces be prepared and placed? Is the media element a promotion or a follow-up? When should collateral material be completed? When should invitations be printed and mailed?

10-STEP STRATEGIC COMMUNICATIONS PLANNING MATRIX

matrix

MATRIX: Action Planning

Step 7-8 — Calendar and Budget

7. *Calendar*   Calendaring should be done with a time-task matrix (such as a Gantt chart) used to plan and strategically integrate the timing of implementation. The calendar should be organized by public and strategy with scheduling for each tactic.

8. *Budget*   Budgets should also be organized by public and strategy. The budget projects the specific cost of each tactic. It should also indicate where costs will be offset by donations or sponsorships. Subtotals should be provided for each strategy and public.

A calendar for implementation is obviously much more detailed than a calendar for a proposed plan. While the latter simply schedules implementation dates, the former requires scheduling of all efforts leading up to the date of implementation.

Budgeting

The budget should also be considered strategically. The issue should not only be total cost but also who should pay and how. Really creative plans find solutions to budgetary limitations that actually result in greater persuasive power. Recruiting volunteers to do work that would have been a budgetary item results not only in lower cost but also in greater support and advocacy from influentials in a community. Building partnerships between organizations — whether business to business or corporate to nonprofit — often strengthens the credibility of the appeal. Combining with other actors in a cooperative community to share costs provides a unity of action that is more persuasive and far reaching than acting unilaterally. Even requesting small contributions from target publics (like $1 admission to an event with the proceeds donated to a relevant local charity) can be effective. Making something free doesn't always make it appealing. In fact, many people consider that something free may not be worth their time. Among certain publics, you are more likely to get attention and participation if there is some monetary investment — no matter how small.

> **Partnership**

A mutually beneficial short- or long-term cooperative relationship to reach common goals.

Your budget should have five columns. The first is actually the public, strategy and tactic under consideration and the second is the detail associated with that (i.e., how many brochures at how much each and any discount percentages or sponsors). The next column is the projected cost, the fair market price of this good or service. The fourth column is the dollar amount of any discount or sponsorship, and the final column is the actual cost to your client or organization (fair market price less the discount or sponsorship).

Budgeting by public, strategy and tactic is particularly important. In your planning it is critical to assess the cost of reaching a particular public for a particular purpose, and then to decide if the expenditure is worth the gain (cost-benefit analysis). If it isn't, then you will need to find a more cost-effective way to reach that public or find another solution that doesn't require their cooperation. Executives will be appreciative of that kind of analysis.

Nevertheless, don't automatically reject a public because of cost. Be creative in finding ways to do what you have planned in more frugal ways. Also, engage in partnerships. They are win-win relationships and in many ways even more important than cost savings.

SUMMARY

Strategic planning does not end at tactics. Your approach to calendaring and budgeting must also be strategic. Tactics should be timed to gain maximum benefit from other tactics in the plan and from external events and annual community calendars. Strategic budgeting allows you to creatively manage cost while leveraging other relationships. The calendar and budget should be just as much a part of your strategic and creative planning as are the other elements of the plan.

CHAPTER EIGHT EXERCISES

1. Examine a local annual event and identify what publics are being targeted. Sketch out the calendar for preparations and tactics. What are all the elements of the event including partnerships, media and collateral materials? Design a calendar that incorporates the preparation and implementation of every element of the event by public, and examine what the lead time would need to be for each tactic.

2. Make some phone calls to cost out the elements of the above event. Categorize the budgetary items by public to determine a cost per public. Identify where the organizers might have negotiated discounts or contributions and where partnerships have mitigated the cost

TEACHING CASE: The Case of the Caustic Cloud

MATRIX: Action Planning
Step 7 — Calendar

Public: G.C. residents affected by spray

		6-May	7-May	8-May	9-May	10-May	11-May
Strategy	Ensure affected individuals are properly cared for through personal contact						
Tactics	Personal visit from company executive		X--------	X			
	Executive report on care of affected individuals			X			
	Send follow-up information to doctors and EMTs						
	Establish/maintain 24-hour helpline			X-----------			
	Medical reimbursement			X-----------			
	Provide gift certificate		X--------	X			
	Follow-up phone call						
Strategy	Maintain esteem by full disclosure through local media						
Tactics	COO guest on Dan Barber talk show			X			
	Full-page ad in Sunday Squawker					X	

Public: G.C. medical professionals

		6-May	7-May	8-May	9-May	10-May	11-May
Strategy	Provide information through personal contact and collateral material						
Tactics	Personal visit to physicians and EMTs		X-----------				
	Send follow-up information to doctors and EMTs						
	Establish/maintain 24-hour helpline			X-----------			

Public: G.C. Town Council

		6-May	7-May	8-May	9-May	10-May	11-May
Strategy	Ensure council feels Spruced Up has responded appropriately through influentials and personal contact						
Tactics	Respond quickly to request to attend council meeting		X				
	Spruced Up executive meet with city manager			X			
	Provide city manager with information on incident			X			
	COO appear at council meeting for Q&A						X
	Aggricultural professor comments on safety						X
	COO follow-up phone call to council members						

Public: Spruced Up employees

		6-May	7-May	8-May	9-May	10-May	11-May
Strategy	Have COO provide information and disclosure through company meetings						
Tactics	Announce two company meetings to explain incident	X					
	Management greet employees as they arrive at meeting			X			
	COO explains situation/opens up Q&A			X			
	Announce 24-hour helpline and restricted spraying hours			X			
	Invite employees to attend the town council meeting			X			
	Online query for stock price	X-----------					

SAMPLE CAMPAIGN

Note: This calendar example is abbreviated for space. Not all publics listed in the sample case are included.
Your calendar should include strategies and tactics for each public.

12-May	13-May	14-May	15-May	16-May	17-May	18-23 May	24-31 May	June	July	Aug	Sept	Oct.
					X							

--- X

-- X

12-May	13-May	14-May	15-May	16-May	17-May	18-23 May	24-31 May	June	July	Aug	Sept	Oct.
		X										

12-May	13-May	14-May	15-May	16-May	17-May	18-23 May	24-31 May	June	July	Aug	Sept	Oct.
------ X												
					X							

--- X

12-May	13-May	14-May	15-May	16-May	17-May	18-23 May	24-31 May	June	July	Aug	Sept	Oct.

X -- X

12-May	13-May	14-May	15-May	16-May	17-May	18-23 May	24-31 May	June	July	Aug	Sept	Oct.

-- X

TEACHING CASE: The Case of the Caustic Cloud

SAMPLE CAMPAIGN

MATRIX: Action Planning
Step 8 — Budget

Note: This budget example is abbreviated for space. Not all publics listed in the sample case are included. Your budget should include strategies and tactics for each public.

Public	G.C. residents affected by spray	Per Item Cost	Total Projected	Sponsored Credit	Actual Projected
Strategy	**Ensure affected individuals are properly**				
	cared for through personal contact				
Tactics	Personal visit from company executive	$0.00	$0.00	$0.00	$0.00
	Executive report on care of affected individuals	$0.00	$0.00	$0.00	$0.00
	Establish/maintain 24-hour helpline (6 months + first week)		$1,644.00	$0.00	$250.00
	Medical reimbursement packet (40 each)	$0.80	$32.00	$0.00	$32.00
	Gift Certificate (40 each)	$50.00	$2,000.00	$1,400.00	$600.00
	Follow-up phone call	$0.00	$0.00	$0.00	$0.00
	Strategy subtotal				*$882.00*
	Public subtotal				$882.00
Public	**G.C. medical professionals**				
Strategy	**Provide information through personal**				
	contact and collateral material				
Tactics	Personal visit to physicians and EMTs	$0.00	$0.00	$0.00	$0.00
	Information packets and mailing (45 copies)	$1.40	$63.00	$0.00	$63.00
	Strategy subtotal				*$63.00*
	Public subtotal				$63.00
Public	**G.C. voters**				
Strategy	**Maintain esteem by full disclosure**				
	through local media				
Tactics	COO guest on Dan Barber talk show	$0.00	$0.00	$0.00	$0.00
	Full-page ad in Sunday Squawker	$500.00	$500.00	$0.00	$500.00
	Strategy subtotal				*$500.00*
	Public subtotal				$500.00
Strategy	**Maintain high public approval through disclosure,**				
	incident management and Q&A at Town Meeting				
Tactics	COO and two execs answer questions	$0.00	$0.00	$0.00	$0.00
	Explain efforts to care for 40 citizens affected	$0.00	$0.00	$0.00	$0.00
	Provide information on 24-hour helpline	$0.00	$0.00	$0.00	$0.00
	Communicate company research efforts/accident	$0.00	$0.00	$0.00	$0.00
	Provide calendar of aerial spraying schedule	$0.00	$0.00	$0.00	$0.00
	Announce limited spraying hours (not after 7:30 a.m.)	$0.00	$0.00	$0.00	$0.00
	Provide summary of operations/community contributions	$0.00	$0.00	$0.00	$0.00
	Hire local research firm to measure perceptions (2 studies)	$3,000.00	$6,000.00	$0.00	$6,000.00
	Strategy subtotal				*$6,000.00*
	Public subtotal				$6,500.00
Public	**G.C. Town Council**				
Strategy	**Ensure council feels Spruced Up has responded**				
	appropriately through influentials and personal contact				
Tactics	Respond quickly to request to attend council meeting	$0.00	$0.00	$0.00	$0.00
	Spruced Up executive meet with city manager	$0.00	$0.00	$0.00	$0.00
	Provide city manager with information on incident	$1.40	$1.40	$0.00	$1.40
	COO appear at council meeting to answer questions	$0.00	$0.00	$0.00	$0.00
	COO follow-up phone call to council members	$0.00	$0.00	$0.00	$0.00
	Strategy subtotal				*$1.40*
	Public subtotal				$1.40
	CAMPAIGN TOTAL				$7,946.40

REFERENCES AND ADDITIONAL READINGS

TechTarget, Inc. (2004). *Gantt Chart.* whatis.techtarget.com/definition/0,,sid9_gci331397,00.html

IMPLEMENTATION AND COMMUNICATIONS MANAGEMENT

"There is a logic of language and a logic
of mathematics. The former is supple
and lifelike, it follows our experience."

— Thomas Merton (1915–1968)

American Monk, Writer and Poet

LEARNING IMPERATIVES

▸ To understand the use of the strategic calendar in managing the tactics for each public and across all publics

▸ To learn to synthesize a plan into a table and check its logic

▸ To understand the importance of measurement and flexibility in the process of implementation

Two of the most valuable tools for managing the implementation of a plan are the strategically planned calendar and the communication confirmation table. The calendar keeps all strategies and tactics for all publics coordinated and on schedule. The communication confirmation table helps you check to make sure you are accomplishing what your analysis and plan said you needed to accomplish with each public to reach the goal. Nevertheless, remember this is a planning matrix; you should complete every step of the planning — through evaluation criteria and tools — before you begin to implement the plan. Once you have done that, use the calendar and the communication confirmation table as your management maps.

Managing by calendar

> **Communication Confirmation Table**

A visual tool used to validate the logic of a communications plan.

To manage a project well, you must be able to visualize the outcome in your head. You must be able to see how an effort comes together to communicate messages to an individual public and across publics. The Gantt chart format for a calendar helps you identify tasks and preparation by public throughout the entire timeframe of the project or campaign. You can manage (or delegate management) by public if needed. The same format allows you to identify a selected timeframe and consider every tactic being implemented among all publics within that timeframe. It provides a holistic view of every tactic integrating across all publics; it displays the whole picture. As a management tool, it helps you keep all the balls in the air because you visualize the entirety of events, but still allows you to narrow your focus to one public as needed.

Managing by communication confirmation table

The steps in the planning section of the Strategic Communications Planning Matrix have required an analytical approach to answer these four questions:

1. What needs to be accomplished to achieve the goal?
2. Who needs to be reached and motivated in order to accomplish that?

3. What messages need to be sent to those publics to motivate them through self-interest appeal?
4. How can the messages be sent so our publics will receive them and act upon them?

The planning is analytical and is completed one public at a time using your research and knowledge about a particular public to formulate and deliver messages to that public. Because planning is naturally linear, it is helpful — particularly to students learning the strategic process — to create an abbreviated and more visual tool to validate the viability of the plan and to make sure it follows logically from the analysis of publics. That is the purpose of the communication confirmation table. It presents the logic across a single line of vision to confirm that planning decisions employ good reasoning. By abbreviating your analysis in key words across the matrix categories, the communication confirmation table shows your logic as it answers the four questions above.

The communication confirmation table summarizes the self-interests of a public and shows in the next column how those self-interests are

10-STEP STRATEGIC COMMUNICATIONS PLANNING MATRIX

matrix

MATRIX: Communication

Step 9 — Communication Confirmation

Communication Confirmation The communications confirmation table confirms the logic of the plan by converting it into short statements for each public in tabular form. This format (see below) aids in checking strategies and tactics to make sure they are appropriate to reach the public, that messages appeal to the public's self-interest and that the planning for each public meets the objectives.

Key Public	Self-Interests	Primary Messages	Influentials	Objectives	Strategies	Tactics

incorporated into the message appeal. It identifies from your overall objectives those that this particular public will help you satisfy and uses key words to highlight the strategies and supporting tactics necessary to achieve the objective. Viewing this short-hand version of your plan helps you confirm that the analysis has been applied, that the plan flows logically, that all elements of the matrix action planning process are aligned. It is not unusual for the confirmation table to reveal discrepancies in logic that were not apparent while the plan was being written. Have you selected midday television talk shows to reach high school students? Did you plan to run PSAs during drive time to reach housewives? Have you designed a message about money-saving features to target a public that is less concerned about money and more concerned about safety? Are you using video news releases to send a complicated message better conveyed in newspaper features or op-ed pieces? Check your logic, and then go back and make any appropriate changes before you begin your implementation. As intimated in the quotation at the beginning of the chapter, language is fluid and logical — especially words defining a strategic plan that effectively builds on itself.

Ongoing monitoring and feedback

These two management tools — the strategically planned calendar and the communication confirmation table — add the flexibility that is often missing from the planning process. When you plan the evaluation (the final step in the Strategic Communications Planning Matrix), you will plan for measurement throughout the implementation phase. These measurements provide checkpoints for your progress toward reaching the objectives and the goal. But what if your measurements reveal that you are not on track? Because you have strategically planned a calendar and thoughtfully prepared the communication confirmation table, you have the flexibility to go back to those two documents to rework and refine your plan to get back on track.

The necessary alteration may be as simple as adding or changing a single tactic or as grand as revamping an entire public. The confirmation table also provides the flexibility to quickly add or delete a public. You don't have to rewrite the whole plan. You have a summary of your plan by public, most particularly of the logic of the plan based on your analysis. Use it to determine what you need to change to reach your objectives on time and within budget.

SUMMARY

The communication confirmation table is a planning tool that becomes a management tool once you have begun the actual implementation of your communications plan. As a planning tool, it confirms the logic of your plan for each public according to the analysis completed in your research. As a management tool, it provides the flexibility to change your plan quickly and effectively to make progress toward your objectives. The strategically planned calendar becomes the other key management tool in the implementation process. Use it to manage your plan for each public as well as to manage the whole effort from a macro perspective. In the implementation process, these two management tools provide the capability for measurement and feedback to adjust the plan and keep it on track.

CHAPTER NINE EXERCISES

1. Use one of the partial plans or analyses completed in the exercises from prior chapters and create a communication confirmation table that will help you evaluate the logic of the plan. Make any appropriate corrections.

2. Now select a public that was not selected in the above plan and add them to the confirmation table as a viable part of the plan.

TEACHING CASE: The Case of the Caustic Cloud

MATRIX: Communication

Step 9 — Communication Confirmation

Key Public	Self-Interests	Primary Messages	Influentials
Goose Creek residents affected by the spray	Being healthy and safe; Not being afraid to go outside or let children go outside; Getting their medical bills paid	1) Spruced Up is committed to the safety and well being of our employees and our community 2) Spruced Up regrets any discomfort you've experienced	Physicians, community leaders, family members and close friends
Goose Creek medical professionals	Knowing whether or not the pesticide is harmful; knowing what to do if it happens again; being seen as competent	1) Spruced Up is committed to the safety and well being of our employees and our community	Other doctors, scientific studies/experts, supervisors, professional colleagues
Goose Creek voters	Health and safety; economic security; a good community to raise families	1) Spruced Up is committed to the safety and well being of our employees and our community 2) Spruced Up is proud to be an active part of Goose Creek and its future	Community leaders, family members, fellow workers and friends who are Spruced Up employees
Goose Creek Town Council	Solving the problem amicably with all parties satisfied; appearing competent and working for constituents' best interest; keeping Spruced Up open and profitable as part of the tax base	1) Spruced Up is committed to the safety and well being of our employees and community 2) We are proactively responding to the incident	City manager, constituents, business leaders, academics
Goose Creek employees	Their jobs at Spruced Up and pride in their employer; economic security; health and safety; a good community to raise families	1) Spruced Up is committed to the safety and well being of our employees and our community 2) We're meeting with and making sure anyone exposed is taken care of quickly 3) Spruced Up is proud to be an active part of Goose Creek and its future	Corporate leaders, co-workers, friends, family and community leaders

SAMPLE CAMPAIGN: COMMUNICATIONS CONFIRMATION TABLE

Note: The communications confirmation table confirms the logic of the plan by converting it into short statements for each public in tabular form.

Objectives	Strategies	Tactics
1) Ensure residents affected have been properly cared for	1) Ensure individuals are properly cared for through personal contact	Personal visit from executive, executive report, follow-up medical reimbersement, gift certificate, follow-up call
2) Ensure 95 percent of residents affected are content with company's actions to resolve the incident	2) Maintain high esteem for Spruced Up by full disclosure through the media	COO guest on Dan Barber show, ad in Squawker
4) Ensure medical professionals have instruction for treatment	1) Provide information on the pesticide and procedures for short-term care through personal contact and collateral material	Personal visit to EMTs and physicians, follow-up information, spraying schedule, 24-hour helpline
3) Regain 85 percent level of perception that Spruced Up is a "good" or "very good" community citizen 5) Obtain a 75 percent level of perception that Spruced Up operates safely and responsibly	1) Ensure voters this was an accident and that their safety and welfare are of paramount concern for Spruced Up through mass media 2) Maintain high level of public approval of Spruced Up through full disclosure, incident management and open Q&A at the town council meeting	COO guest on Dan Barber show, ad in Squawker COO open Q&A at meeting, efforts to care for affected residents, 24-hour helpline, research efforts, calendar of spray schedule, change in spraying hours, contributions to the community, hire firm to measure perceptions
3) Regain 85 percent level of perception that Spruced Up is a "good" or "very good" community citizen 5) Obtain a 75 percent level of perception that Spruced Up operates safely and responsibly	1) Ensure vast majority of council members feel Spruced Up has responded appropriately to the incident through influentials and personal contact	Respond quickly to invitation, meet with city manager in advance, provide manager with preview information, COO appear at town meeting, aggricultural professor comment, follow-up phone call
3) Regain 85 percent level of perception that Spruced Up is a "good" or "very good" community resident 5) Obtain a 75 percent level of perception that Spruced Up operates safely and responsibly 6) Mitigate negative effects keep dips in stock price less than 5 percent	1) Complete disclosure to employees about incident to maintain support and trust through a company meeting	Announce company meetings, greet employees, COO explain situation, 24-hour helpline, invite to town meeting, track stock price

EFFECTIVE COMMUNICATIONS MEASUREMENT AND EVALUATION

"Unless evaluation becomes less of a mystery and a more accessible process, it would appear that a generation of better educated practitioners is needed to break the technician mold."

— Tom Watson

Author, "Integrating Planning and Evaluation"

LEARNING IMPERATIVES

▸ To understand the importance of evaluation in demonstrating results

▸ To understand how to plan evaluation that meets the standards set by an organization's management

▸ To understand how to determine evaluation criteria and the appropriate measurement tools

W ith the new vigor with which communications research is finally being pursued, another step in the RACE process moves in to take the "most neglected" title: evaluation. Evaluation has long been cast into the pot with research and, consequently, its specific nature and conduct ignored. In fact, surveys among public relations professionals found that they generally "lacked confidence to promote evaluation methods to employers and clients" (Watson, 2001). Lack of knowledge and understanding of evaluation models and techniques seemed to be the primary reason practitioners did not propose or conduct evaluation.

Nevertheless, how can the organization's communicators hope to be taken seriously if they shrink from measurements of their effectiveness? For too long, the communications function has been viewed as a kind of mystical intangible: intangible methods, intangible effects and intangible results. But no organization focused on building strong relationships with key publics can afford to spend resources on intangibles. We have often claimed that our benefit to the organization was indirect, but that they would really miss us if we weren't there. It is a wonder more organizations haven't taken that challenge.

Organizations — commercial, governmental and nonprofit — are managed to produce results, to accomplish missions. Each function of the organization must be able to demonstrate its contribution to the accomplishment of its mission. The ability to prove results is critical not only for the organization but also for the employees doing the work. It is little reward to work daily in efforts that you cannot be sure are making a contribution.

Evaluation models

The literature of communication contains several models of evaluation. They basically all evaluate success along three standards. The first is success that justifies the budget expenditure. The second is effectiveness of the program itself. The third is whether or not objectives were met. While these standards are all worthwhile, they may leave you and your organization wanting. Put yourself in the chair of the CEO. What is he/she looking for? In a word, results.

Results may mean meeting the objectives, they may mean success that justifies the budget expenditure or they may mean effectively carrying out a program. But what we should focus on as our organization's marketing, public relations and advertising communication specialists is setting objectives that are measured in terms of results, justifying budget expenditures in terms of results, and determining program effectiveness in terms of results.

To simplify the process here, we refer the reader to a model of evaluation constructed by Cutlip, Center and Broom (2000, pp. 436-454). The Preparation, Implementation and Impact (PII) model is a straightforward approach to evaluating communication programs at all required levels. It provides guidelines to evaluate the preparation and planning process within the organization, the tactical implementation and the impact or results of any given effort. In evaluating the planning process, it asks if the research collected was sufficient and complete, if it was organized and analyzed in a way that it could be used effectively, if the process was timely and inclusive, and other key questions that assess whether the process functioned to produce a workable plan to meet the challenge.

Evaluation of the implementation process tracks the success of tactics by counting media placement, event attendance and other such measures of our tactical abilities. The final evaluation is the impact of the program. What were the results? Did the program meet the objectives? Were attitudes, opinions and behaviors changed? And finally, did those changes produce the desired result and satisfy the goal (assuming the objectives were met) within the allocated budget? Evaluation that does not measure end results simply cannot stand the test of today's organizational managers. And communications professionals who cannot demonstrate that their efforts produce the desired results within acceptable expenditures are expendable.

Evaluation is actually relatively easy if it is planned from the beginning of an effort using the Strategic Communications Planning Matrix.

10-STEP STRATEGIC COMMUNICATIONS PLANNING MATRIX

matrix

MATRIX: Evaluation

Step 10 — Evaluation Criteria and Tools

Evaluation Criteria and Tools   Evaluation criteria are the specific measures used to determine the success of each objective. Evaluation tools are the specific methods used to gather the data identified by each criterion. The evaluation tools should be included in the calendar and budget.

Good evaluation owes a lot to good objectives. If the objectives are written as outcomes to be accomplished in order to reach the goal, then the evaluation will be results-oriented and satisfy the organization's management. Two steps must be considered in evaluating any plan. First, by what criteria should we judge success; and second, how are those criteria best measured?

Evaluation criteria

Criteria are automatically set when objectives are set. Objectives are designed to provide direction to planning and to identify the results that determine success. Clients and managers will judge success by the criteria (objectives) you have set. In this step of your plan, you should restate your objectives in terms of success, and designate an appropriate method for measuring each one including a date. For example, if one of your objectives is to increase name recognition of your client from 30 percent to 80 percent, the criteria for success would be written, "Achieve Eighty percent name recognition of the client's name among key publics on June 30."

The successful achievement of all campaign objectives should result in the accomplishment of the goal, which may or may not be directly measurable. If you have followed the strategic planning matrix, accomplishing the overall goal will signify to management that you have achieved success in all three standards identified above. You can justify the expenditure because you reached your goal within proposed budget. You demonstrate effectiveness because your strategies and tactics combined to accomplish the goal. And, you met the campaign objectives which resulted in the accomplishment of the goal.

In addition to evaluating results by measuring performance on each objective, you should establish criteria for evaluation of the effectiveness of your plan and communication tactics. While the ultimate evaluation is results, you are also being personally evaluated by supervisors and clients on your professionalism, creativity and ability to direct a communications effort. You should add evaluation factors that specifically address your success and effectiveness in community relations, media relations or some other skill area. While media placement is not a measure of whether a public received and acted upon a message, it is still a factor to be evaluated within the context of effective of strategies and tactics.

> **Evaluation Criteria**

Standards set to measure success.

Although it is not recommended to set an objective for specific media placements because it tends to demonstrate manipulative tendencies which are expressly forbidden in some codes of ethics (PRSA's specifically), it is perfectly acceptable to set an evaluation criteria that measures your success at placement couched in terms of media relations. While an objective for front-page coverage in the Wall Street Journal may set a manipulative course that is fatal to good relationships with media, evaluation criteria that measures such coverage and placement as a whole across the campaign would examine the quality of the writing, newsworthiness of the information and the adequacy with which you identified and met the needs of media contacts. The first course is manipulative; the second seeks to evaluate and improve media relationships.

Similarly, you may seek to evaluate your performance at staging and promoting events or any other accepted marketing or public relations communication tool. Although these evaluations are not specifically determining whether or not you achieved your objectives, they are crucial to improvement of your communications efforts and demonstrating your expertise, professionalism and value to the client or organization.

Converting your objectives to evaluation criteria is your primary evaluation of results. Additional criteria that address your team's specific capability and expertise are highly useful secondary criteria to measure your effectiveness.

Evaluation tools

Each objective must be converted to an evaluation criterion and each criterion must be measurable by an evaluation tool. Measurement tools are essentially research tools. They are the same kinds of methodologies used in research but focused on evaluation. They may include surveys or measure sales or count votes. But you will also tally results: dollars raised or saved, legislative bills passed or failed and other concrete outcomes. The rules of research apply in evaluation, more particularly because the evaluation of your communications effort then becomes part of the background for subsequent efforts.

> **Evaluation Tools**

Methods used to gather data needed to assess whether or not evaluation criteria were met.

Typically, evaluation measurements require a benchmark measurement prior to the program, during the program or both. Without adequate planning for the evaluation process, the benchmarks are often not taken in the beginning, resulting in no data for comparison. Unless you know where you started, you cannot determine how far you've come.

Although measurement tools are essentially the same as research methods, many research organizations have specialized in evaluative methods. It would be wise to access the web sites and newsletters on evaluation and measurement produced by specialty firms like KD Paine and Partners. While evaluation tools for some objectives may be obvious, others may require complicated formulas that would, for example combine measures of sales, media placements and trade show referrals in some kind of sliding scale that measures the effect of marketing communications and media relations on product sales.

Clearly articulated evaluation tools must include the source of information and how it will be obtained. Include all necessary tasks when describing the evaluation tool for each criterion. If you are measuring the criterion mentioned above, your evaluation tool would read something like this: "Conduct a random, statistically viable, telephone survey of the key public population June 28–30, 2004 to determine what percent recognize the client's name." This data could then be compared to the survey conducted at the beginning of the campaign, which indicated 30 percent name recognition for the client.

Calendaring and budgeting the evaluation

The evaluation process points out the necessity of reviewing your calendar and budget to ensure that all evaluation tools are scheduled. You can designate a separate section of the calendar and budget to specifically address the planned evaluation. A wiser choice might be to include evaluation as part of the planned strategies and tactics for each public. Only with this kind of planning can you ensure that appropriate benchmark research is done in the beginning and throughout the campaign to compare with evaluation research. It also enables you to incorporate appropriate evaluation in the detailed planning for tactics. For example, if you need to measure the number of attendees at events, or number of visitors to a trade show display, you will build into the tactic a method for tracking those numbers. Trying to guesstimate such figures later only causes your evaluation to be inadequate and your claim to success suspect. Finally, including the evaluation tools in the calendar and budget for each public ensures that the funding is available for this critical function.

SUMMARY

Communications and marketing professionals cannot expect to be taken seriously unless they positively demonstrate the results of their efforts. Measuring the effectiveness of communications efforts can be a straightforward process if you use the Strategic Communications Planning Matrix. The matrix focuses your efforts to set objectives that are the outcomes which will combine to reach the end result desired. Evaluation of the objectives should be as strategic a function as any part of the process. Objectives become the evaluation criteria and must meet the highest standards of evaluation measurement. Your planning will also facilitate setting criteria to measure the effectiveness of the communications strategies and tactics.

Tools for measuring success are basically the same as the methodologies used in research. Nevertheless, many professional research firms now specialize in evaluative research and can design specific tools for your needs. Make sure to include the evaluation process in your tactics and in the calendar and budget for each public so this critical process is not overlooked.

CHAPTER TEN EXERCISES

1. Ask a local nonprofit to share with you the objectives in an old
   strategic plan and check to see if evaluation measurement is included in the plan. Ask about the process for evaluating success and
   assess whether the tools used were appropriate to determine if the
   goal was truly achieved.

2. Examine several of the research methodologies identified in Chapter
   Three and determine how each could be converted to an evaluation
   methodology.

3. Do a Web search for research companies and find those that adver-
   tise evaluation measurement. Try to find specific descriptions of
   those measurements on their sites. Also search for communications
   research and/or evaluation newsletters that are available on the
   Web.

TEACHING CASE: The Case of the Caustic Cloud

MATRIX: Evaluation

Step 10 — Evaluation Criteria and Tools

SAMPLE CAMPAIGN

Objective 1

Criteria:

- All Goose Creek residents affected by the insecticide were properly cared for by May 7.

Tool:

- Ask each executive/manager who meets with affected residents to report on the condition and care of each individual.

Objective 2

Criteria:

- 95 percent of residents affected by the insecticide (38 of the 40) were content with the company's actions to resolve the incident by Friday, May 14.

Tool:

- Have company officials ask affected residents how well they feel the company has responded to their needs and resolved the incident during follow up telephone calls on Friday, May 14.

Objective 3

Criteria:

- 85 percent of the Goose Creek population perceive Spruced Up as a "good" or "very good" community resident on May 31 and again on October 31.

Tool:

- Hire a local research firm to conduct a random survey of Goose Creek residents on May 31 and again on October 31.

Objective 4

Criteria:

- Treatment instructions and background information on the insecticide are distributed to the 45 general practice physicians and EMTs in Goose Creek by Friday, May 21.

Tool:

- Determine if communications staff mailed medical treatment instructions, background information on the spray and a letter from the company to the 45 identified general practice physicians and EMTs by May 18 so it will arrive on or before May 21.

Objective 5

Criteria:

- 75 percent level of perception that Spruced Up operates safely and responsibly regarding employees and the community on May 31 and again on October 31.

Tool:

- Ask the local research firm hired for objective 3 to include a question about Spruced Up operating safely and responsibly on the survey conducted May 31 and October 31.

Objective 6

Criteria:

- Keep the overall decline in Spruced Up's share price to less than 5 percent through June 5 (measured against the pre-incident price of $32).

Tool:

- Have a member of the communications staff access the company's closing stock price online each day and record this figure each day through June 5 or ask the company's investor relations department to provide a 30-day history of stock performance on June 5.

REFERENCES AND ADDITIONAL READINGS

Cutlip, S. M., Center, A. H., & Broom, G. M. (2000). *Effective Public Relations*. (8th ed.). Upper Saddle River, N.J.: Prentice Hall.

KD Paine and Partners. *The Measurement Standard*. www.measuresof-success.com.

Newsom, D., Turk, J. V., & Kruckeberg, D. (2004). *This Is PR: The Realities of Public Relations*. (8th ed.). Belmont, Calif.: Wadsworth Publishing Company.

Watson, T. (2001). "Integrating planning and evaluation: Evaluating the public relations practice and public relations programs." In Heath, R.L. *Handbook of Public Relations*. Thousand Oaks, Calif.: Sage Publications, Inc., pp. 259-268.

chapter 1

EXECUTIVE SUMMARIES AND BUSINESS PRESENTATIONS

"The ability to present is probably the number one skill lacking today. If you can't present well, you're not going to move up in the company."

— Cindy Peterson

Founder of Presentations for Results, a coaching and consulting firm in Boise, Idaho

LEARNING IMPERATIVES

▶ To understand the components and characteristics of effective executive summaries

▶ To understand how to create and give a business presentation that achieves positive results

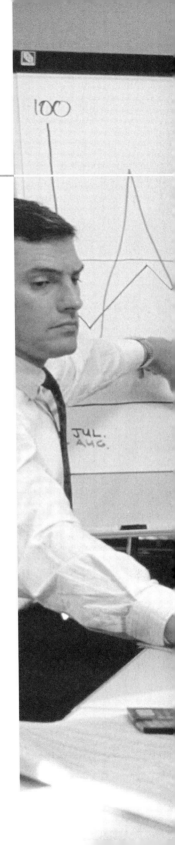

T he reality of our fast-paced business environment today is that few executives have the time or patience to read lengthy reports. In fact, nearly all written material targeted at executives today contains a short executive summary. Hopefully someone on the project team will read the entire report, or in your case the communications plan, but that cannot be guaranteed. The only two probable points of exposure to your plans, campaigns or ideas are the executive summary and the business or client presentation. If these are engaging and to the point, an executive might take the time to look deeper into your plan. If not, you will lose his/her attention and support.

The primary key to success for both executive summaries and business presentations is a strategic planning approach. With a goal in mind and specific objectives for the summary or presentation to accomplish, analyze the public(s) to be addressed and their self-interest messages. Then design your summary or presentation to deliver the messages and lead your audience (perhaps only one key decision maker) to the conclusions you want it to reach.

Knowing your audience has little time, you must get to the key points and solutions quickly while capturing and retaining interest. You must show the logic and the creativity that make the proposal workable. Give just enough detail to sell the plan but not so much as to lose the interest of the target audience. Always include the cost in terms of time and resources (money). Remember that an executive decision maker typically has only two questions that matter to him/her:

1. Is this the best solution or plan (i.e., is there really a need and will it work)?
2. How much will it cost?

To convince the executive to spend time and money on your plan, you must address the core of the challenge or opportunity and the macro-level logic, creativity and appropriateness of the solution proposed. Your grand idea may be in the form of branding, identification with a key societal issue, a change in the logo or slogan, a new focus on community relations or a number of other overarching ideas. Just remember that executives usually have a broader, more holistic view of problems, opportunities and programs. They want to see the grand solution and creative integration of that solution across organizational functions and publics. They also want to know if it is the most cost effective approach to the situation and why they should support the plan. Remember, in order for them to internalize your plan, you must first capture their attention.

Executive summaries

A typical executive summary should be no more than four pages; two to three pages is best. It needs to be written directly to the target audience so it will be brief, comprised of short sentences and bullet points. It must be concise, focusing on solutions and referring to additional details in appropriate sections of the report or plan. It should also be written with words and phrases that invoke visual images of the proposed plan.

> Executive Summary

A concise overview of a document's key points and conclusions targeted to key decision makers.

A good executive summary has five basic characteristics.

1. It immediately engages the attention of the reader. Either by an incisive restatement of the problem or challenge, a vision of what could be created or some other attention-getting device, the executive summary must grab the reader and entice him/her to read on.

2. It provides a broad solution to a problem that integrates across the organization and its publics and/or creatively takes advantage of an opportunity. The executive summary must provide just enough creative detail to keep the reader engaged but not so much that he/she will lose interest.

3. It is written with words and phrases that will enable the executive to actually visualize the plan including the creative work that will secure the attention of targeted publics.

4. It provides concise rationale for acceptance of the solution.

5. It identifies the cost of the plan and puts it in the context of what it will cost not to accept the plan.

Business or client presentations

A presentation of your solution or plan is a multi-sensory version of an executive summary. It must contain the same five components listed above to be successful. While in an executive summary, you write in a way that stimulates a visual picture of your proposed effort, a business presentation by its nature is visual. The visual elements create their own impressions regarding consistency, dependability and competency of the team. They must be very carefully considered and developed to support your approach, not detract from it.

No matter how much time you have to make your presentation, you must capture the attention of your audience in the first few seconds. Establish the need and the broad solution immediately. Then sketch in the details as time — and interest — permits. Make sure to show creative work — slogans, logos, visual tactics — to engage and excite the target audience, but don't continue describing details after interest in them wanes. Get back quickly to the rationale for selecting this plan and the cost of doing so. Also address the cost of not embracing your solution. Then end on a positive note and with the only wise course of action — hiring you.

Some general principles for success follow.

- Keep the end result in mind at all times. The goal is to gain approval and selection of your plan by the decision makers. Everything you do and say in the presentation must be focused on that goal.
- Focus on establishing a relationship with the key decision maker whether he/she is a client or an executive in your organization.
- Timing is important. Most presentations should be short, concise and to the point. Long presentations often lose the audience. Set a time limit for each discussion point in the presentation and stick to it. Keep the presentation moving and the ideas flowing.
- Use logical and customized organization. Use a research-based, analytical approach to problem solving that the client will understand. Focus on opportunities and solutions. Customize the presentation to meet the self-interests and needs of the target audience. Figure 11.1

figure **11.1**

Sample Organization of a Business Presentation

- Introduce yourself and review the agenda.
- Review the opportunities and problems, demonstrating understanding of the potential client's position through research.
- Present your unique approach for solving the problem.
- State the objectives and publics/messages necessary to accomplish them.
- Show some of the creative work. Planning typically has no visual appeal. It must be accompanied by creative work to sell your solution.
- Overview the budget using graphic displays.
- Provide the rationale for implementing the plan, as well as the inherent difficulties and the cost of not accepting your proposal.
- Summarize the campaign and make the final pitch.

provides a sample organization for a business presentation, but remember to tailor it to your specific audience. Use examples relevant to the target audience's experience.

- Be prepared. Organize well. Use appealing visual aids. Rehearse thoroughly. An audience can always tell when someone is unprepared. Further, your ability to improvise when unexpected problems arise (such as your software not being compatible with the provided technical equipment) is directly related to how well prepared you are. Don't expect to be able to ad lib in an emergency if you haven't thoroughly prepared and practiced.

Using presentation technology

In today's high-tech environment, expectations for professionalism are also very high. But high-tech presentations have their pitfalls. Computer-designed and driven presentations can be very impressive. But when the technology fails, for whatever reason, the failure reflects on the presenter. While a great presentation can demonstrate the creativity, capability and innovativeness of a team, a poor presentation can ruin any chance of success.

Technical difficulties are unacceptable. If you are using technology of any kind in a presentation, make sure you know the equipment, how to operate it and how to fix it. Make sure every link and program is compatible. Make sure the presentation area has sufficient power outlets and is wired to support the technology. Arrive early to set up and test the equipment. Bring spare cords, bulbs and other small replacement parts and connectors. Always be prepared well enough to give your presentation without the visuals if necessary.

Recognize also that technology has a tendency to reduce and sometimes eliminate the personal connection between the presenter and the client or executive. The presenter must be conscious of the relationship and work to maintain the personal connection. When possible, use a remote or have someone help you advance slides. Cut the invisible tether that keeps so many people tied to a podium or laptop by moving around, using hand gestures and pointing out significant information or visuals on the screen.

The presentation is an opportunity to interact with the client or executive and begin to build trust. Technology should support but never drive a presentation. Presentations should always be driven by purpose and content as outlined above. Nevertheless, in today's business climate, a good presentation is your key to opening the door. A bad presentation means your ideas may never see the light of day.

SUMMARY

Executive summaries and business presentations are the key channels of communication for almost every public relations or marketing plan. No matter how revealing the research, no matter how creative and ingenious the strategic plan, no change will occur unless we effectively communicate the plan or solution to the decision makers and demonstrate the criticality of their expending resources on this plan or solution.

As with all communication, our target audience must first be persuaded to pay attention to the message and then be persuaded to act on the content. Persuading decision makers to use our solutions requires the same two-step process. We have to gain their attention and then their approval.

In our fast-paced world, executive summaries and business presentations are the key to getting the decision makers to pay attention and more deeply examine a proposal. They should be approached with the same care and analysis we used in our planning. When done right, these brief overviews will open many doors.

CHAPTER ELEVEN EXERCISES

1. Take a trip to the nearest library and look for published reports that have executive summaries. They may be reports of research studies or even white papers. Examine a number of executive summaries and evaluate their effectiveness in drawing you into the details in the document.

2. Select any of the plans you have prepared for the exercises in other chapters of this book and create a short presentation that would engage a decision maker and cause him/her to listen to your ideas. Follow the steps in figure 11.1 and make sure you have an attention-getting tactic at the beginning of the presentation.

3. Visit other classes or environments within which presentations are being given. Do your own analysis of their effectiveness. What techniques worked well and why? What did not work and what would you have done differently?

REFERENCES AND ADDITIONAL READINGS

Bienvenu, S. (1999). *The Presentation Skills Workshop: Helping People Create and Deliver Great Presentations*. New York: AMACOM.

Boylan, B. (2001). *What's Your Point?: The 3-Step Method for Making Effective Presentations*. Avon: MA: Adams Media Corporation.

Leech, T. (2004). How to prepare, stage, and deliver winning presentations. New York: AMACOM.

chapter **12**

ETHICS AND PROFESSIONALISM

"A little integrity is better than any career."

— Ralph Waldo Emerson (1803–1882)

American Poet

LEARNING IMPERATIVES

▶ To understand the values and ethical standards upon which to base decisions and behavior

▶ To be cognizant of professional codes of ethics and resolve to abide by them

▶ To understand the characteristics of professionalism and begin to develop behaviors consistent with those characteristics

▶ To appreciate the contributions of diverse individuals and adopt an attitude of acceptance

No text on public relations, communications and marketing techniques and practice would be complete without a discussion of ethics and professional behavior. Our current environment, with such high levels of mistrust for most business organizations, exacerbates the built-in mistrust of any kind of persuasive communication or advocacy. Nonetheless, advocacy is a critical function in a free market economy and a free society. Without advocacy, people are unaware of the full range of choices available to them from consumer products to political organizations. Because some organizations have abused the public trust by using manipulative communication and marketing practices and sometimes even deceit, communicators today are often labeled "flacks" or "spin doctors," implying the less than trustworthy practices of advocating questionable causes and twisting truth. Because of past abuses perpetrated by a few, almost all organizations, corporations and institutions face an uphill battle to gain the trust of their publics.

ETHICS

The ethics and behavior of organizations and individuals have come to the forefront in terms of the expectations of an organization's stakeholders. According to Wilcox, Ault and Agee:

> Ethics refers to the value system by which a person determines what is right or wrong, fair or unfair, just or unjust. It is expressed through moral behavior in specific situations. An individual's conduct is measured not only against his or her own conscience but also against some norm of acceptability that has been societally, professionally, or organizationally determined (1989, p. 117-118).

As the statement implies, ethical decisions are made at a number of different levels. At the highest level, every society has an implied ethical standard. Nevertheless, societal standards of ethics often deteriorate to become the equivalent of legal standards. The danger is that the ethical bottom line tends to become whatever is legal. With trust at a premium now in our society, the second level of ethical standard-setting is in organizations that have formulated their own ethical codes based on core corporate or organizational values. The goal is to guide employees to comply in programs, procedures and practices. To be credible, the values and codes must permeate the organization's communication practices.

At the third level, communications and marketing professionals may choose to subscribe to professional codes of behavior like those provided by the American Marketing Association (AMA), the American Advertising Federation (AAF) or the Public Relations Society of America (PRSA). (See Appendix C: Professional Codes of Ethics.) Finally, underlying each of these ethical levels are personal standards of behavior based on individual value systems.

Ideally, ethical guidelines at the different levels would reinforce each other. In practice, there may be conflicts to be resolved. In today's environment, ethical behavior is widely recognized as a necessary element of professionalism.

> Ethics

Personal and professional value systems and standards that underlie decisions and behavior.

Organizational ethics

As addressed in the first chapter, the issue for organizations today is "transparency." In fact, only the terminology is new. The issue for organizations has always been openly aligning their behavior and their communication with a set of core values that are societally accepted. According to Stoker and Rawlins (2004):

> By revealing the organization's motives, the [organization] becomes accountable to the public. Transparency then becomes self-regulating, encouraging organizations to choose only practices they could publicly justify. By being transparent, the organization puts its credibility on the line by aligning its communication with its ethics.

Gertz (1998) goes a step further by providing two moral rules that must be inviolate. The first is "do not disable" (p. 163). To disable is to diminish a person's ability to choose or act voluntarily. People have a right to the information they need to make reasoned, rational decisions for their own lives. The second rule is "do not deprive of freedom" (p. 164). This rule requires organizations to disclose any information on practices that may affect stakeholders. Gertz includes in this rule any action that would limit someone's ability to act freely, depriving him/her of control over personal actions.

Gertz applies some additional moral rules to transparency: don't deceive, don't cheat, keep promises, obey laws and do your duty (p. 216). Stoker and Rawlins (2004) comment that "these rules directly apply to the communication process. It would be hard to imagine transparency without abiding by these rules. But these are the [minimum] expectations for [communications professionals]."

> **Ethical Codes**

Written and formalized standards of behavior used as guidelines for decision making.

Codes of ethics and professional standards

According to public relations professional Davis Young, the keys to resolving the ethical issues confronting us can be found in five hypotheses.

1. Ethical choices most often appear in gray areas. They are seldom black or white.
2. We usually act in keeping with the letter of the law, but violating the spirit of the law is the typical source of ethical problems.
3. The true objective of any communications effort is to enhance perceptions of trust. All else comes from that foundation.
4. The effectiveness of individual communicators is directly proportional to the extent they are trusted.
5. You cannot be forced to lose your values. They are only lost if you choose to relinquish them.

Understanding the source of most ethical dilemmas may help us to avoid them. As a guide, most professional associations have established codes of ethical behavior (such as the examples in Appendix C) to which their members subscribe. But professional ethical codes are not without problems. By their nature, such codes tend to establish the basest acceptable behavior, bordering on legality rather than morality. They share the dilemma mentioned above that what is legal becomes the ethical bottom line. In the professional environment, what's legal does not always equate with what is ethical. Yet, in the attempt to regulate the behavior of professionals, we often resort either to what is legal or to what is minimally acceptable in society. Over time, such standards tend to reduce the overall level of ethical practice to that minimally acceptable expectation. To quote James E. Faust in an address given to law students in 2003:

> There is a great risk of justifying what we do individually and professionally on the basis of what is "legal" rather than what is "right. ..." The philosophy that what is "legal" is also "right" will rob us of what is highest and best in our nature. What conduct is actually "legal" is, in many instances, way below the standards of a civilized society... If [we] accept what is legal as [our] standard of personal or professional conduct, [we] will rob [ourselves] of that which is truly noble in [our] personal dignity and worth.

Further, it is usually quite difficult for a professional organization to enforce a code of ethics and identify credible punishment for infractions. Much has been written about ethical codes and their problems. Nevertheless, professionally it is deemed important for organizations to establish ethical codes for their members. Such codes are seen as critical for maintaining professional status, respect and legitimacy. They are also guidelines to entry-level professionals seeking to establish their own ethical standards based on a personal value system. Most professional codes of ethics incorporate stated values that include truth, honesty, fairness, good taste and decency. Basing behavior on these values will always provide a solid foundation of personal ethics for any communications professional.

Personal ethics and decision making

Our personal ethics are based on our system of values and beliefs. As was discussed in the chapter on persuasion, values and beliefs are the building blocks for attitudes which direct behavior. Although a very personal determination, our values and ethics are heavily influenced by our culture and background. In American culture, truth, freedom, independence, equity and personal rights are highly valued and contribute to the formulation of most of our value systems and resultant ethical standards. But another important influence on our value systems is our personal and societal definition of success.

In the late 1980s, Amitai Etzioni, having just completed a book on ethics, prepared to teach the subject to students at Harvard Business School. After a semester of effort, he lamented that he had been unable to convince classes full of MBA candidates "that there is more to life than money, power, fame and self-interest." Etzioni's experience is disconcerting but not surprising. And he would undoubtedly find much the same situation today. Our society has put such an emphasis on money, power and fame as primary measures of success that these factors have become the decision-making criteria for generations of professionals. Yet those same professionals, at the ends of their careers (and usually in commencement speeches to graduating college students), regret not having spent enough time with family or serving the community. Even our analysis of self-interests of publics should lead us to the conclusion that money, power and fame are usually secondary motivators when placed next to important life issues.

Perhaps our personal definitions of success and the pressure to reach the perceived societal definition of success have caused us to neglect those things in life that really matter. Those definitions necessarily affect our ethical standards and decisions. It would, therefore, seem important to take another look at our measure of personal success, and re-establish basic values to shape moral and ethical behavior. Ralph Waldo Emerson's definition of success (figure 12.1) may be a viable starting point.

figure 12.1

An Enduring Definition of Success

To laugh often and love much; to win the respect of intelligent persons and the affection of children; to earn the approbation of honest citizens and to endure the betrayal of false friends; to appreciate beauty; to find the best in others; to give of one's self; to leave the world a bit better, whether by a healthy child, a garden patch, or a redeemed social condition; to have played and laughed with enthusiasm and sung with exultation; to know that even one life has breathed easier because you have lived, this is to have succeeded.

— Ralph Waldo Emerson, 1803–1882

Consistent with contemporary measures of success, most decisions to behave unethically seem to be based primarily on financial considerations, and secondarily on power considerations. Most professionals find the temptation to behave unethically becomes overwhelming only when money (or the loss of it) is the decision factor. The more there is to lose financially, the greater the temptation to behave contrary to what the individual and organization know to be ethical. When your ability to support and feed your family and keep a roof over their heads is threatened, you become more open to an unethical alternative.

Once you have compromised, you can expect the demand for compromise to continue. Even changing jobs doesn't necessarily free you. Whatever reputation you establish will follow you to at least some degree for the rest of your professional life. And you will personally have to deal with your own assessment of your character as a person and as a professional. In the communications profession where personal credibility and trustworthiness is an imperative, reputation can mean the difference between success and failure. Figure 12.2 identifies Davis Young's suggestions to enhance your credibility in professional dealings.

All professional codes and standards aside, ethics come down to our personal decisions of appropriate behavior. Six simple rules may help you

---

figure 12.2

Enhancing Personal Credibility and Trustworthiness

- Avoid over promising.
- Set parameters for program expectations in advance and agree on measurements. Embrace accountability.
- Put as much emphasis on full and accurate disclosure as you do on timely disclosure.
- Align your programs and yourself with the public interest.
- Place more emphasis on substance and less on bells and whistles.
- Go to great lengths to avoid the appearance of impropriety.
- Recognize there are no quick, easy answers or magic solutions to tough communication problems.
- Keep learning. Professional development never stops.
- Always take the high road.
- Confront ethical issues by placing them in the context of long-term interests of clients or employers.
- Never hide from the media.
- When in doubt, don't.

— Davis Young

---

to protect yourself against situations which will compromise your ethics, and thus your professionalism.

1. **Make your ethical decisions now**. Remember Nancy Reagan's antidrug campaign to combat drug abuse among America's youth? "Just Say No" was an attempt to convince young people to decide against drug use before they were in a peer pressure situation that would perhaps cause them to succumb. You can make the same kind of decision about ethical conduct. Examine your value system and define your personal and professional ethics now. Examine case studies of ethical dilemmas and make decisions about what your own conduct will be. It is much easier to stick to ethical decisions you have already made based on personal and professional values than it is to make those decisions in the face of pressure and financial need.

2. **Develop empathy**. Remember the golden rule. Walk a mile in someone else's shoes and treat others as you would expect to be

treated. Don't judge others too harshly, and lend a helping hand. You may be fortunate not to have faced their dilemmas, but it may only be a matter of time. A little empathy and compassion goes a long way, and increases the chances of receiving compassion and assistance when you need it.

3. **Take the time to think things through**. Don't be railroaded or rushed into making decisions that may have a dramatic impact on your professional future. When you are pressured to make a quick decision about something that sounds shady, the warning bells should ring. Chances are that if you feel rushed when making an ethical decision, you are being railroaded into doing something unethical and unwise, something you would not do if you had more time to think it through.

4. **Identify behavior as what it really is**. Lying, cheating and stealing by any other names are still lying, cheating and stealing. In today's complex business environment, we have an incredible ability to sanitize issues and rationalize behavior by using less poignant terms like "white lies" or "half-truths" or "omission" or "creative storytelling." But deception of any kind is lying; winning by anything but honest and ethical means is cheating; and appropriating anything that does not rightfully belong to you or your employer is stealing. Applying the terms that most people agree are prohibited by both personal and professional standards will help you make ethical decisions in complex or confusing situations.

5. **Recognize that every action and decision has an ethical component**. Ethical dilemmas seldom emerge suddenly. They are the culmination of several seemingly innocuous decisions and actions leading to the point of ethical crisis. Every decision you make has an ethical component even if it is not immediately obvious. Make sure to review the ethical ramifications of actions and decisions along the way. Project where a given decision will lead. Doing so will help you avoid many ethical crises that might otherwise "sneak up" on you.

6. **Establish a freedom fund**. With the first check from your first job, start a savings account to which you contribute each time you are

paid. In the beginning, you may not be able to afford more than five or ten dollars a pay period, but it is imperative that you habitually contribute to your freedom fund. As was noted above, most unethical behavior is a result of feeling you simply cannot afford to behave otherwise. You have financial obligations in life, and losing your job may mean you will lose your car or your home or that you won't be able to feed your family. If you are asked to do something that violates your personal or a professional code of ethics, you should first try to reason or negotiate not to do it. If you are unable to convince your employer, a freedom fund allows you to quit a job rather than compromise standards and jeopardize your professional reputation.

Initially, plan to accumulate the equivalent of three to six months net salary in a freedom fund. As you are promoted to higher professional levels, raise the balance to a year's net income. A freedom fund is designed to pay the bills until you find another job. The greater your professional stature, the longer you should expect to look before finding an acceptable position. Plan accordingly, and never withdraw money from your freedom fund for anything else. If you do, it won't be there when you need it. In today's environment, chances are that at some point you will need to rely on your freedom fund to preserve your ethical standards.

CHARACTERISTICS OF PROFESSIONALISM

Professional reputation is one of the few enduring possessions. Businesses may come and go. Circumstances may at times cause difficulties in your career. Your professional success is dependent upon building a good reputation.

Obviously, ethical behavior is one of the most important attributes of a solid professional. But it is not the only attribute. In fact, there must be hundreds, if not thousands, of lists of characteristics and attributes necessary for professional survival. A categorization of these attributes may help us understand all the areas that deserve attention.

Personal and professional development

A professional should never stop learning. Formal and informal means of education are continually available. Strengthen your skills and keep up with changes and innovations, particularly in the area of technology. Read profusely both in and out of the field. One of the reasons behind the broad liberal arts curriculum in communication programs is the need for communicators and business professionals to be familiar with other areas of learning. The skills needed to communicate come from your communication curriculum. Background in what you will be communicating comes from other fields of knowledge.

Obtain membership in at least one professional association and actively pursue the educational opportunities offered. Read the newspaper and the professional journals. Read the important new books that everyone is reading. Read national magazines that broaden your knowledge of current events and world information. You will be interacting with people in personal, professional and social situations. It is imperative that you be able to converse about current events, new discoveries, important studies and research, politics, sports, entertainment and other topics. Knowing your profession thoroughly will not alone impress the decision makers you need to influence to gain approval for projects or just to keep your job.

Learn from your colleagues and fellow professionals. Be actively involved in professional organizations that provide networking opportunities. Call professionals you meet to gain information and advice. Meet them regularly for lunch. Congratulate them on successes and awards. Send them appropriate notes of congratulations, thanks and encouragement. Send out lots of Christmas cards. Keep your network vital and alive by developing relationships that demonstrate your care and respect for others.

Finally, don't be afraid to ask questions. Have confidence in yourself, your knowledge and your ability but remain humble and teachable. Overconfidence often masks incompetence. Don't be afraid to admit you have more to learn.

> Professionalism

Characteristics and behavior befitting a professional.

Work habits and job performance

Know your own strengths and weaknesses and own up to your mistakes. Otherwise, you'll never overcome your challenges. Prioritize tasks, allocate time and work within constraints. Don't be concerned with the number of hours worked, but with the results and successes. Be goal-oriented, not just task-oriented. Pay attention to detail and always deliver work on time. Be absolutely dependable.

If you want to be promoted, do your job well and then help do the job of the person you would like to replace. Help that person whenever possible. When people are promoted, they often have a hand in selecting a replacement. Make yourself the obvious choice.

Personal conduct

Always act in a professional manner and dress professionally. Be aware of what goes on around you. Observe procedures and power structures (formal and informal) and work within them. Always be ethical and never allow yourself to be persuaded to compromise your personal standards. The respect of others is directly proportional to your respect for yourself. Work toward a balance in your life. Don't live to work or you'll be too stressed to maintain other vital relationships in life. If all you have in life is your job, you might be good at what you do, but you'll be very dull. Cultivate other interests and relationships.

Human relations

A few years ago, Ann Landers provided a concise perspective in one of her columns:

> When you get right down to it, good manners are nothing more than being thoughtful and considerate of others. They are the principal lubricant of the human machinery we use when we interact with others.

Be personable and likeable. Learn to work well with people, treating them as equals. Work with and respect administrative assistants and other staffers. They can help you succeed or cause you to fail. Develop relationships that win loyalty and dedication. Know people's names (and the proper spelling) and use them. Be a mentor to newcomers.

Keep a sense of humor and of perspective. Don't hold grudges and stay out of office politics for at least the first year of employment. It will take that long to figure out the informal power and communications structure. Never allow yourself to believe the job couldn't be done without you. Remember that cooperative effort is the key to success. Always be grateful and show that gratitude openly and often. Give others credit freely for their contributions.

Consider the advice of Strategic Public Relations Counsel Craig Miyamoto, APR, at a PRSA conference in 1998. He identified "The Five Gs" of success:

1. **Good work**. Strive for only the best quality.
2. **Generosity**. Be generous with your time, money and praise.
3. **Gratitude**. Be grateful to others. Few people are solely responsible for their own success.
4. **Guts**. Have the courage to work hard and take on the difficult tasks. Take some risks.
5. **Glory**. Set your sights high. Go for the glory.

EMBRACING DIVERSITY

In today's world, both ethics and professionalism demand that we embrace diversity. Because issues of diversity in our society have come to the fore as trendy and politically correct, detractors may scorn their importance. More damaging though are those who have taken up the cause because it is trendy, rather than because it is morally right and a critically important part of the essence of our humanity.

Often, we wrongly equate diversity with equal employment opportunity and hiring quotas, failing to recognize that diversity celebrates the differences in all people, uniting them for better solutions and a brighter future. Harnessing diversity in our organizations and communities means creating an environment in which all individuals, regardless of difference, can work toward reaching their personal potential while serving the common good. Diversity does not focus just on race or gender. It addresses the contributions all individuals have to make because of their differences, not in spite of them. Nelson Mandela, in his 1994 inaugural speech, commented on individual ability and contribution:

> Our deepest fear is not that we are inadequate. Our deepest fear is that we are powerful beyond measure. It is our light, not our darkness, that most frightens us. We ask ourselves, who am I to be brilliant, gorgeous, talented and fabulous? Actually, who are you not to be? You are a child of God. Your playing small doesn't serve the world. There's nothing enlightened about shrinking so that other people won't feel insecure around you. We were born to make manifest the glory of God that is within us. It's not just in some of us; it's in everyone. And as we let our own light shine, we unconsciously give other people permission to do the same. As we are liberated from our own fear, our presence automatically liberates others.

> Diversity

Appreciating differences in culture, gender, race, background and experience.

Diversity demands we examine privilege and accept the responsibility that comes with that privilege. It requires that we set aside "tolerance" in preference for acceptance. It requires that we not identify one right way, one mainstream to which all others must conform, but that we recognize a myriad of viable paths to a solution. It means we must set aside ethnocentrism and learn to appreciate the variety of our world and its inhabitants.

In the workplace, issues of diversity become even more critical. In today's environment, employers seek not only trained and skilled individuals; they are looking for versatility, flexibility and skill in operating in diverse environments. They require not only job skills, but skills in communication and human relations. Preparing for the workforce, especially as a communicator, means preparing for work in diverse environments with individuals who are different in many ways, among them culture, race, gender, religion, physical ability, age and socioeconomic status. Some guidelines to developing characteristics to embrace diversity follow.

- **Understand yourself and your history**. The first step to embracing diversity is to understand yourself and the part played in your life by culture. Culture largely determines behavior. When we accept something as correct, right or proper, we have usually made a cultural judgment. Understand also the privileges and opportunities you have been afforded that have contributed to the person you are now. Recognize that with those privileges come responsibilities, and own up to those responsibilities. Also identify situations in which you were disadvantaged and how they have contributed to who you are. Rather than feeling self-pity, use those circumstances to develop empathy for others. We have all experienced both privilege and disadvantage to some degree. Reaching out to join cooperatively in the elimination of disadvantages of any kind is a positive way to deal with our own disadvantages.

- **Shed the guilt and stop the blame**. One of the biggest barriers to embracing diversity is guilt. Guilt is manifested in defensive postures. "It's not my fault," is heard all too often when we deal with issues of diversity. But in most cases you are not being blamed. Learn to recognize a statement of fact without trying to ascribe blame. It is a fact that certain groups in our society have been disadvantaged in ways that have been difficult to overcome. Supporting their efforts is not an admission of guilt. It is an attempt to prevent further pain and suffering by helping overcome disadvantages, regardless of their cause.

   On the other hand, do not become engaged in blaming behaviors. It does no good to blame people and drive them into a defensive posture. Blame and guilt are divisive not unifying or productive.

- **Minimize ethnocentrism**. Although ethnocentrism is typically manifested between national cultures, it is present within nations as well. Ethnocentrism, or identifying our own particular culture and circumstance as the ideal to which all others should strive, is like wearing blinders. Different doesn't mean wrong or less effective. It just means different. Just as there is not only one right answer in creatively solving problems, there is not just one "right" culture. Appreciate your own culture but recognize it is not better, just different than others.

- **Avoid stereotypes**. Stereotyping is sometimes a useful tool, but when we talk about diversity it is almost always harmful. Don't assume stereotypical characteristics about people with whom you have not worked or become acquainted. Also avoid the tendency to classify people as valuable members of a team just because of their membership in a particular group that may be a target public. All trained communicators should be able to marshal the resources and research to target any public.

  A few years ago, a New York cosmetic company announced the appointment of an African-American woman to head its public relations effort. Since the majority of its sales efforts targeted African-American women, the company felt she was the perfect candidate for the job. Would the company fire that woman and hire someone else if the market changed? White males are typically seen as capable of targeting any group, regardless of color, gender or any other characteristic. Are other individuals, with the same training, capable only of communicating with publics who bear their similar characteristics? Of course not.

- **Appreciate different ways of doing things**. Learn not only that there is more than one right answer or way to accomplish something but also that different ways of doing something may have advantages not evident at first glance. Appreciate that using different approaches may enhance the creativity of the whole team. And, recognize that sometimes a different approach has a contribution to make that standard methods could not. Western medicine is a typical example of ethnocentrism and stereotype which has hindered the widespread use of less traumatic treatments that work. Eastern-trained healers who work with the nervous system, the body's electrical impulses and pressure points have been successful time and again at curing ailments Western medicine has pronounced incurable. Yet few Western medical professionals recognize that other cultures have, over the centuries, come up with their own answers to medical problems.

- **Recognize professionalism and ability**. Stereotypes often prevent us from recognizing the skills and competence of individuals. Professional communications and marketing skills are not genetic. If we begin to look at colleagues as fellow professionals instead of classifying them by their differences, we will find we have more in common than we thought.

- **Learn to develop relationships with individuals**. Begin to see people as individuals: living, breathing and pursuing a quality of life similar to that which you pursue. Friendships begin when people take the time to get to know one another as human beings. Ask questions if you are uncertain of how to behave. Whereas "Blacks" used to be appropriate terminology, many now refer to themselves as African-Americans. Many Native Americans prefer to be addressed by tribal affiliation. Hispanics include Puerto Ricans, Mexicans and Mexican-Americans, to name only a few. Ask people how they define themselves and then show respect for the individual by adopting that definition in your interactions with them. It is the same personal respect you would wish to be accorded.

In the marketing and communications professions, more often than not, we work in teams. Seldom is a solution developed or implemented by one person in isolation from others. Learning to harness diversity means learning to let differences work for you, allowing diversity to enhance solutions and performance. In today's world, those who excel professionally will be those who have learned to appreciate and embrace diversity.

SUMMARY

It is only logical to conclude our examination of strategic communications planning with a discussion of professionalism and ethical practice. Without these elements, no communications effort will succeed over the long term. Successful communication is based on trust, and trust is built by exhibiting professional and ethical behavior. Ethics are based on individual and group value systems (ethical codes) governing acceptable behavior. Value systems must place a premium not only on ethical behavior but also on diversity. True professionals exhibit a sincere commitment to an environment in which all may reach their potential while contributing to the overall goals.

CHAPTER TWELVE EXERCISES

1. Do some thinking about your own personal value system and how it will drive your ethical choices in the professional world. Develop your own definition of success and identify the ethical standards it implies.

2. Open a savings account designated as your freedom fund.

3. Initiate a serious discussion with one or two other colleagues or friends about diversity. Explore your similarities and your differences. Speak honestly about your privilege or how you have been advantaged as well as your disadvantages.

REFERENCES AND ADDITIONAL READINGS

Etzioni, A. (1989). "Money, power and fame." *Newsweek*. 18 September, p. 10.

Faust, J.E. (2003). "Be healers." Address given to the J. Reuben Clark Law School at Brigham Young University, Provo, Utah, 28 February.

Gertz. B. (1998). *Morality: Its Nature and Justification*. New York: Oxford.

Howard C. and Mathews, W. (1994). *On Deadline: Managing Media Relations* (2nd ed.). Prospect Heights, Ill.: Waveland Press.

Stoker, K. and Rawlins, B. (2004). "Light and air hurt no one: The moral and practical imperative for transparency." Paper presented at the International Public Relations Research Conference, Miami, Fla., 10-14 March.

Tannen, D. (1994). "Gender games." *People*. 10 October, pp. 71-74.

Wilcox, D.L., Ault, P.H., & Agee, W.K. (1989). *Public Relations: Strategies and Tactics* (2nd ed.). New York: Harper and Row.

Young, D. (1987). "Confronting the ethical issues that confront you." Address given at the 40th Annual PRSA National Conference in Los Angeles, 8-11 November.

APPENDIX A

Teaching Case

TEACHING CASE: The Case of the Caustic Cloud

This teaching case was developed to help students internalize the 10-step Strategic Communications Planning Matrix. A description of the case problem is given here along with the completed research section (background, situation analysis, and core problem/opportunity). Through this teaching case you will learn how to build a complete campaign, for any marketing or communications opportunity/problem, as you compare each step of the matrix with the example illustrated in the teaching case.

CASE DESCRIPTION

Spruced Up is one of the largest tree farm companies in the United States. The company operates nine farms in Washington, Oregon and California. It had revenues of $950 million in 2003 with $8 million in profits. The company is publicly traded on the New York Stock Exchange (NYSE) under the symbol NYSE:TREE.

Although started in 1952, Spruced Up has experienced rapid growth during the past decade as a result of an explosion in housing construction and landscaping. The company's stock has grown an average of 14 percent annually during the past five years and is actively traded. Part of Spruced Up's appeal to investors has been its proactive environmental policies.

The company had a very favorable reputation in the communities in which it operates until a mysterious cloud appeared over Goose Creek, Ore. While conducting routine aerial pesticide application at the company's largest farm, unexpected wind gusts carried a cloud of pesticide over a portion of the town. The incident occurred in the early afternoon on Wednesday, May 5, 2004, and has the town's residents in a fevered pitch. Roughly 40 people, mostly elderly and school children, reported respiratory distress the day of and several days following the incident. The Goose Creek Town Council has called an emergency meeting for May 10 and has summoned the company's CEO to respond to community outrage.

Goose Creek, a community of 60,000 residents, is also home to an extension campus of the state agricultural university with 3,500 students, many of whom are involved in pest control research. Spruced Up's Goose Creek farm employs approximately 4,000 people from the town and surrounding communities.

The company follows strict procedures for aerial insecticide spraying. Spruced Up is particularly careful that the insecticide used and the method of application does not pose a threat to employees or residents. Weather conditions are closely monitored — particularly wind velocity and direction — to contain insecticide application to Spruced Up properties. Community exposure to insecticide from any of the farms is rare. Only one other incident has been reported in the past 10 years. The other incident occurred in 1993 when a pilot inadvertently dropped spray on a small community in Northern California.

Although aerial spraying is routinely used on all Spruced Up farms, the company fears local outrage may affect its operations throughout Oregon and California. Spruced Up believes aerial insecticide application to be not only the most thorough but also the most cost effective way to protect its trees from deadly infestations.

MATRIX: Research
Steps 1-3 — Background, Situation Analysis, Core Problem/Opportunity

SAMPLE CAMPAIGN

Note: This background example is abbreviated for space. Background research should not be unduly limited. Nevertheless, only directly relevant information should be included in the background text of your strategic plan. Additional charts, graphs and other information should be included. Profiles of potential publics should contain relevant demographics and psychographics such as opinions, attitudes, beliefs, behaviors, lifestyles and information sources.

BACKGROUND

Spruced Up is a significant employer in Goose Creek, Ore. The company employs roughly 15 percent of the town's adult working population. Spruced Up has also been active in the community supporting activities such as Little League baseball, the women's shelter and the state's agricultural college. In addition, the company has donated all of the shrubs and trees for Goose Creek's new Tucker Memorial Park sports complex completed in late April 2004.

Spruced Up is a vibrant, fast-growing company with headquarters in Eugene, Ore. The company has recorded a profit every year since it went public in 1998. Spruced Up stock is traded on the New York Stock Exchange under the symbol NYSE: TREE. The company recorded profits of $8 million on revenue of $950 million in 2003. Annual share growth has averaged 14 percent. The stock is currently trading at $32 per share and does not appear to have been affected by the May 5 incident. One of the factors contributing to the company's fast growth has been a strong demand for landscape and reforestation as a result of a healthy new home construction market in the United States. Low mortgage rates continue to brace the construction industry against a four-year economic downturn.

Spruced Up is viewed favorably by most environmental groups active in the area. The company has won praise for its low-impact approach to the environment. Its use of organic fertilizers has been the focus of several industry articles and even highlighted in a 2001 Wall Street Journal cover story. The company is the largest supplier of reforestation seedlings in the Northwest. Spruced Up stock is held in several "green," environmentally conscious, mutual funds.

The insecticide used by Spruced Up on May 5 is a mildly toxic preventative agent that is relatively new in the industry. Warning labels indicate the possibility of respiratory distress and caution against human exposure. Nevertheless, extensive testing has shown the active ingredients to be relatively harmless to humans in their diluted state. Spruced Up's procedures for aerial spraying require all employees to remain indoors during application. An official notification of aerial spraying dates is routinely posted in the local newspaper 10 days prior to spraying. It is also placed in the monthly city newsletter sent to all Goose Creek households.

Agricultural scientists on the extension campus are divided with regard to the safety of the insecticide in question when used in aerial application. Not much conclusive research has been done on this particular product. While no one believes it to be dangerous to the majority, some suspect that exposure by those with weaker immune systems may cause long-term health concerns.

Nonetheless, Spruced Up's internal scientists and agricultural specialists believe aerial spraying of this insecticide to be the least toxic, most cost-effective way to prevent infestation that could cause the loss of entire crops during the next several years.

Three physicians in Goose Creek treated 40 individuals who had respiratory difficulties subsequent to the incident. None of the cases posed long-term health concerns. All but two of those affected were released without need for medication or follow-up care. An elderly gentleman and an eight-year-old girl were treated for asthma-like symptoms. Both now appear to be symptom-free.

A short article about the May 5 incident has appeared in the local newspapers in two other communities where Spruced Up has farm operations. Neither of the stories received front-page coverage. The incident was mentioned briefly on the local Dan Barber radio talk show on Thursday morning, but not much detail was given and no calls were taken on the subject because not enough was known and Barber didn't think is was fair to delve into commentary on the story with so few facts. The story in the Goose Creek Squawker, the local paper with a circulation of 8,000, was on the front page of the Thursday morning edition without comment from Spruced Up because the story occurred right on deadline. A follow-up story is set to run on Friday morning with information on the pesticide and comment from Spruced Up, and with updated information on the medical condition of those affected. The derogatory comments of a member of the town council regarding Spruced Up's careless pursuit of profits will also be in the story. By Thursday afternoon, the Squawker had received an unprecedented 35 letters-to-the-editor complaining about Spruced Up's disregard for their employees and local residents. Three of the letters are set to run in the Friday morning edition.

Profiles of potential publics

Local media

Goose Creek has one daily newspaper, the Goose Creek Squawker, which ran a front page story without Spruced Up's comment on Thursday morning. They have a follow-up story scheduled for Friday morning's edition that is more balanced as it reports the innocuous nature of the pesticide and Spruced Up's comments as well as an update on the medical conditions of the 40 victims. The story does quote a town councilwoman criticizing Spruced Up for a "profits over people" mentality. The 8,000 circulation hits over half the households and most of the businesses in Goose Creek.

There are three local radio stations that receive good listenership from Goose Creek and surrounding areas. One is a news/talk format that captures the attention of most of the local business and professional people, community leaders, senior citizens and the academics. A second station is a teen music format and the third is a 60s and 70s music station that draws from Goose Creek residents, parents and blue collar workers (including Spruced Up's employees) who don't listen to talk radio. This station has a very short local news show every hour from 6–9 a.m., at noon and from 4–7 p.m. It didn't have the story on Wednesday, and didn't get it on the air for the morning or noon broadcasts Thursday. It may or may not hit the evening broadcasts on Thursday, but will probably be on the air by Friday.

A talk show host on the talk radio station, Dan Barber, deals with local community and political issues including the environment on his morning show. While the news of the aerial spraying incident hit too late for him to pull together intelligent commentary for a Thursday program, he did mention the incident. We can assume that as a result most of the community leaders, business and professional people, senior citizens (some of whom were affected) and college professors know about the incident either from the newspaper or from radio.

The three television stations that cover the Goose Creek area are from a significant population center (200,000 people) about 80 miles away. Goose Creek gets little local news coverage from two of them, but most people tune into the nightly news on one of the three stations. The one station that does provide some news coverage of Goose Creek picked up the aerial spraying story and will have a reporter at the town council meeting on Monday night.

Other media are in the form of newsletters. One is from the City of Goose Creek and goes monthly to all households in the city limits. Another goes monthly to members of the local chamber of commerce. The third significant newsletter is a small weekly publication that goes to employees at the agricultural college.

With the exception of television media, other media outlets are typically cooperative because they are always looking for content. They have provided positive coverage of Spruced Up's community involvement. Nevertheless, people with news typically have to come to them because they are short staffed and don't have a lot of time to dig it out or investigate a story.

Current relationship:
- Cooperative

Influentials:
- For the mass media, their audiences
- For newsletters, their gatekeepers (publishers) and audiences/members

Self-interests:
- Scooping other media
- Being financially viable by getting news that their viewers, listeners and subscribers want and need
- Doing as little work as possible to get information

Financial and trade media

Financial and trade media are simply interested in Spruced Up as a company and in its products. The aerial spraying incident would make news only if it was thought to threaten revenue, profits or stock price. These are the media Spruced Up deals with most and their relationships are based on trust. Spruced Up is always open about its financial picture and its niche is in a pretty stable industry. These media would have no reason to pick up the story or even want it unless it had created a problem that could have financial or business ramifications. If the incident is smoothed over quickly and completely, no disclosure to these media would be expected.

Current relationship:
- Cooperative business relationship, mutual respect

Influentials:
- Their audience, industry analysts, fund managers

Self-interests:
- Getting the story first and right
- Being financially viable by getting news that their subscribers want and need
- Being independent of the source
- Being considered the best source for financial and trade news

Industry analysts/fund managers

As with the financial media, this story would not be of much interest to the industry analysts and fund managers unless the situation got out of hand and threatened the company's financial stability or ability to do business. This public is interested in the financial picture and profitability. They are concerned with the validity of the stock price and the growth of profits. Currently this situation shows no potential of threatening either.

Current relationship:
- They know Spruced Up and respect its stability

Influentials:
- Professional colleagues and financial media

Self-interests:
- Getting the analysis right, choosing the right stocks
- For fund managers, making profit for clients
- Professional stature

Spruced Up shareholders

Shareholders come in a few varieties. The shares held in mutual funds (the so-called "green" funds) are controlled by the fund managers discussed previously. About 22 percent of Spruced Up stock is held in these funds. There will be no need for any advisory or communication with this public unless the situation becomes litigious.

Another category of shareholder is the individual investor. Some in this category have purchased the stock for their portfolio because they either know the company well and trust its track record, or because they know how to do research and diversify their portfolio by selecting sound investments in many industries. Either type of investor knows the company well and will not be unduly alarmed by the aerial spraying incident, although they will monitor the outcome closely if they hear about it. They are a steady kind of investor rather than a nervous investor. They will watch the company's response if they have picked up on the news, but would not be concerned unless the incident got out of hand. Although some may live in the area, most are probably from other communities and have not received any news about the incident. Only 7 percent of the stock is spread among this kind of small individual investor.

In this group you also have the large investors, those who control large blocks of the stock and who are personally known to and cultivated by the management of Spruced Up because they are major investors. The senior management of Spruced Up at the headquarters in Eugene maintain frequent contact with these individuals and many are also professional colleagues. Approximately 23 percent of the stock of Spruced Up is controlled by four such large investors. These large investors would typically view the aerial spraying incident with little interest, understanding that it will be successfully handled locally because the company's reputation for environmental care is exceptional, and the nature of the pesticide and incident are so innocuous there really shouldn't be a problem.

The senior management of Spruced Up, including the chairman of the board who started the company and the current CEO, his son, owns 27 percent of the stock. Because they are corporate executives, they will be concerned, but they were also immediately notified of the incident, all relevant information and the actions proposed to contain and resolve the challenge presented. They elected not to send any of their corporate communications staff to assist the local staff, demonstrating complete trust in the ability of local staff and management to handle the situation.

The final group of stockholders is employees and retired employees who have purchased stock through employee stock purchase opportunities as part of their retirement plan. They own 21 percent of the stock. This group of stockholders might be a bit more concerned than the other stockholders and any rush to sell would result in a fall in the stock price. This is definitely a group that needs some information from the company. Most would be considered routinely within the employee public, but those who are retired would not receive information targeted just at employees. Rash decisions to sell on their part may cause the company broader problems in the financial community. The employees' analysis will describe them in more detail and provide the necessary analysis on information sources, influentials, current relationship and self-interests. The retirees would fall into the category of senior citizens, but may need to be targeted separately because their concerns would go beyond being affected by the spray. They would have more financial concerns.

In general, shareholders would be a significant public for Spruced Up to target if concern from other publics and the spraying incident in general are not effectively addressed and resolved. However, if Spruced Up can handle the crisis in a professional manner, it is probably not necessary to target this public initially.

Current relationship:
- They know and like us because we make money for them

Influentials:
- Fund managers discussed above
- Individual investors are influenced by industry analysts and financial media as well as by fellow investors and Spruced Up management
- Large investors are influenced by Spruced Up corporate executives, financial analysts, fellow investors and colleagues
- Employee investors are influenced by corporate executives, fellow employees and employee investors
- Retired employee investors are influenced by corporate executives, fellow retirees and current employees

Self-interests:
- Making a profit
- A viable, secure, moderate growth investment for retirement

Spruced Up employees

The local farm employees about 4,100 people from Goose Creek and surrounding rural areas. Of that, 1,000 are seasonal employees, mostly students working in the summer. Of the permanent employees, 25 percent are shareholders through the employee stock purchase plan. Spruced Up pays decent wages for farm work. It doesn't pay as well as logging or the mills, but the work is not nearly as grueling and is much safer than the other industries. Among the permanent employees, overall job satisfaction (which includes wages) was at 75 percent in an employee survey done last year. The seasonal employees rated job satisfaction at 82 percent. In the same survey, 92 percent of Spruced Up employees considered the company to be a "good" or "very good" community citizen.

That survey also measured the level of trust of employees for local management and it was a 4.2 on a scale of one to five with five being absolute trust in all matters. The trust comes from more than just working at the company. Most of the managers at this farm have been promoted from within the ranks. Even the chief operating officer (COO) is a local boy who began working at this farm to put himself through a forestry degree at the local college. The company later sent him to Eugene to work in the headquarters office while he completed an MBA (which the company paid for) at the University of Oregon. He came back three years later as a senior manager and worked his way up to COO. He is well respected and well liked. Many consider him a friend.

Most of the permanent employees are raising families in Goose Creek. They have the same concerns and networks as residents and parents, but they have the added benefit of being tied into the company grapevine. Because they love their jobs and love their company, they are good representatives for Spruced Up in the community.

Employees are fully aware of the policy that all employees must remain indoors during aerial spraying of the crops. They understand that the pesticide is not toxic, but that it could cause some problems if directly exposed. Nevertheless, many fudge a bit on the policy, waiting until the last possible moment with the plane overhead before dashing indoors. Many have breathed the spray and consider it harmless. Nevertheless, they are concerned that the company needs to do right by the people who were affected by the spray so that they can continue to be proud employees. As blue-collar workers, most get their information from the oldies radio station and the local newspaper. More importantly, they get information about Spruced Up from work and information about how the community feels from friends and neighbors who are anxious to talk to them because they are Spruced Up employees.

Current relationship:
- Cordial, both parties satisfied with regular transactions

Influentials:
- Government contracting and regulators, their own stockholders, their own clients
- Local direct purchasers influenced like other Goose Creek residents

Self-interests:
- Getting the best price for quality seedlings and plantings
- Maintaining the source of supply

Goose Creek residents affected by spray

The residents affected by the spray include the elderly and young children, both of whom are more susceptible to respiratory distress. The public of concern regarding the young children is their parents. Only 15 of those affected were children, 12 elementary school age and three in junior high school. The other 25 were elderly residents. There is no clear evidence that the asthma-like symptoms were caused by the spray, but it is assumed that the short-term rise in respiratory emergencies and the aerial spraying accident are linked.

All but two of those affected were released without medication or necessary follow-up care. The other two were kept under observation for a couple of hours and provided with an inhaler to use as needed to reduce the irritation of nasal passages and lungs. Both patients appear to be fine. In spite of the minimal side effects, the parents of the children affected and the elderly residents affected are extremely concerned. They were assured by physicians there would probably be no side effects, but they are still a bit frightened from the experience of not being able to breathe well for several minutes. They fear that a more serious incident would cause more debilitating effects. They understand that this was an accident, but they don't think Spruced Up should be using any kind of chemicals that would cause any ill effects if an accident occurs. They don't want Spruced Up's business to be affected by this because they know people who depend on their jobs there. But they are also afraid. They want some assurances and they don't think it's fair that they had to pay medical expenses (even if some were just insurance co-pays) and emergency room charges because of Spruced Up's mistake. They are not inclined to sue, but do think some compensation is in order. Some had to actually leave work and are out sick/family time off because of it.

The elderly residents and parents are typical members of the Goose Creek community. They get their information in the same way as other residents. Influentials for this public are their family members, their family doctors and their community leaders. Most of the members of this public are personally acquainted with one or more members of the town council. They trust their community leaders to do the best for the residents of Goose Creek, but they will be at the town meeting and closely watching the outcome. They want some answers and assurances of their own.

Current relationship:
- Tentative
- Have viewed Spruced Up as a good community resident but are now concerned, afraid and need some answers

Influentials:
- Physicians, community leaders, family members and close friends

Self-interests:
- Being healthy and safe
- Not being afraid to go outside or to let children go outside
- Getting their medical bills paid

Goose Creek doctors and EMTs

There are 35 general practice physicians and 10 licensed EMTs in Goose Creek. This number includes emergency room physicians. Further, the Goose Creek Fire Department has three stations in the city. Only one of the three responded to emergency calls following the incident. The medical community in town is led by a handful of older doctors who have practiced in Goose Creek for 25–30 years, some of whom were actually reared there. A few are younger doctors who came to Goose Creek because it was an area that needed doctors but had a hard time keeping them. The small town atmosphere may be a great place to raise kids, but no doctor will ever get rich here. Nevertheless, the doctors are among the highest socioeconomic group in Goose Creek. Just over 50 percent of this group has lived in Goose Creek less than five years. Nearly 40 percent do not intend to stay for an extended period of time. By nature, the local doctors tend not to panic, and the three who treated people after the aerial spraying incident assured their patients there would be no adverse effects. Two of the three who treated people are emergency room physicians. Six of those affected were either treated on site or taken to the emergency room by EMTs connected with the local fire department.

Doctors obviously have a higher level of education than the norm, having attended both college and medical school. They typically keep up on the medical literature, particularly that provided by pharmaceutical sales representatives and others like them who bring specific information directly to the doctor. They will investigate an ailment if they are uncertain of its ramifications and that investigation typically begins by calling a colleague who might know the answer. They will respond well to any responsible information provided by Spruced Up about the pesticide used and the potential adverse effects and proper treatments.

As a group, the general practice physicians are completely unconcerned with the incident. The emergency room doctors and the EMTs are more concerned, but primarily they just want to be prepared to treat patients in any similar incident in the future. They are radio news listeners (primarily the local news/talk station) and read the newspaper. They are typically uninvolved in community affairs or events because of limited time. Their opinion leaders are their spouses and professional colleagues.

Current relationship:
- Good, but a bit strained because of some lack of information

Influentials:
- For the doctors, each other and scientific studies/experts
- For EMTs, their supervisors and professional colleagues

Self-interests:
- Knowing whether or not the pesticide is harmful
- Knowing what to do if it happens again
- Being seen as competent

Goose Creek Town Council

The town council has five members elected for rotating terms of five years each. Two members — one a banker and one a plumber — are from leading families in town and are well-known and well-respected. They have both been re-elected to the council several times and have the longest history of service in this capacity. Another council member is a botany professor at the college who applied for the faculty position so he could raise his kids in a small town with traditional values. He is perhaps the least-known member of the council because he has no family ties in town beyond his immediate family.

The newest member of the council is a mother and housewife who has been active in the PTA and in community volunteerism and was encouraged by friends and neighbors to run for the council. She was a popular candidate and won by a wide margin. The remaining member of the council owns a local lumber mill. He worked in the mill part-time to put himself through school in forest engineering at the local college. He saved his money since he was a kid and purchased some property at a low price while he was in college. A few years later he sold the timber on the property and made a handsome profit, which allowed him to make a substantial down payment on the mill.

The council members are elected officials who serve in their spare time for a modest stipend. They officially direct the full-time city manager and city employees. They are sincerely interested in the best interests of the community and are truly community servants. Nevertheless, all enjoy their status as respected community leaders to greater or lesser degrees. They are often in the public eye and rather enjoy the acclaim they get from friends and neighbors from that status. They are particularly supportive of local business because they recognize the necessity of the tax base to support local schools and employers to keep unemployment down and the economy functioning. But, they also want a safe community free from the social problems experienced in the cities.

The banker and the plumber always vote as a block on the council, and they are always pro-business. The botany professor is relatively new to the council but also tends to vote quite conservatively. The former PTA leader is conservative on most issues but is an ardent defender of the children and disadvantaged in the community. She is the one who made the derogatory comments to be published Friday morning in the Goose Creek Squawker.

The mill owner is a "pull yourself up by your bootstraps" kind of guy who likes low taxes. He supports a strong educational system, but he believes parents have the lion's share of the responsibility to make sure their kids get a good education. He and the PTA leader often disagree; he thinks she is a "bleeding heart liberal." Their influentials include the city manager (because he is an information source and has the institutional memory), their constituents (friends and neighbors) and local business leaders. They read the local newspaper, listen to local radio and are consumers of national media, but they also stay connected to local information through the city newsletter, the Chamber of Commerce newsletter and the college employee newsletter. They are tied into various local grapevines and generally are the first to know of local happenings and local opinion.

Current relationship:
- Basically cooperative, but now a bit tentative
- Willing to cooperate, but need to see evidence of responsible action

Influentials:
- City manager, constituents, business leaders, academics

Self-interests:
- Solving the problem amicably with all parties feeling satisfied
- Appearing to be competent and working for the constituents' best interest
- Keeping Spruced Up open and profitable as part of the tax base

Goose Creek voters/residents

Goose Creek is the kind of a small town with traditional values where people are long-time residents; they are born, work and retire in Goose Creek or the surrounding communities. Goose Creek voters are residents who are very active in the community and frequently attend city council meetings and most town events. They feel a sense of pride in their community and want the town to remain safe and prosperous. They make extra efforts to ensure they are informed of what's going on in the community so they can vote appropriately and get involved whenever possible. Few people are new to Goose Creek, although some have moved in for employment at the Spruced Up farm and the agricultural college. That means many of the residents are related to each other either immediately or by extension. The elderly residents that were affected by the spray may not only be concerned for their own welfare; they may also be concerned that their grandchildren may be affected by subsequent accidents. It is the kind of town where every one knows everyone else in their neighborhoods and church groups because they all grew up together or went to school together or played on sports teams with or against each other. A few family names have dominated local activities and local politics. The Tuckers, Brooks, Bakers, Huddlestons, Martins, Gowens and Pynes have family members throughout the community. They have family members who work for Spruced Up, own their own small businesses, work in the local financial industry and at the college. And Joe Baker, a local banker, and Wilson Pyne, a local plumber, are on the town council.

Goose Creek is a blue-collar town. Nevertheless, it is also a very conservative, non-union community, rare for Oregon metropolitan areas but typical of its more rural locales. Most of the residents work at the Spruced Up farm or in the lumber industry in some way. Some are loggers and some are mill workers. A few of the rural residents are farmers who understand the need for the application of pesticides and are familiar with the safety of the pesticide used by Spruced Up. The majority of Goose Creek residents are in the lower ranges of middle income families ($40,000 to $60,000 a year per household). While the university employs about 500 workers, only 280 are academics. The remaining 220 are in the middle income range and relate well to the blue-collar logging and farming community; in fact, most have spouses or relatives working in those other industries. Nearly 75 percent of Goose Creek adults consider themselves Republican (whether or not registered). The remainder lean Democratic, primarily the more liberal academics and those employed in nonprofit and social service sectors. Of the 60,000 residents, about 40 percent are children under the age of 18. Goose Creek has two small high schools, three junior high schools and several elementary schools.

Most residents appreciate the community involvement and support from Spruced Up. They recognize it as a stable and valued employer and community resident. Some vaguely recall the incident in 1993, but don't remember any details because it didn't happen in this community and there was no real fallout from the incident. It really didn't cause much controversy. In a survey conducted last year, 85 percent of Goose Creek residents thought Spruced Up was a "good" to "very good" community resident.

Most Goose Creek adults read the local newspaper and listen to local radio. Other community information sources include networks through church groups, neighborhoods, families and workplaces. Again, the key work places include the logging companies, lumber mills, the Spruced Up farm and the college. The local chamber of commerce is a key information source for local business people.

The incident has the residents and voters concerned and a bit frightened. They are concerned that they may become victims of caustic pesticide in the future, but they are willing to give Spruced Up a chance to respond to community concerns. They will be listening and watching to see what Spruced Up has to say and what they do to make things right by those affected by the accident.
Current relationship:
- Good, but they have some questions to be answered

Influentials:
- Community leaders, family members, fellow workers and friends who are Spruced Up employees

Self-interests:
- Health and safety
- Economic security
- A good community to raise families

Goose Creek parents

Goose Creek parents are profiled well by the profile of voters and residents. The 60,000 population of Goose Creek represents 12,000 households and 9,000 of those include at least one parent and one child. Of those, 77 percent have two parents in the home. Average number of children under the age of 18 in a home is three. The vast majority of the parents work. In nearly 80 percent of households with two parents, both work either full or part time.

Parents are more than a little concerned for the vulnerability of their children to respiratory distress resulting from exposure to Spruced Up's pesticide applications, and fear long-term consequences. Nevertheless, most have mixed emotions because fully 80 percent of households are partially or entirely supported by employment in the timber industry either by direct employment or employment in support industries such as at the Spruced Up farm. They don't want to lose their jobs, but they want their kids to be safe. They may be skeptical, but they are willing to give Spruced Up an opportunity to correct the situation. Parent's ranking of Spruced Up on last year's community resident survey was identical to overall residents. In fact, parents are nearly identical in all ways to residents except the level of concern is a bit elevated.

Current relationship:
- Tentative
- They fear for the safety of their children

Influentials:
- Community leaders, family members, fellow workers and friends who are Spruced Up employees

Self-interests:
- Health and safety of their children
- Economic security
- A good community to raise families

Goose Creek academics

The small community of academics (280 teachers and professors) actually poses little threat to Spruced Up farms. A small, but vocal, group are environmentalists and "tree huggers" that have continually attacked the local logging industry with the result that the majority of townspeople ignore their rants. They have not targeted Spruced Up in the past because they provide seedlings for replanting, although they don't really support it either because it feeds the timber industry. They are not counted among more mainstream environmentalists who have praised Spruced Up's environmental consciousness.

Far more credible in Goose Creek and in the majority on the faculty of the college are the academics who specialize in the agricultural industry. They are perceived as more down to earth and reasonable. They are trusted by the townspeople and could be considered opinion leaders for this particular issue. The survey a year ago found 60 percent of the academics believed Spruced Up to be a "good" to "very good" community resident. A professor of botany at the college is on the town council. Spruced Up has actually contributed a couple of million dollars to support faculty research in agriculture, particularly forestry and botany, and for student scholarships.

By nature, the academics in the last category are not eloquent or even vocal. They typically stay out of political issues and are more interested in their kids' high school football or basketball season. The typical academic in this category is male (age 35-55) and married with an average of three children, at least one approaching or in high school. They earn approximately 15 percent more than the average Goose Creek resident, but invest their earnings back into their homes and families rather than on luxury items. Many have a family history in Goose Creek, having been raised here and returned to work at the university after receiving academic credentials. They get their local information from the newspaper and radio, and through the grapevine. The television stations available locally are from the larger population center (a city of 200,000) 80 miles away from Goose Creek. The stations rarely carry Goose Creek news, although one did cover the aerial spraying accident and will have a reporter at the town meeting on Monday, May 10.

The environmentalist academics are typically young (age 28-35) and teach in the liberal arts and humanities. Most are unmarried or married to another environmentalist academic and have few if any children. They are typically new to Goose Creek (within the last five years) and have chosen this community because of its woodland setting. These individuals have set themselves apart from the local residents, considering most to be uneducated "hicks." These individuals are the source of many of the letters to the local newspaper, but they are also key consumers of the paper. They do not listen to local radio, preferring an NPR station. They are heavy consumers of national media, both newspapers and cable news channels.

Current relationship:

- Strong because Spruced Up supports the university

Influentials:
- University officials, colleagues, family members, community leaders

Self-interests:
- Professional stature
- A good community to raise families, as well as health and safety of children
- Economic security

Senior citizens

Seniors in Goose Creek have typically spent their lives here. They are shirt-tail relatives to almost everyone in the community in one way or another. Nearly all have children and grandchildren who live here as well. They are also connected throughout the community and know each other well because they've spent a lifetime with these same friends and neighbors in Goose Creek. Because of their history here, they are strongly connected to the traditional logging and lumber industries, and nearly 30 percent are retired or have a spouse that retired from the local Spruced Up farm and hold its stock as part of their retirement funds.

The senior citizens value Spruced Up's community-mindedness. They are aware of their modest contribution to help build the local senior center and are reminded of it every time they go to play Bingo in the Spruce Activity Hall at the center. In last year's survey 89 percent of seniors considered Spruced Up a "good" or "very good" community resident. Nevertheless, this public is seriously distressed from this incident. It isn't so much anger at Spruced Up as it is a fear of their vulnerability. Word has passed quickly through the grapevine at the senior center, through church groups, families and neighborhoods that the majority of those affected were seniors. Even though they know the pesticide isn't deadly because they've been around long enough to know Spruced Up couldn't and wouldn't use it if it were, they also realize that older people often die from ailments that have little or no effect on younger people. They fear for their lives. They know the spraying must continue if Spruced Up's farm is to be productive. They fear there is nothing that can be done to prevent them from being sickened or possibly killed by it.

While most of this public reads the newspaper, their most credible sources are talk radio and the senior grapevine that stretches through the senior center, churches and neighborhoods. They aren't going to oppose Spruced Up, but they see the spraying as just one more thing in the air that causes them respiratory difficulty. And most seniors recognize that respiratory difficulty is the bane of old age, and the ultimate cause of most deaths among seniors.

Current relationship:
- Fatalistic, they support us, but fear our practices

Influentials:
- Each other, family members, the two town council members who are from local families (Baker and Pyne)

Self-interests:
- Health and safety, as well as a safe place for their children and grandchildren
- Economic security
- Meaningful golden years

Other communities with Spruced Up farms

Although no two communities are completely alike, seven of Spruced Up's nine farms are in towns very similar to Goose Creek. The other two farms are in more populated areas. If the aerial spraying incident is handled quickly and effectively, the company's other farms will experience no difficulties from it. If the situation gets out of hand, then each of these communities will need to be considered individually. Most likely, media relations will be the extent of the effort needed. Nevertheless, if more in-depth efforts are needed to regain the loyalty of these communities, many of the strategies for publics and supporting tactics could be borrowed from Goose Creek, as could some of the collateral material.

SITUATION ANALYSIS

Spruced Up is a vibrant, fast-growing company that enjoys a positive reputation in the communities within which it operates. It also has a solid reputation as an industry leader and pioneer in safety and environmental practices. To maintain this strong financial position and reputation, the company must quickly and responsibly respond to those affected by the May 5 incident. The problem occurred when a cloud of pesticide intended for Spruced Up's nearby tree farm was inadvertently blown over a portion of Goose Creek. This is the first aerial spraying accident the company has experienced in 10 years and did not result in any lasting heath concerns. However, the local community is worried about the company's potential to inflict future harm on local residents.

Failure to adequately diffuse the situation could result in a reversal of public support and a weakening of Spruced Up's financial position. If the company fails to be perceived as concerned about Goose Creek residents and does not act to prevent future incidents, then it may lose support from its employees and public support in all of the communities in which it operates. Related difficulties could include hiring challenges, employee dissatisfaction, loss of investor confidence, customer concerns, increased costs, lawsuits and diminished revenues.

CORE PROBLEM/OPPORTUNITY

To maintain its growth and financial strength, Spruced Up must quickly address community concerns in Goose Creek about the safety of its operations and communicate its ongoing commitment to its employees and the communities where it operates.

GOAL AND OBJECTIVES

Goal

Spruced Up's goal is to maintain its positive reputation in Goose Creek and its growth and financial strength by quickly addressing community and employee concerns related to the safety of its operations.

Objectives

1. Ensure that all Goose Creek residents affected by the insecticide have been properly cared for by Friday, May 7.
2. Ensure that 95 percent of Goose Creek residents affected by the insecticide (or their parents) are content with the company's actions to resolve the incident by Friday, May 14.
3. Regain 85 percent level of perception that Spruced Up is a "good" or "very good" community resident by May 31 and again by October 31.
4. Distribute short-term treatment instructions and background information about the spray to the 45 general physicians, emergency room doctors and EMTs in the Goose Creek area by Friday, May 21.
5. Obtain a 75 percent level of perception that Spruced Up operates "safely" and "responsibly" regarding employees and the community by May 31 and again by October 31.
6. Mitigate negative effects to Spruced Up's financial position by keeping overall dips in the company's stock price to less than 5 percent for at least 30 days following the incident (stock was trading at $32 at the market close on May 4).

KEY PUBLICS AND MESSAGES

Goose Creek residents affected by the spray

This public needs to be satisfied that they are not at personal risk from this incident and the company's ongoing operations. We need their satisfaction to maintain the high perception ratings we have received from the community. If they believe they have been dealt with fairly, they will become advocates for Spruced Up, rather than opponents.

Primary message:
- Spruced Up is committed to the safety and well being of our employees and our community.

Secondary message:
- The procedures in place for safety have worked well at this farm since it was established.
- Industry studies show the pesticide to be safe. Tests have shown this pesticide to have less toxicity than any other pesticide on the market.
- We will research why our weather information was not sufficient in this case and evaluate alternative sources of information.
- We encourage you to watch the monthly newsletter for advanced notifications of routine aerial spraying.
- As a courtesy and to minimize the risk of human exposure, we are making a commitment to conduct aerial spraying only between sunrise and 7:30 a.m.

Primary message:
- Spruced Up regrets any discomfort you've experienced.

Secondary message:
- We have created a procedure to reimburse you for your medical costs.
- Submit the forms we are leaving with you and the company will send you a check within a few days.
- Call the company executive who visited you directly if you have additional questions or problems resulting from this incident.
- EMTs and physicians in the area are being sent information on how to provide short-term treatment in the unlikely event this would ever happen again.
- We recognize that the spray incident may have inconvenienced you and want to give you something for your trouble. We are leaving you a gift certificate for a live tree or cut Christmas tree from the Spruced Up farm.

Goose Creek EMTs and physicians

It needs to be reinforced to this public that Spruced up is committed to its employees and the community and would not do anything that would cause harm. This public needs to be assured that the spray poses little medical danger. They also need to feel prepared to deal with the situation and to provide short-term treatment if the incident were to be repeated or if residents were to be exposed to the spray from other agricultural operations in the area. If they feel they have all the information they need to handle the current and possible future situations, they will continue to be supportive of Spruced Up.

Primary message:
- Spruced Up is committed to the safety and well being of our employees and community.

Secondary message:
- Spruced Up will share with you research showing the pesticide to be safe.
- Although it is unlikely something like this will happen again, we want you to feel prepared to treat patients that might be exposed to the insecticide through any number of agricultural operations in the area. We are therefore sending you short-term treatment recommendations as well as background on the spray.
- Resources are available to you, including a 24-hour phone line, should you have further questions about the insecticide or any of the company's activities.

Goose Creek voters

This public is familiar with Spruced Up as a significant employer and contributor to the economy. They are interested in the company's response and expect them to effectively manage the situation. If their concerns regarding future incidents can be addressed, they will maintain favorable views of the organization and recognize its many positive contributions to Goose Creek.

Primary message:
- Spruced Up is committed to the safety and well being of our employees and community.

Secondary message:
- Spruced Up has a proven safety record — only one other very minor spraying accident has occurred in the past 10 years.
- Spruced Up uses the safest chemicals available. The pesticide used is the least toxic of any solution available on the market.
- Spruced Up carefully examined insecticide research — some of which was conducted at the

local college — to ensure there would not be any detrimental affects to anyone exposed to the pesticide.

- We encourage you to monitor the routine notifications of future sprayings in the town newsletter and on the company's Internet site.
- We are investigating weather information systems to see if alternative systems would give us more accurate readings of wind conditions.
- As a courtesy and to minimize the risk of human exposure, we are making a commitment to conduct aerial spraying only between sunrise and 7:30 a.m.
- We are also adding a 24-hour helpline to answer questions and provide basic company information.

Primary message:

- Spruced Up is proud to be an active part of Goose Creek and its future.

Secondary message:

- We love being a part of this community.
- Spruced Up is a significant employer in Goose Creek. The company employs roughly 15 percent of the town's adult working population.
- Spruced Up continues to be an active supporter of community activities such as Little League baseball, the women's shelter and the state's agricultural college.
- We're looking forward to the grand opening of Tucker Memorial Park and will be there to help you celebrate on July Fourth.

Goose Creek Town Council

This public wants to see Spruced Up successful and profitable because of its contribution to the community in terms of tax dollars, jobs and charitable involvement. They need to be reminded of those contributions now more than ever. They do, however, feel a strong responsibility to their constituents and want to see Spruced Up act in a responsible manner to those affected by the incident. They want Goose Creek to be a safe place and will need to see evidence that Spruced Up is taking measures to ensure this end. If the council is convinced Spruced Up is taking responsibility for its actions and that affected constituents are being treated, support from the group towards Spruced Up will continue.

Primary message:

- Spruced Up is committed to the safety and well being of our employees and community.

Secondary message:
- Spruced Up has a proven safety record — only one other very minor spraying accident has occurred in the past 10 years.
- Spruced Up uses the safest chemicals available. The pesticide used is the least toxic of any solution available on the market.
- Spruced Up carefully examined insecticide research — some of which was conducted at the local college — to ensure there would not be any detrimental affects to anyone exposed to the pesticide.
- We encourage you to monitor the routine notifications of future sprayings in the town newsletter and on the company's Internet site.
- We are investigating weather information systems to see if alternative systems would give us more accurate readings of wind conditions.
- As a courtesy and to minimize the risk of human exposure, we are making a commitment to conduct aerial spraying only between sunrise and 7:30 a.m.
- We are also adding a 24-hour helpline to answer questions and provide basic company information.
- Spruced Up continues to be an active supporter of community activities such as Little League baseball, the women's shelter and the state's agricultural college.
- We're looking forward to the grand opening of Tucker Memorial Park. We're excited to be there with you on July 4.

Primary message:
- We are proactively responding to the spray incident.

Secondary message:
- Company officials have personally visited each of the 40 people affected by the spray.
- We are reimbursing individuals affected by the spray for their medical expenses and any lost work time in the two days following the incident.
- We are also providing the families of those treated for respiratory distress with a Spruced Up gift certificates for the inconvenience the incident may have caused.
- Spruced Up is sending physicians and EMTs short-term medical treatment and background information on the insecticide.
- We have established a 24-hour helpline for anyone with questions related to the spray incident or the company's general operations.
- We are working with the local media to provide information concerning the pesticide and our commitment to the safety of our employees and our community.

- A company scientist is visiting personally with the EMTs and physicians who treated people exposed to the spray to make sure they have all the information they need to follow up patients and to prepare for an unlikely future event of this kind.

Primary message:
- Spruced Up's business success is a major factor in the economic prosperity of Goose Creek.

Secondary message:
- Spruced Up is the single largest tax-payer in Goose Creek.
- The company employs approximately 4,000 people from Goose Creek and the surrounding communities.
- Roughly 20 percent of all money circulating through Goose Creek businesses originates with Spruced Up and its employees.

Spruced Up employees

Employees trust the company and value their jobs. They know the company is strong on safety and sometimes goes to the extreme to protect them. They are likely to get questions from friends and neighbors in Goose Creek about the insecticide incident. They want Spruced Up to resolve the situation and maintain a high-level of trust from residents so they can continue to feel proud about where they work. If this public sees the positive evidence of Spruced Up's efforts, they will maintain their high level of support and trust in their employer.

Primary message:
- Spruced Up is committed to the safety and well being of our employees and community.

Secondary message:
- Spruced Up has a proven safety record — only one other very minor spraying accident has occurred in the past 10 years.
- Spruced Up uses the safest chemicals available. The pesticide used is the least toxic of any solution available on the market.
- Before choosing a new insecticide last year, the company researched all products available and determined that the product used on May 5 was the safest to humans and one of the most effective against harmful insects.
- We do not fault any company employee for the May 5 incident. It was an accident caused by unreliable weather data.
- We will research why our weather information was not sufficient in this case and evaluate alternative sources of information.

- As a courtesy and to minimize the risk of human exposure, we are making a commitment to conduct aerial spraying only between sunrise and 7:30 a.m.
- Please use the 24-hour helpline to report any problems or submit your ideas for company improvements.

Primary message:
- We're meeting with and making sure anyone exposed to the insecticide is taken care of quickly.

Secondary message:
- Individuals experiencing any kind of problems from exposure to the spray have been visited personally by a member of Spruced Up's executive team.
- The insecticide does not pose any serious long-term health risks — independent research supports this claim.
- EMTs and physicians in the area will be sent medical treatment information detailing active ingredients and short-term treatment suggestions for patients exposed to the insecticide.

Primary message:
- Spruced Up is proud to be an active part of Goose Creek and its future.

Secondary message:
- We love being a part of this community.
- You make up approximately 15 percent of the town's adult working population.
- We continue to be an active supporter of community activities such as Little League baseball, the women's shelter and the state's agricultural college.
- We hope you and your families will join company and community officials at the grand opening of Tucker Memorial Park on the Fourth of July.

STRATEGIES AND TACTICS

Goose Creek residents affected by the spray

Strategy one:
- Ensure that each person affected by the spray is being properly cared for through personal contact with a company representative.

Tactics:

1. On Thursday (or Friday) send a senior company official to meet with those affected by the spray to extend regrets and see if they need additional help. Provide a direct home and office phone number for the company official in case additional questions arise.

2. Explain the incident more fully and communicate the company's safety record and procedures. Also explain the company's new commitment to further minimize public exposure by not spraying after 7:30 a.m.

3. Ask each executive/manager who meets with affected residents to submit a report by the end of the day May 7 giving the condition and care of each individual.

4. Send follow-up information about the insecticide not previously available to the doctors including any symptoms that could indicate a reaction and immediate care instructions. Also provide the approximate schedule of aerial spraying and a 24-hour phone number to call for information or to talk to a company official. (This toll-free phone line should be established at headquarters and manned at all times by communications staffers in the first full week after the incident. After that, it could be staffed in off hours by an answering service that would take a message for a response the following business day.)

5. Send medical reimbursement forms with company officials to leave with those affected by the spray. Explain how they can recoup medical exam, short-term treatment and lost work costs directly related to the spray incident.

6. Make sure company representatives take a gift certificate for a live tree or cut Christmas tree to each family of those affected by the spray incident.

7. Have company officials follow-up by phone on Friday, May 14 with each person to see if any issues are unresolved and if those affected by the spray are content with the company's response (evaluation tool).

Strategy two:

- Maintain the high level of esteem for Spruced Up by full disclosure of the incident through local mass media:

Tactics:

1. Place the COO as a guest on Dan Barber's Friday morning talk show to discuss the aerial spraying incident and take questions and give answers regarding the incident, the company's safety record and procedures, and the harmlessness of the pesticide. Also explain the commitment not to spray after 7:30 a.m.

2. Purchase a full-page ad in the Sunday Squawker for an open letter to Goose Creek residents that explains the incident, provides full information on the pesticide and re-emphasizes

Spruced Up's commitment to the community and its employees. Provide information about the 24-hour helpline.

Goose Creek medical professionals

Strategy one:
- Provide detailed information on the pesticide used by Spruced Up and industry-recommended procedures for emergency and short-term care through personal contact and collateral material.

Tactics:
1. Within one week of the incident, send a company scientist and a communications staff member to meet with the EMTs and three physicians that treated residents exposed to the insecticide.
2. Mail information about the pesticide along with a letter from the company, information on the company's aerial spraying procedures and medical treatment suggestions to the 45 EMTs and physicians in the area on Tuesday, May 18 to ensure its arrival by May 21 (evaluation tool).
3. Remind medical personnel in the letter that the aerial spraying schedule is printed in the local community newsletter and published on the company's web site. Also provide them with the 24-hour helpline number.

Goose Creek voters

Strategy one:
- Ensure residents that the incident was an accident because of an unexpected wind gust, but that their safety and the welfare of the community are of paramount concern to Spruced Up through local mass media.

Tactics:
1. Place the COO as a guest on Dan Barber's Friday morning talk show to discuss the aerial spraying incident and take questions and give answers regarding the incident, the company's safety record and procedures, and the harmlessness of the pesticide. Also explain the commitment not to spray after 7:30 a.m.
2. Buy a full-page ad in the Sunday Squawker for an open letter to Goose Creek residents that explains the incident, provides full information on the pesticide and re-emphasizes

Spruced Up's commitment to the community and its employees. Provide information about the 24-hour helpline.

Strategy two:

- Maintain the high level of public approval of Spruced Up through full disclosure, incident management and open Q&A at the town council meeting.

Tactics:

1. The COO and two local senior executives (one a communications executive) will be present and will respond openly and honestly to all questions and concerns.
2. Explain Spruced Up's efforts to take care of the 40 residents that reported short-term respiratory problems associated with the pesticide.
3. Provide information about the new 24-hour helpline.
4. Communicate the company's efforts to research and select a safe pesticide. Reiterate the fact that the incident was an accident caused by very strong, unexpected winds.
5. Provide a calendar of approximate dates and times of aerial spraying and remind council members and residents attending that this information is printed in the Goose Creek community newsletter as well as published on Spruced Up's web site.
6. Announce the change in spraying procedures that will limit spraying to the hours between sunrise and 7:30 a.m.
7. Provide a summary of facts about Spruced Up's operations including its contributions to the community, impact on jobs and the local economy and charitable work. Reiterate the company's commitment to employees and the communities in which it operates.
8. Hire a local research firm to conduct a survey of residents/voters on May 31 to determine the level of perception that Spruced Up is a "good" or "very good" community resident (evaluation tool).
9. Include question(s) on the May 31 survey to measure level of perception that Spruced Up operates "safely" and "responsibly" regarding employees and the community (evaluation tool).
10. Conduct a follow-up survey on October 31 to measure level of perception that Spruced Up is a "good" or "very good" community resident and that it operates "safely" and "responsibly" regarding employees and the community (evaluation tool).

SAMPLE CAMPAIGN: CALENDAR

		6-May	7-May	8-May	9-May	10-May	11-May
Public	**G.C. residents affected by spray**						
Strategy	Ensure affected individuals are properly cared for through personal contact						
Tactics	Personal visit from company executive		X--------	X			
	Executive report on care of affected individuals			X			
	Send follow-up information to doctors and EMTs						
	Establish/maintain 24-hour helpline			X--------	--------	--------	--------
	Medical reimbursement			X--------	--------	--------	--------
	Provide gift certificate		X--------	X			
	Follow-up phone call						
Strategy	Maintain esteem by full disclosure through local media						
Tactics	COO guest on Dan Barber talk show			X			
	Full-page ad in Sunday Squawker					X	
Public	**G.C. medical professionals**						
Strategy	Provide information through personal contact and collateral material						
Tactics	Personal visit to physicians and EMTs		X--------	--------	--------	--------	--------
	Send follow-up information to doctors and EMTs						
	Establish/maintain 24-hour helpline			X--------	--------	--------	--------
Public	**G.C. Town Council**						
Strategy	Ensure council feels Spruced Up has responded appropriately through influentials and personal contact						
Tactics	Respond quickly to request to attend council meeting		X				
	Spruced Up executive meet with city manager			X			
	Provide city manager with information on incident			X			
	COO appear at council meeting for Q&A						X
	Aggricultural professor comments on safety						X
	COO follow-up phone call to council members						
Public	**Spruced Up employees**						
Strategy	Have COO provide information and disclosure through company meetings						
Tactics	Announce two company meetings to explain incident	X					
	Management greet employees as they arrive at meeting			X			
	COO explains situation/opens up Q&A			X			
	Announce 24-hour helpline and restricted spraying hours			X			
	Invite employees to attend the town council meeting			X			
	Online query for stock price	X--------	--------	--------	--------	--------	--------

Note: This calendar example is abbreviated for space. Not all publics listed in the sample case are included.
Your calendar should include strategies and tactics for each public.

12-May	13-May	14-May	15-May	16-May	17-May	18-23 May	24-31 May	June	July	Aug	Sept	Oct.
					X							
												X
							X					
		X										

12-May	13-May	14-May	15-May	16-May	17-May	18-23 May	24-31 May	June	July	Aug	Sept	Oct.
X												
				X								
												X

12-May	13-May	14-May	15-May	16-May	17-May	18-23 May	24-31 May	June	July	Aug	Sept	Oct.
X					X							

12-May	13-May	14-May	15-May	16-May	17-May	18-23 May	24-31 May	June	July	Aug	Sept	Oct.
							X					

Goose Creek Town Council

Strategy one:
- Ensure that the majority of council members feel Spruced Up has responded appropriately to the pesticide incident through influentials and personal contact with council members.

Tactics:
1. Respond quickly to the city council's request to attend the next council meeting and answer any preliminary questions over the phone.
2. Have a Spruced Up executive meet with the city manager in advance of the council meeting to gain his/her support of the company's actions to handle the incident.
3. Provide the city manager with early information about the pesticide, the aerial spraying, the company's response to those affected, change in spraying hours, the 24-hour helpline and a list of company executives who will attend the meeting.
4. Have the company COO appear at the council meeting to explain the company's actions in person and to respond, along with other company experts, to questions from the council and residents.
5. Ask one of the agricultural professors who worked on pesticide research at the local college to attend the council meeting and comment on the pesticide's safety.
6. Have the COO follow up with a phone call to each council member within a week of the town meeting to address any additional questions or concerns members may have.

Spruced Up employees at Goose Creek

Strategy one:
- Have the well-respected COO provide accurate information and complete disclosure about the pesticide cloud to Spruced Up employees, and thereby maintain their support and trust, through company meetings.

Tactics:
1. Announce to employees that two company meetings will be held — one in the morning and one in the afternoon — on Friday, May 7 for all full-time and part-time employees to explain what caused the pesticide cloud and the company's response.
2. Have company management greet employees as they arrive for the meeting.
3. Have the COO explain the situation and open up the meeting for questions to be answered by the COO and Spruced Up management involved with the situation.

SAMPLE CAMPAIGN: BUDGET

Note: This budget example is abbreviated for space. Not all publics listed in the sample case are included. Your budget should include strategies and tactics for each public.

Public	G.C. residents affected by spray	Per Item Cost	Total Projected	Sponsored Credit	Actual Projected
Strategy	Ensure affected individuals are properly				
	cared for through personal contact				
Tactics	Personal visit from company executive	$0.00	$0.00	$0.00	$0.00
	Executive report on care of affected individuals	$0.00	$0.00	$0.00	$0.00
	Establish/maintain 24-hour helpline (6 months + first week		$1,644.00	$0.00	$250.00
	Medical reimbursement packet (40 each)	$0.80	$32.00	$0.00	$32.00
	Gift Certificate (40 each)	$50.00	$2,000.00	$1,400.00	$600.00
	Follow-up phone call	$0.00	$0.00	$0.00	$0.00
	Strategy subtotal				*$882.00*
	Public subtotal				**$882.00**
Public	G.C. medical professionals				
Strategy	Provide information through personal				
	contact and collateral material				
Tactics	Personal visit to physicians and EMTs	$0.00	$0.00	$0.00	$0.00
	Information packets and mailing (45 copies)	$1.40	$63.00	$0.00	$63.00
	Strategy subtotal				*$63.00*
	Public subtotal				**$63.00**
Public	G.C. voters				
Strategy	Maintain esteem by full disclosure				
	through local media				
Tactics	COO guest on Dan Barber talk show	$0.00	$0.00	$0.00	$0.00
	Full-page ad in Sunday Squawker	$500.00	$500.00	$0.00	$500.00
	Strategy subtotal				*$500.00*
	Public subtotal				**$500.00**
Strategy	Maintain high public approval through disclosure,				
	incident management and Q&A at Town Meeting				
Tactics	COO and two execs answer questions	$0.00	$0.00	$0.00	$0.00
	Explain efforts to care for 40 citizens affected	$0.00	$0.00	$0.00	$0.00
	Provide information on 24-hour helpline	$0.00	$0.00	$0.00	$0.00
	Communicate company research efforts/accident	$0.00	$0.00	$0.00	$0.00
	Provide calendar of aerial spraying schedule	$0.00	$0.00	$0.00	$0.00
	Announce limited spraying hours (not after 7:30 a.m.)	$0.00	$0.00	$0.00	$0.00
	Provide summary of operations/community contributions	$0.00	$0.00	$0.00	$0.00
	Hire local research firm to measure perceptions (2 studies)	$3,000.00	$6,000.00	$0.00	$6,000.00
	Strategy subtotal				*$6,000.00*
	Public subtotal				**$6,500.00**
Public	G.C. Town Council				
Strategy	Ensure council feels Spruced Up has responded				
	appropriately through influentials and personal contact				
Tactics	Respond quickly to request to attend council meeting	$0.00	$0.00	$0.00	$0.00
	Spruced Up executive meet with city manager	$0.00	$0.00	$0.00	$0.00
	Provide city manager with information on incident	$1.40	$1.40	$0.00	$1.40
	COO appear at council meeting to answer questions	$0.00	$0.00	$0.00	$0.00
	COO follow-up phone call to council members	$0.00	$0.00	$0.00	$0.00
	Strategy subtotal				*$1.40*
	Public subtotal				**$1.40**
	CAMPAIGN TOTAL				**$7,946.40**

SAMPLE CAMPAIGN: COMMUNICATION CONFIRMATION TABLE

Key Public	Self-Interests	Primary Messages	Influentials
Goose Creek residents affected by the spray	Being healthy and safe; Not being afraid to go outside or let children go outside; Getting their medical bills paid	1) Spruced Up is committed to the safety and well being of our employees and our community 2) Spruced Up regrets any discomfort you've experienced	Physicians, community leaders, family members and close friends
Goose Creek medical professionals	Knowing whether or not the pesticide is harmful; knowing what to do if it happens again; being seen as competent	1) Spruced Up is committed to the safety and well being of our employees and our community	Other doctors, scientific studies/experts, supervisors, professional colleagues
Goose Creek voters	Health and safety; economic security; a good community to raise families	1) Spruced Up is committed to the safety and well being of our employees and our community 2) Spruced Up is proud to be an active part of Goose Creek and its future	Community leaders, family members, fellow workers and friends who are Spruced Up employees
Goose Creek Town Council	Solving the problem amicably with all parties satisfied; appearing competent and working for constituents' best interest; keeping Spruced Up open and profitable as part of the tax base	1) Spruced Up is committed to the safety and well being of our employees and community 2) We are proactively responding to the incident	City manager, constituents, business leaders, academics
Goose Creek employees	Their jobs at Spruced Up and pride in their employer; economic security; health and safety; a good community to raise families	1) Spruced Up is committed to the safety and well being of our employees and our community 2) We're meeting with and making sure anyone exposed is taken care of quickly 3) Spruced Up is proud to be an active part of Goose Creek and its future	Corporate leaders, co-workers, friends, family and community leaders

Objectives	Strategies	Tactics
1) Ensure residents affected have been properly cared for	1) Ensure individuals are properly cared for through personal contact	Personal visit from executive, executive report, follow-up medical reimbersement, gift certificate, follow-up call
2) Ensure 95 percent of residents affected are content with company's actions to resolve the incident	2) Maintain high esteem for Spruced Up by full disclosure through the media	COO guest on Dan Barber show, ad in Squawker
4) Ensure medical professionals have instruction for treatment	1) Provide information on the pesticide and procedures for short-term care through personal contact and collateral material	Personal visit to EMTs and physicians, follow-up information, spraying schedule, 24-hour helpline
3) Regain 85 percent level of perception that Spruced Up is a "good" or "very good" community citizen

5) Obtain a 75 percent level of perception that Spruced Up operates safely and responsibly | 1) Ensure voters this was an accident and that their safety and welfare are of paramount concern for Spruced Up through mass media

2) Maintain high level of public approval of Spruced Up through full disclosure, incident management and open Q&A at the town council meeting | COO guest on Dan Barber show, ad in Squawker

COO open Q&A at meeting, efforts to care for affected residents, 24-hour helpline, research efforts, calendar of spray schedule, change in spraying hours, contributions to the community, hire firm to measure perceptions |
| 3) Regain 85 percent level of perception that Spruced Up is a "good" or "very good" community citizen

5) Obtain a 75 percent level of perception that Spruced Up operates safely and responsibly | 1) Ensure vast majority of council members feel Spruced Up has responded appropriately to the incident through influentials and personal contact | Respond quickly to invitation, meet with city manager in advance, provide manager with preview information, COO appear at town meeting, aggricultural professor comment, follow-up phone call |
| 3) Regain 85 percent level of perception that Spruced Up is a "good" or "very good" community resident

5) Obtain a 75 percent level of perception that Spruced Up operates safely and responsibly

6) Mitigate negative effects keep dips in stock price less than 5 percent | 1) Complete disclosure to employees about incident to maintain support and trust through a company meeting | Announce company meetings, greet employees, COO explain situation, 24-hour helpline, invite to town meeting, track stock price |

4. Announce the new 24-hour helpline and the restricted spraying hours.

5. Invite all employees to attend the town council meeting.

6. Ask a communications staff member to track Spruced Up's stock price through June 5 or obtain a 30-day stock history report from the company's investor relations department (evaluation tool).

CAMPAIGN: EVALUATION CRITERIA AND TOOLS

Objective 1

Criteria:

- All Goose Creek residents affected by the insecticide were properly cared for by May 7.

Tool:

- Ask each executive/manager who meets with affected residents to report on the condition and care of each individual.

Objective 2

Criteria:

- 95 percent of residents affected by the insecticide (38 of the 40) were content with the company's actions to resolve the incident by Friday, May 14.

Tool:

- Have company officials ask affected residents how well they feel the company has responded to their needs and resolved the incident during follow up telephone calls on Friday, May 14.

Objective 3

Criteria:

- 85 percent of the Goose Creek population perceive Spruced Up as a "good" or "very good" community resident on May 31 and again on October 31.

Tool:

- Hire a local research firm to conduct a random survey of Goose Creek residents on May 31 and again on October 31.

Objective 4

Criteria:

- Treatment instructions and background information on the insecticide are distributed to the 45 general practice physicians and EMTs in Goose Creek by Friday, May 21.

Tool:

- Determine if communications staff members mailed medical treatment instructions, background information on the spray and a letter from the company to the 45 identified general practice physicians and EMTs by May 18 so it will arrive on or before May 21.

Objective 5

Criteria:

- 75 percent level of perception that Spruced Up operates safely and responsibly regarding employees and the community on May 31 and again on October 31.

Tool:

- Ask the local research firm hired for objective 3 to include a question about Spruced Up operating safely and responsibly on the survey conducted May 31 and October 31.

Objective 6

Criteria:

- Keep the overall decline in Spruced Up's share price to less than 5 percent through June 5 (measured against the pre-incident price of $32).

Tool:

- Have a member of the communications staff access the company's closing stock price online each day and record this figure each day through June 5 or ask the company's investor relations department to provide a 30-day history of stock performance on June 5.

APPENDIX B

Copy Outlines

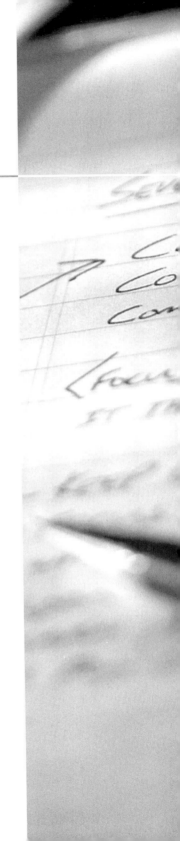

COPY OUTLINE — BACKGROUNDER/BRIEF HISTORY

Key public (audience) including current level of understanding of product/service:

Secondary publics (audiences), if any:

Action desired from public(s):

How that action ties to the primary public's self-interest:

Issue:

Primary messages: (usually 2-5, short statements/selling points to be conveyed)
Secondary messages: (bulleted supporting data, facts, cases, testimonials, etc.)

1. Primary Message:

Secondary:
-
-
-

2. Primary Message:

Secondary:
-
-
-

3. Primary Message:

Secondary:
-
-
-

Influentials (third-party opinion leaders who may influence the key public):

How they will be used to influence the key public (testimonials, examples, etc.):

Proposed backgrounder/brief history title:

Proposed photos/graphics (if any):

Method and timing of distribution (Internet, mail, fax, etc.):

Follow-up (if any):

Timeline/deadline:

COPY OUTLINE — BILLBOARD/POSTER

Key public (audience) including current level of understanding of product/service:

Secondary publics (audiences), if any:

Action desired from public(s):

How that action ties to the primary public's self-interest:

Overriding Message:

Primary messages: (usually 2-5, short statements/selling points to be conveyed)
Secondary messages: (bulleted supporting data, facts, cases, testimonials, etc.)

1. Primary Message:

Secondary:
- •
- •
- •

2. Primary Message:

Secondary:
- •
- •
- •

3. Primary Message:

Secondary:
- •
- •
- •

Influentials (third-party opinion leaders who may influence the key public):

How they will be used to influence the key public (testimonials, examples, etc.):

Slogan or tagline:

Proposed graphics:

Size of billboard or poster:

Location of billboard/posters:

Method and timing of distribution:

Print quantity and number of colors (poster):

Timeline/deadline:

COPY OUTLINE — BROCHURE

Key public (audience) including current level of understanding of product/service:

Secondary publics (audiences), if any:

Action desired from public(s):

How that action ties to the primary public's self-interest:

Primary messages: (usually 2-5, short statements/selling points to be conveyed)
Secondary messages: (bulleted supporting data, facts, cases, testimonials, etc.)

1. Primary Message:

Secondary:
- •
- •
- •

2. Primary Message:

Secondary:
- •
- •
- •

3. Primary Message:

Secondary:
- •
- •
- •

Influentials (third-party opinion leaders who may influence the key public):

How they will be used to influence the key public (testimonials, examples, etc.):

Proposed cover title and cover copy:

Proposed cover photos/graphics (if any):

Method and timing of distribution (self-mailer, point of purchase display, etc.):

Brochure size and paper (weight, finish, etc.):

Print quantity and number of colors:

Other graphics to be used (other than cover):

Timeline/deadline:

COPY OUTLINE — DIRECT MAIL PIECE

Key public (audience) including current level of understanding of product/service:

Secondary publics (audiences), if any:

Action desired from public(s):

    How that action ties to the primary public's self-interest:

Overriding message and tone:

Proposed p.s.:

Primary messages: (usually 2-5, short statements/selling points to be conveyed)
    Secondary messages: (bulleted supporting data, facts, cases, testimonials, etc.)

    1. Primary Message:

    Secondary:
-
-
-

    2. Primary Message:

    Secondary:
-
-
-

    3. Primary Message:

    Secondary:
-
-
-

Influentials (third-party opinion leaders who may influence the key public):

    How they will be used to influence the key public (testimonials, examples, etc.):

Proposed cover title and cover copy:

Proposed cover photos/graphics (if any):

Source of mailing list:

Mailer size and paper (weight, finish, etc.):

Print quantity and number of colors:

Other graphics to be used (other than cover):

Timeline/deadline:

COPY OUTLINE — FACT SHEET

Key public (audience) including current level of understanding of product/service:

Secondary publics (audiences), if any:

Action desired from public(s):

　　How that action ties to the primary public's self-interest:

Overriding Message:

Primary messages: (usually 2-5, short statements/selling points to be conveyed)
　　Secondary messages: (bulleted supporting data, facts, cases, testimonials, etc.)

　　1. Primary Message:

　　Secondary:　　•
　　　　　　　　　•
　　　　　　　　　•
　　2. Primary Message:

　　Secondary:　　•
　　　　　　　　　•
　　　　　　　　　•
　　3. Primary Message:

　　Secondary:　　•
　　　　　　　　　•
　　　　　　　　　•

Influentials (third-party opinion leaders who may influence the key public):

　　How they will be used to influence the key public (testimonials, examples, etc.):

Proposed graphics/charts (if any):

Method and timing of distribution (Internet, media kits, w/letter, etc.):

Follow-up (if any):

Finished size and paper (weight, finish, etc.):

Print quantity and number of colors:

Timeline/deadline:

COPY OUTLINE — FEATURE STORY

Key public (audience) including current level of understanding of product/service:

Secondary publics (audiences), if any:

Action desired from public(s):

    How that action ties to the primary public's self-interest:

Proposed theme:

Proposed headline:

Proposed lead:

Primary messages: (usually 2-5, short statements/selling points to be conveyed)
    Secondary messages: (bulleted supporting data, facts, cases, testimonials, etc.)

    1. Primary Message:

    Secondary: •
                    •
                    •

    2. Primary Message:

    Secondary: •
                    •
                    •

    3. Primary Message:

    Secondary: •
                    •
                    •

Influentials (third-party opinion leaders who may influence the key public):

    How they will be used to influence the key public (testimonials, examples, etc.):

Proposed photos/graphics (if any):

Desired length (number of words or pages):

Method and timing of distribution (e-mail, fax, etc.):

Specific media to receive story:

Follow-up with media:

Timeline/deadline:

COPY OUTLINE — LETTER TO THE EDITOR

Key public (audience) including current level of understanding of product/service:

Secondary publics (audiences), if any:

Action desired from public(s):

How that action ties to the primary public's self-interest:

News reference (previous story and date it appeared or current issue):

Primary messages: (usually 2-5, short statements/selling points to be conveyed)
Secondary messages: (bulleted supporting data, facts, cases, testimonials, etc.)

1. Primary Message:

Secondary: •
•
•

2. Primary Message:

Secondary: •
•
•

3. Primary Message:

Secondary: •
•
•

Influentials (third-party opinion leaders who may influence the key public):

How they will be used to influence the key public (testimonials, examples, etc.):

Proposed length (newspaper's suggested word count):

Method of distribution (editor's name and address):

Timeline/deadline:

Note: Use a typical letter format complete with your signature.

COPY OUTLINE — MEDIA KIT

Key public (audience) including current level of understanding of product/service:

Secondary publics (audiences), if any:

Action desired from public(s):

　　How that action ties to the primary public's self-interest:

Influentials (third-party opinion leaders who may influence the key public):

　　How they will be used to influence the key public (testimonials, examples, etc.):

Special event or reason to send the kit:

Proposed contents (fact sheet, executive bios, backgrounders, photos, etc.) and how they appeal to the key public's self-interests (each communications piece should have its own copy outline).

　　a.

　　b.

　　c.

　　d.

　　e.

Proposed packaging (folder, box, envelope, etc.):

Packaging graphics (logo, photo, etc.):

Method and timing of distribution (sent with story, handed out at event, etc.):

Print quantity:

Specific media to receive kit:

Follow-up with media (if any):

Timeline/deadline:

COPY OUTLINE — NEWSLETTER

Key public (audience) including current level of understanding of product/service:

Secondary publics (audiences), if any:

Action desired from public(s):

    How that action ties to the primary public's self-interest:

Influentials (third-party opinion leaders who may influence the key public):

    How they will be used to influence the key public (testimonials, examples, etc.):

Overall tone:

Masthead text and graphics:

Proposed lead story:

Proposed lead story graphics:

Regular features or sections (special columns, reports and letters) and how they appeal to the key public's self-interests (each feature and news story should have its own copy outline).

    a.

    b.

    c.

    d.

Other stories or articles (again, each should have its own copy outline):

Other photos/graphics:

Method and timing of distribution (self-mailer, Internet, handed delivered, etc.):

Finished size, number of pages, and paper (weight, finish, etc.):

Print quantity and number of colors:

Timeline/deadline:

COPY OUTLINE — NEWS PITCH

Key public (audience) including current level of understanding of product/service:

Secondary publics (audiences), if any:

Action desired from public(s):

> How that action ties to the primary public's self-interest:

News hook:

Story headline:

Story lead:

Primary messages: (usually 2-5, short statements/selling points to be conveyed)
> Secondary messages: (bulleted supporting data, facts, cases, testimonials, etc.)

> 1. Primary Message:

> Secondary:
> -
> -
> -

> 2. Primary Message:

> Secondary:
> -
> -
> -

> 3. Primary Message:

> Secondary:
> -
> -
> -

Influentials (third-party opinion leaders who may influence the key public):

> How they will be used to influence the key public (testimonials, examples, etc.):

Proposed photos/charts to accompany story (if any):

Method and timing of distribution (e-mail, fax, etc.):

Specific media to receive pitch:

Follow-up with media (if any):

Timeline/deadline:

COPY OUTLINE — NEWS RELEASE

Key public (audience) including current level of understanding of product/service:

Secondary publics (audiences), if any:

Action desired from public(s):

    How that action ties to the primary public's self-interest:

News hook:

Proposed headline:

Proposed lead:

Primary messages: (usually 2-5, short statements/selling points to be conveyed)
    Secondary messages: (bulleted supporting data, facts, cases, testimonials, etc.)

    1. Primary Message:

    Secondary:
-
-
-

    2. Primary Message:

    Secondary:
-
-
-

    3. Primary Message:

    Secondary:
-
-
-

Influentials (third-party opinion leaders who may influence the key public):

    How they will be used to influence the key public (testimonials, examples, etc.):

Proposed photos/charts (if any):

Method and timing of distribution (e-mail, fax, etc.):

Specific media to receive release:

Follow-up with media (if any):

Timeline/deadline:

COPY OUTLINE — OP-ED PIECE

Key public (audience) including current level of understanding of product/service:

Secondary publics (audiences), if any:

Action desired from public(s):

    How that action ties to the primary public's self-interest:

Overriding message and tone:

Primary messages: (usually 2-5, short statements/selling points to be conveyed)
    Secondary messages: (bulleted supporting data, facts, cases, testimonials, etc.)

    1. Primary Message:

    Secondary:
-
-
-

    2. Primary Message:

    Secondary:
-
-
-

    3. Primary Message:

    Secondary:
-
-
-

Influentials (third-party opinion leaders who may influence the key public):

    How they will be used to influence the key public (testimonials, examples, etc.):

Proposed headline:

Proposed lead:

Method distribution (e-mail, fax, mail, etc.):

Specific media to receive piece:

Follow-up with media (if any):

Timeline/deadline:

COPY OUTLINE — PRINT ADVERTISEMENT

Key public (audience) including current level of understanding of product/service:

Secondary publics (audiences), if any:

Action desired from public(s):

    How that action ties to the primary public's self-interest:

Overriding message and tone:

Primary messages: (usually 2-5, short statements/selling points to be conveyed)
    Secondary messages: (bulleted supporting data, facts, cases, testimonials, etc.)

    1. Primary Message:

    Secondary:
-
-
-

    2. Primary Message:

    Secondary:
-
-
-

    3. Primary Message:

    Secondary:
-
-
-

Influentials (third-party opinion leaders who may influence the key public):

    How they will be used to influence the key public (testimonials, examples, etc.):

Proposed ad graphics:

Slogan or tagline (if any):

Target publication(s):

Ad size, format and number of colors:

Timeline/deadline:

COPY OUTLINE — PUBLIC SERVICE ANNOUNCEMENT (PSA)

Key public (audience) including current level of understanding of product/service:

Secondary publics (audiences), if any:

Action desired from public(s):

    How that action ties to the primary public's self-interest:

Overriding message and tone:

Format (jingle, single voice, dialogue, etc.):

Primary messages: (usually 2-5, short statements/selling points to be conveyed)
    Secondary messages: (bulleted supporting data, facts, cases, testimonials, etc.)

    1. Primary Message:

    Secondary:
-
-
-

    2. Primary Message:

    Secondary:
-
-
-

    3. Primary Message:

    Secondary:
-
-
-

Influentials (third-party opinion leaders who may influence the key public):

    How they will be used to influence the key public (testimonials, examples, etc.):

Production format and length (script, recording, 30 sec., 60 sec., etc.):

Production quantity:

Specific media to receive spot:

Follow-up with media (if any):

Timeline/deadline:

COPY OUTLINE — RADIO ADVERTISEMENT

Key public (audience) including current level of understanding of product/service:

Secondary publics (audiences), if any:

Action desired from public(s):

    How that action ties to the primary public's self-interest:

Overriding message and tone:

Format (jingle, single voice, dialogue, etc.):

Primary messages: (usually 2-5, short statements/selling points to be conveyed)
    Secondary messages: (bulleted supporting data, facts, cases, testimonials, etc.)

    1. Primary Message:

    Secondary:
-
-
-

    2. Primary Message:

    Secondary:
-
-
-

    3. Primary Message:

    Secondary:
-
-
-

Influentials (third-party opinion leaders who may influence the key public):

    How they will be used to influence the key public (testimonials, examples, etc.):

Production format and length (script, recording, 30 sec., 60 sec., etc.):

Slogan or tagline if any:

Production quantity:

Target stations:

Timeline/deadline:

COPY OUTLINE — SPEECH

Key public (audience) including current level of understanding of product/service:

Secondary publics (audiences), if any:

Action desired from public(s):

    How that action ties to the primary public's self-interest:

Speaker: Event:

Length:

Overriding message and tone:

Opening attention getting device (humor, story, statistics, etc.):

Primary messages: (usually 2-5, short statements/selling points to be conveyed)
    Secondary messages: (bulleted supporting data, facts, cases, testimonials, etc.)

    1. Primary Message:

    Secondary:
-
-
-

    2. Primary Message:

    Secondary:
-
-
-

    3. Primary Message:

    Secondary:
-
-
-

Influentials (third-party opinion leaders who may influence the key public):

    How they will be used to influence the key public (testimonials, examples, etc.):

Proposed title:

Visuals to be used (if any):

Conclusion or summary:

Timeline/deadline:

COPY OUTLINE — TELEVISION ADVERTISEMENT

Key public (audience) including current level of understanding of product/service:

Secondary publics (audiences), if any:

Action desired from public(s):

    How that action ties to the primary public's self-interest:

Overriding message and tone:

Format (jingle, voice over, situation, etc.):

Primary messages: (usually 2-5, short statements/selling points to be conveyed)
    Secondary messages: (bulleted supporting data, facts, cases, testimonials, etc.)

    1. Primary Message:

    Secondary:
-
-
-

    2. Primary Message:

    Secondary:
-
-
-

    3. Primary Message:

    Secondary:
-
-
-

Influentials (third-party opinion leaders who may influence the key public):

    How they will be used to influence the key public (testimonials, examples, etc.):

Proposed visuals:

Production length (30 sec., 60 sec., etc.):

Slogan or tagline (if any):

Production quantity:

Target stations:

Timeline/deadline:

COPY OUTLINE — VIDEO/DVD

Key public (audience) including current level of understanding of product/service:

Secondary publics (audiences), if any:

Action desired from public(s):

How that action ties to the primary public's self-interest:

Overriding message/theme and tone:

Primary messages: (usually 2-5, short statements/selling points to be conveyed)
Secondary messages: (bulleted supporting data, facts, cases, testimonials, etc.)

1. Primary Message:

Secondary:
-
-
-

2. Primary Message:

Secondary:
-
-
-

3. Primary Message:

Secondary:
-
-
-

Influentials (third-party opinion leaders who may influence the key public):

How they will be used to influence the key public (testimonials, examples, etc.):

Proposed title and cover copy:

Proposed photos/graphics for the case (if any):

Proposed length:

Method and timing of distribution (Internet streaming, mailed to homes, shown at venue, etc.):

Production quantity and format:

Timeline/deadline:

COPY OUTLINE — VIDEO NEWS RELEASE (VNR)

Key public (audience) including current level of understanding of product/service:

Secondary publics (audiences), if any:

Action desired from public(s):

How that action ties to the primary public's self-interest:

Overriding message and tone:

Proposed headline:

Proposed lead:

Primary messages: (usually 2-5, short statements/selling points to be conveyed)
Secondary messages: (bulleted supporting data, facts, cases, testimonials, etc.)

1. Primary Message:

Secondary:
-
-
-

2. Primary Message:

Secondary:
-
-
-

3. Primary Message:

Secondary:
-
-
-

Influentials (third-party opinion leaders who may influence the key public):

How they will be used to influence the key public (testimonials, examples, etc.):

Proposed visuals:

Desired length (number of seconds, minutes):

Method and timing of distribution (satellite, mail):

Specific media to receive story:

Follow-up with media:

Timeline/deadline:

COPY OUTLINE — WEB SITE

Key public (audience) including current level of understanding of product/service:

Secondary publics (audiences), if any:

Action desired from public(s):

　　How that action ties to the primary public's self-interest:

Overriding message and tone:

Design elements (logos, pictures, colors, etc.):

Primary messages for the home page:

　　1. Primary Message:

　　2. Primary Message:

　　3. Primary Message:

Primary navigation categories and sub-categories (indicate how they appeal to the key public's self-interest):

A.
　　a.
　　b.
　　c.
B.
　　a.
　　b.
　　c.
C
　　a.
　　b.
　　c.
D.
　　a.
　　b.
　　c.

List databases that will need to be connected (electronic sources):

Planned publicity to drive traffic to URL:

Timeline/deadline:

APPENDIX C

Professional Codes of Ethics

CODE OF ETHICS — PUBLIC RELATIONS SOCIETY OF AMERICA

PREAMBLE

**Public Relations Society of America
Member Code of Ethics 2000**

- Professional Values
- Principles of Conduct
- Commitment and Compliance

This Code applies to PRSA members. The Code is designed to be a useful guide for PRSA members as they carry out their ethical responsibilities. This document is designed to anticipate and accommodate, by precedent, ethical challenges that may arise. The scenarios outlined in the Code provision are actual examples of misconduct. More will be added as experience with the Code occurs.

The Public Relations Society of America (PRSA) is committed to ethical practices. The level of public trust PRSA members seek, as we serve the public good, means we have taken on a special obligation to operate ethically.

The value of member reputation depends upon the ethical conduct of everyone affiliated with the Public Relations Society of America. Each of us sets an example for each other — as well as other professionals — by our pursuit of excellence with powerful standards of performance, professionalism and ethical conduct.

Emphasis on enforcement of the Code has been eliminated. But, the PRSA Board of Directors retains the right to bar from membership or expel from the Society any individual who has been or is sanctioned by a government agency or convicted in a court of law of an action that is in violation of this Code.

Ethical practice is the most important obligation of a PRSA member. We view the Member Code of Ethics as a model for other professions, organizations and professionals.

PRSA MEMBER STATEMENT OF
PROFESSIONAL VALUES

This statement presents the core values of PRSA members more broadly, of the public relations profession. These values provide the foundation for the Member Code of Ethics and industry standard for the professional practice of public These values are the fundamental beliefs that guide our and decision-making process.We believe our professional are vital to the integrity of the profession as a whole.

Advocacy

- We serve the public interest by acting as responsible advocates for those we represent.
- We provide a voice in the marketplace of ideas, facts and viewpoints to aid informed public debate.

Honesty

- We adhere to the highest standards of accuracy and truth in advancing the interests of those we represent and in communicating with the public.

Expertise

- We acquire and responsibly use specialized knowledge and experience.
- We advance the profession through continued professional development, research and education.
- We build mutual understanding, credibility and relationships among a wide array of institutions and audiences.

Independence

- We provide objective counsel to those we represent.
- We are accountable for our actions.

Loyalty

- We are faithful to those we represent, while honoring our obligation to serve the public interest.

Fairness

- We deal fairly with clients, employers, competitors, peers, vendors, the media and the general public.
- We respect all opinions and support the right of free expression.

PRSA CODE PROVISIONS
FREE FLOW OF INFORMATION

Core Principle

- Protecting and advancing the free flow of accurate and truthful information is essential to serving the public interest and contributing to informed decision making in a democratic society.

Intent

- To maintain the integrity of relationships with the media, government officials and the public.
- To aid informed decision-making.

Guidelines

A member shall:

- Preserve the integrity of the process of communication.
- Be honest and accurate in all communications.
- Act promptly to correct erroneous communications for which the practitioner is responsible.
- Preserve the free flow of unprejudiced information when giving or receiving gifts by ensuring that gifts are nominal, legal and infrequent.

Examples of Improper Conduct Under This Provision

- A member representing a ski manufacturer gives a pair of expensive racing skis to a sports magazine columnist, to influence the columnist to write favorable articles about the product.
- A member entertains a government official beyond legal limits and/or in violation of government reporting requirements.

COMPETITION

Core Principle

- Promoting healthy and fair competition among professionals preserves an ethical climate while fostering a robust business environment.

Intent

- To promote respect and fair competition among public relations professionals.

- To serve the public interest by providing the widest choice of practitioner options.

Guidelines

A member shall:
- Follow ethical hiring practices designed to respect free and open competition without deliberately undermining a competitor.
- Preserve intellectual property rights in the marketplace.

Examples of Improper Conduct Under This Provision
- A member employed by a "client organization" shares helpful information with a counseling firm that is competing with others for the organization's business.
- A member spreads malicious and unfounded rumors about a competitor in order to alienate the competitor's clients and employees in a ploy to recruit people and business.

DISCLOSURE OF INFORMATION

Core Principle
- Open communication fosters informed decision making in a democratic society.

Intent
- To build trust with the public by revealing all information needed for responsible decision making.

Guidelines

A member shall:
- Be honest and accurate in all communications.
- Act promptly to correct erroneous communications for which the member is responsible.
- Investigate the truthfulness and accuracy of information released on behalf of those represented.
- Reveal the sponsors for causes and interests represented.
- Disclose financial interest (such as stock ownership) in a client's organization.
- Avoid deceptive practices.

Examples of Improper Conduct Under This Provision
- Front groups: A member implements "grass roots" campaigns or letter-writing campaigns to legislators on behalf of undisclosed interest groups.
- Lying by omission: A practitioner for a corporation knowingly fails to release financial information, giving a misleading impression of the corporation's performance.

- A member discovers inaccurate information disseminated via a web site or media kit and does not correct the information.
- A member deceives the public by employing people to pose as volunteers to speak at public hearings and participate in "grass-roots" campaigns.

SAFEGUARDING CONFIDENCES

Core Principle
- Client trust requires appropriate protection of confidential and private information.

Intent
- To protect the privacy rights of clients, organizations and individuals by safeguarding confidential information.

Guidelines
A member shall:
- Safeguard the confidences and privacy rights of present, former and prospective clients and employees.
- Protect privileged, confidential or insider information gained from a client or organization.
- Immediately advise an appropriate authority if a member discovers that confidential information is being divulged by an employee of a client company or organization.

Examples of Improper Conduct Under This Provision
- A member changes jobs, takes confidential information and uses that information in the new position to the detriment of the former employer.
- A member intentionally leaks proprietary information to the detriment of some other party

CONFLICTS OF INTEREST

Core Principle
- Avoiding real, potential or perceived conflicts of interest builds the trust of clients, employers and the publics.

Intent
- To earn trust and mutual respect with clients or employers.
- To build trust with the public by avoiding or ending situations that put one's personal or

professional interests in conflict with society's interests.

Guidelines

A member shall:

- Act in the best interests of the client or employer, even subordinating the member's personal interests.
- Avoid actions and circumstances that may appear to compromise good business judgment or create a conflict between personal and professional interests.
- Disclose promptly any existing or potential conflict of interest to affected clients or organizations.
- Encourage clients and customers to determine if a conflict exists after notifying all affected parties.

Examples of Improper Conduct Under This Provision

- The member fails to disclose that he or she has a strong financial interest in a client's chief competitor.
- The member represents a "competitor company" or a "conflicting interest" without informing a prospective client.

ENHANCING THE PROFESSION

Core Principle

- Public relations professionals work constantly to strengthen the public's trust in the profession.

Intent

- To build respect and credibility with the public for the profession of public relations.
- To improve, adapt and expand professional practices.

Guidelines

A member shall:

- Acknowledge that there is an obligation to protect and enhance the profession.
- Keep informed and educated about practices in the profession to ensure ethical conduct.
- Actively pursue personal professional development.
- Decline representation of clients or organizations that urge or require actions contrary to this Code.
- Accurately define what public relations activities can accomplish.

- Counsel subordinates in proper ethical decision making.
- Require that subordinates adhere to the ethical requirements of the Code.
- Report ethical violations, whether committed by PRSA members or not, to the appropriate authority.

Examples of Improper Conduct Under This Provision

- A PRSA member declares publicly that a product the client sells is safe, without disclosing evidence to the contrary.
- A member initially assigns some questionable client work to a non-member practitioner to avoid the ethical obligation of PRSA membership.

RESOURCES

Rules and Guidelines

The following PRSA documents, available in The Blue Book, provide detailed rules and guidelines to help guide your professional behavior:

- PRSA Bylaws
- PRSA Administrative Rules
- Member Code of Ethics

If, after reviewing them, you still have a question or issue, contact PRSA headquarters as noted below.

QUESTIONS

The PRSA is here to help. Whether you have a serious concern or simply need clarification, contact Judy Voss at judy.voss@prsa.org.

PRSA MEMBER CODE OF ETHICS
PLEDGE

I pledge:

To conduct myself professionally, with truth, accuracy,
fairness and responsibility to the public;
to improve my individual competence and advance the
knowledge and proficiency of the profession through
continuing research and education;
and to adhere to the articles of the Member Code
of Ethics 2000 for the practice of public relations as adopted
by the governing Assembly of the
Public Relations Society of America.

I understand and accept that there is a consequence for
misconduct, up to and including membership revocation.

And, I understand that those who have been or are sanctioned by a
government agency or convicted in a court of law of an action that
is in violation of this Code may be barred from membership or
expelled from the Society.

_____

Signature

_____

Date

CODE OF ETHICS — AMERICAN MARKETING ASSOCIATION

Members of the American Marketing Association are committed to ethical professional conduct. They have joined together in subscribing to this Code of Ethics embracing the following topics:

RESPONSIBILITIES OF THE MARKETER

Marketers must accept responsibility for the consequences of their activities and make every effort to ensure that their decisions, recommendations and actions function to identify, serve and satisfy all relevant publics: customers, organizations and society.

Marketers' Professional Conduct must be guided by:
1. The basic rule of professional ethics: not knowingly to do harm;
2. The adherence to all applicable laws and regulations;
3. The accurate representation of their education, training and experience; and
4. The active support, practice and promotion of this Code of Ethics.

Honesty and Fairness

Marketers shall uphold and advance the integrity, honor and dignity of the profession by:
1. Being honest in serving consumers, clients, employees, suppliers, distributors and the public;
2. Not knowingly participating in conflict of interest without prior notice to all parties involved; and
3. Establishing equitable fee schedules including the payment or receipt of usual, customary and/or legal compensation for marketing exchanges.

Rights and Duties of Parties in the Marketing Exchange Process

Participants in the marketing exchange process should be able to expect that
1. Products and services offered are safe and fit for their intended uses;
2. Communications about offered products and services are not deceptive;
3. All parties intend to discharge their obligations, financial and otherwise, in good faith; and
4. Appropriate internal methods exist for equitable adjustment and/or redress of grievances concerning purchases.

It is understood that the above would include, but is not limited to, the following responsibilities of the marketer:

In the area of product development and management:
- disclosure of all substantial risks associated with product or service usage;
- identification of any product component substitution that might materially change the product or impact on the buyer's purchase decision;
- identification of extra cost-added features.

In the area of promotions:
- avoidance of false and misleading advertising;
- rejection of high-pressure manipulations, or misleading sales tactics;
- avoidance of sales promotions that use deception or manipulation.

In the area of distribution:
- not manipulating the availability of a product for the purpose of exploitation;
- not using coercion in the marketing channel;
- not exerting undue influence over the reseller's choice to handle a product.

In the area of pricing:
- not engaging in price fixing;
- not practicing predatory pricing;
- disclosing the full price associated with any purchase.

In the area of marketing research:
- prohibiting selling or fund-raising under the guise of conducting research;
- maintaining research integrity by avoiding misrepresentation and omission of pertinent research data;
- treating outside clients and suppliers fairly.

Organizational Relationships

Marketers should be aware of how their behavior may influence or impact the behavior of others in organizational relationships. They should not demand, encourage or apply coercion to obtain unethical behavior in their relationships with others, such as employees, suppliers, or customers.

1. Apply confidentiality and anonymity in professional relationships with regard to privileged information;

2. Meet their obligations and responsibilities in contracts and mutual agreements in a timely manner;

3. Avoid taking the work of others, in whole, or in part, and representing this work as their own or directly benefiting from it without compensation or consent of the originator or owner; and

4. Avoid manipulation to take advantage of situations to maximize personal welfare in a way that unfairly deprives or damages the organization of others.

Any AMA member found to be in violation of any provision of this Code of Ethics may have his or her Association membership suspended or revoked.

AMERICAN MARKETING ASSOCIATION
CODE OF ETHICS FOR MARKETING ON THE INTERNET

Preamble

The Internet, including online computer communications, has become increasingly important to marketers' activities, as they provide exchanges and access to markets worldwide. The ability to interact with stakeholders has created new marketing opportunities and risks that are not currently specifically addressed in the American Marketing Association Code of Ethics. The American Marketing Association Code of Ethics for Internet marketing provides additional guidance and direction for ethical responsibility in this dynamic area of marketing. The American Marketing Association is committed to ethical professional conduct and has adopted these principles for using the Internet, including on-line marketing activities utilizing network computers.

General Responsibilities

Internet marketers must assess the risks and take responsibility for the consequences of their activities. Internet marketers' professional conduct must be guided by:

1. Support of professional ethics to avoid harm by protecting the rights of privacy, ownership and access.

2. Adherence to all applicable laws and regulations with no use of Internet marketing that would be illegal, if conducted by mail, telephone, fax or other media.

3. Awareness of changes in regulations related to Internet marketing.
4. Effective communication to organizational members on risks and policies related to Internet marketing, when appropriate.
5. Organizational commitment to ethical Internet practices communicated to employees, customers and relevant stakeholders.

Privacy

Information collected from customers should be confidential and used only for expressed purposes. All data, especially confidential customer data, should be safeguarded against unauthorized access. The expressed wishes of others should be respected with regard to the receipt of unsolicited e-mail messages.

Ownership

Information obtained from the Internet sources should be properly authorized and documented. Information ownership should be safeguarded and respected. Marketers should respect the integrity and ownership of computer and network systems.

Access

Marketers should treat access to accounts, passwords and other information as confidential, and only examine or disclose content when authorized by a responsible party. The integrity of others' information systems should be respected with regard to placement of information, advertising or messages.

ADVERTISING ETHICS & PRINCIPLES — AMERICAN ADVERTISING FEDERATION

Truth

Advertising shall tell the truth, and shall reveal significant facts, the omission of which would mislead the public.

Substantiation

Advertising claims shall be substantiated by evidence in possession of the advertiser and advertising agency, prior to making such claims.

Comparisons

Advertising shall refrain from making false, misleading or unsubstantiated statements or claims about a competitor or his/her products or services.

Bait Advertising

Advertising shall not offer products or services for sale unless such offer constitutes a bona fide effort to sell the advertising products or services and is not a device to switch consumers to other goods or services, usually higher priced.

Guarantees and Warranties

Advertising of guarantees and warranties shall be explicit, with sufficient information to apprise consumers of their principal terms and limitations or, when space or time restrictions preclude such disclosures, the advertisement should clearly reveal where the full text of the guarantee or warranty can be examined before purchase.

Price Claims

Advertising shall avoid price claims which are false or misleading, or saving claims which do not offer provable savings.

Testimonials

Advertising containing testimonials shall be limited to those of competent witnesses who are reflecting a real and honest opinion or experience.

Taste And Decency

Advertising shall be free of statements, illustrations or implications which are offensive to good taste or public decency.

* Adopted by the American Advertising Federation Board of Directors, March 2, 1984, San Antonio.

GLOSSARY
OF TERMS

GLOSSARY OF TERMS

Analytical Process

A process in which action in each step is determined by the information acquired and decisions made in previous steps.

Attitudes

Collections of beliefs organized around a focal point that predisposes behavior.

Beliefs

Inferences we make about ourselves and the world around us.

Brainstorming

A structured group creative exercise to generate as many ideas as possible in a specified amount of time.

Channel

The conduit or medium through which messages are sent to a specific public to accomplish a specific purpose.

Communication Confirmation Table

A visual tool used to validate the logic of a communications plan.

Confidence Level

The percentage of certainty that the results of a survey would be the same if replicated.

Copy Outline

An analytical tool that extends strategic planning to creation of effective tactics.

Creativity

The process of looking outside ourselves and our routine to discover new ideas and innovative solutions.

Crisis Management

The process of anticipating and preparing to mediate problems that could affect an organization's environment and profitability.

Demographic Data

Information used to segment publics according to tangible characteristics such as age, gender and socioeconomic status.

Disinformation

Information that is intentionally inaccurate or misleading.

Diversity

Appreciating differences in culture, gender, race, background and experience.

Ethics

Personal and professional value systems and standards that underlie decisions and behavior.

Ethical Codes
Written and formalized standards of behavior used as guidelines for decision making.

Evaluation Criteria
Standards set to measure success.

Evaluation Tools
Methods used to gather data needed to assess whether or not evaluation criteria were met.

Executive Summary
A concise overview of a document's key points and conclusions targeted to key decision makers.

Focus Group Research
Moderator-led discussions with fewer than 15 participants providing in-depth information on attitudes and behaviors.

Formal Research
Data gathering structured according to accepted rules of research.

Frame of Reference
The collection of experiences, knowledge, culture and environment that forms our perceptual screen.

Goal
The result or desired outcome that solves a problem, takes advantage of an opportunity or meets a challenge.

Interactivity
The degree to which the tactic provides interaction between the sender of the message and the receiver.

Intervening Public
An individual or public used as a message channel to reach and influence a key public.

Issue Management
A long-range approach to identifying and resolving issues before they become problems or crises.

Key Public/Audience
Segmented groups of people whose support and cooperation are essential to the long-term survival of an organization or the short-term accomplishment of its objectives.

Misinformation
Information that is unintentionally inaccurate or misleading.

Nonsampling Error
A mistake made in selecting the sample and designing and implementing the questionnaire.

Objective
Specific, measurable statements of what needs to be accomplished to reach the goal.

Opinion leader
A trusted individual to whom one turns for advice because of his/her greater knowledge or experience regarding the issue at hand.

Panel Study
Respondents who have agreed to be surveyed repeatedly over time to track opinion and attitude change.

Partnership
A mutually beneficial short- or long-term cooperative relationship to reach common goals.

Personal Drop-off
Personally delivering a survey for later pick-up or mailing.

Persuasion
Disseminating information to appeal for a change in attitudes, opinions and/or behavior.

Planning
The process of using research to chart the step-by-step course to solve a problem, take advantage of an opportunity or meet a challenge.

Primary Messages
Sound bite statements that encompass what you need the public to do and an appeal to the public's self-interest to act.

Primary Research
Firsthand information gathered specifically for your current purpose.

Product Page
A cover page to introduce the communication product to the client, demonstrating its strategic design and use.

Professionalism
Characteristics and behavior befitting a professional.

Psychographic Data
Information used to segment publics according to values, attitudes and lifestyles.

Public Opinion
Attitudes expressed by a majority of people in a particular group about an issue that affects them.

Public Relations
An organization's efforts to establish and maintain mutually beneficial relationships in order to communicate and cooperate with the publics upon whom long-term success depends.

Purposive Sampling

Identifying and surveying opinion leaders to determine attitudes and behaviors.

Relationship Building

A return to the roots of human communication and persuasion that focuses on personal trust and mutual cooperation.

Research

Gathering information to clarify an issue and solve a problem

Research-based

When decision making in the planning and implementation process is based on the acquisition, interpretation and application of relevant facts.

Sampling Error

Measured as margin of error, it indicates the possible percentage variation of the sample data from the whole population.

Secondary Messages

Bulleted details that include facts, testimonials, examples, etc. that support a primary message.

Secondary Research

Information previously assimilated for other purposes that can be adapted to your needs.

Segmentation

Defining and separating publics by demographics and psychographics to ensure more effective communication.

Selective Perception

The inherent human function of selecting from the millions of daily stimuli only those messages one chooses to perceive.

Selective Retention

The inherent human function of selecting from the hundreds of stimuli perceived only those messages one chooses to retain.

Slogan or Theme

Short, catchy phrase that integrates primary messages and appeals to the broad interests of many key publics.

Strategic Communications Planning

An approach to communications planning that focuses actions on the accomplishment of organizational goals.

Strategic Cooperative Communities

Relationship-based interaction among all members of a community to achieve individual and collective goals.

Strategic Function

One that contributes significantly to the accomplishment of an organization's mission and goals.

Strategic Management

The process of evaluating all proposed action by focusing on organizational goals, usually defined in short-term contributions to the bottom line.

Strategies

Public-specific approaches to achieve objectives.

Stratified Sampling

Selecting the sample to ensure proportionate representation of segments within the universe.

Tactics

Strategy-specific communication products that carry the message to key publics.

Tag Line

A slogan or summarizing theme that appears at the end of an advertisement.

Triggering Event

An event that transforms readiness to act into actual behavior.

Trust

An emotional judgment of a person's credibility and performance on issues of importance.

Values

Core beliefs or beliefs central to an individual's cognitive system.

INDEX

INDEX